Weaving Libraries into the Web

The year 1997 found the members of the OCLC (Online Computer Library Center) cooperative in an expansive mood. More than 1,000 library leaders attended the OCLC President's Luncheon in San Francisco, where they celebrated OCLC's 30th anniversary. There were more than 25,000 libraries participating in the cooperative, including nearly 3,000 libraries in 62 countries outside the U.S., and the WorldCat database contained more than 37 million bibliographic records.

Over the next ten years, the global digital library would indeed emerge, but in a form that few could have predicted. Against a backdrop of continuous technological change and the rapid growth of the Internet, the OCLC cooperative's WorldCat database continued to grow and was a central theme of the past decade.

As the chapters in this book show, OCLC's chartered objectives of furthering access to the world's information and reducing the rate of rising library costs continue to resonate among libraries and librarians, as the OCLC cooperative enters its fifth decade.

This book was published as a special issue of the *Journal of Library Administration.*

Jay Jordan became the fourth president in OCLC's 38-year history in May 1998. He came to OCLC after a 24-year career with Information Handling Services, an international publisher of databases, where he held a series of key positions in top management, including President of IHS Engineering. He is active in professional organizations, including the American Library Association and the Special Libraries Association. He is a Fellow of the Standards Engineering Society.

Weaving Libraries into the Web

OCLC 1998-2008

Edited by Jay Jordan

Routledge
Taylor & Francis Group
LONDON AND NEW YORK

First published 2011
by Routledge

2 Park Square, Milton Park, Abingdon, Oxon, OX14 4RN
Simultaneously published in the USA and Canada
by Routledge
711 Third Avenue, New York, NY 10017

Routledge is an imprint of the Taylor & Francis Group, an informa business

First issued in paperback 2011

This book is a reproduction of the *Journal of Library Administration*, vol. 49, issue 6 & 7. The Publisher requests to those authors who may be citing this book to state, also, the bibliographical details of the special issue on which the book was based

Typeset in Garamond by Value Chain, India

British Library Cataloguing in Publication Data
A catalogue record for this book is available from the British Library

ISBN13: 978-0-415-57690-1 (hbk)
ISBN13: 978-0-415-51866-6 (pbk)

Contents

ABSTRACTS

Biographical Sketch of Frederick G. Kilgour Librarian, Educator, Entrepreneur, 1914–2006

Excerpted from NextSpace, the OCLC Newsletter, *No. 3, October 2006.*

The article traces the career of Frederick G. Kilgour (1914–2006), who is widely recognized as one of the leading figures in 20thcentury librarianship. He founded the Ohio College Library Center (OCLC) and from 1967 to 1981 was its first president and chief executive officer, presiding over OCLC's rapid growth from an intrastate network to an international network. In 1971, under Kilgour's leadership, OCLC introduced an online shared cataloguing system and an online union catalog (WorldCat) that is today the world's foremost bibliographic database. In 1978, he created the OCLC Office of Research, and in 1979, under his direction, OCLC launched its online interlibrary loan system. The author of 205 scholarly papers, Kilgour received numerous awards and honors over the course a career that took him from Harvard University Library, to the Office of Strategic Services in World War II, to Yale Medical Library, to OCLC, and finally, to the University of North Carolina at Chapel Hill, where he spent his final years on the faculty of the School of Information and Library Science as a Distinguished Research Professor.

Governing a Global Cooperative

LARRY P. ALFORD

The governance of the Online Computer Library System (OCLC) is understood best by placing it in the context of the arrangements that are typical for non-profit corporations organized within the United States to meet a public purpose. There are some provisions for OCLC's governance structures that are specific to the laws of Ohio, where OCLC was founded and where its principal offices remain.

A Brief History of the OCLC Members Council

GEORGE NEEDHAM AND RICH VAN ORDEN

On May 19, 2009, the Online Computer Library Center (OCLC) Members Council held its 90th and final meeting. It was the end of an era that began in 1977, when the Ohio College Library Center changed its name to OCLC and adopted a new governance structure that extended membership in the cooperative to libraries outside Ohio. In the ensuing 30 years, libraries around the world elected 450 delegates to attend three Council meetings each year at OCLC.

RLG and OCLC: Combined for the Future

LIZABETH WILSON, JAMES NEAL, JAMES MICHALKO AND JAY JORDAN

On July 1, 2006, The Research Libraries Group, Inc. (RLG) and the Online Computer Library System (OCLC) combined their organizations and resources. RLG's products and services were integrated with OCLC's, and RLG's program initiatives went forward within an expanded OCLC Research division. This was a historic moment for libraries and research institutions consonant with the incredible changes in the information environment that had been underway during the previous decade. The expansion of WorldCat that resulted and the renewed attention given to research libraries by OCLC in the merger has positively impacted libraries around the globe.

OCLC in the Asia Pacific Region

ANTHONY W. FERGUSON AND ANDREW WANG

This essay provides an overview of both the accomplishments and difficulties faced by OCLC as it has expanded in the vast Asia Pacific region. It describes the organizational changes as they evolved as this previously North American collaborative organization expanded westward and details initiatives pursued in each of the Asia Pacific countries where it has operated. Finally, it examines the five major challenges yet facing OCLC in the region: the lack of bibliographic name authority files, competing classification systems, competing MARC cataloging formats, the perceived high costs associated with participating OCLC programs and services, and the need for local vernacular products in addition to those developed largely for the North American and European markets.

History and Activity of OCLC in Canada

DANIEL BOIVIN

Canada has always been an important and natural trading partner for the United States, and this was reflected within the library field when a Canadian library, the Alberta Alcoholism and Drug Abuse Commission (AADAC) became an Online Computer Library Center (OCLC) member in 1979. This was OCLC's first member library outside the United States.

OCLC in Europe, the Middle East and Africa, 1998–2008

JANET LEES

This article is a continuation of the article of the same name by Christine Deschamps who described the evolution of OCLC in Europe 1981–1997. This article continues the story for the period 1998–2008 and covers the expansion of OCLC services to the Middle East and Africa. It also includes the organizational, governance and product portfolio developments for this period under the global leadership of Jay Jordan.

OCLC in Latin America and the Caribbean: A Chronology

LAWRENCE OLSZEWSKI

From one library in 1995 to 884 in 2008, the number of Online Computer Library Center (OCLC) libraries in Latin American and the Caribbean has grown significantly. They are presently active in 27 countries and territories. The following chronology highlights not only the significant achievements since 1997 that OCLC has made in providing products and services to the region but also the contributions the libraries in the region have made to OCLC in providing input and advice to the governance and product development.

The OCLC Network of Regional Service Providers: The Last Ten Years

BRENDA BAILEY-HAINER

Developed in the early 1970s, the alliance between the Online Computer Library Center (OCLC) and its regional service providers is a strategic partnership that has survived for over 30 years. Originally created by OCLC to help it efficiently reach out to libraries in other states beyond its initial Ohio focus, this alliance is now starting to transform into a new structure. This new structure as well as other changes in the relationship between OCLC and its partners will have an impact upon all of the organizations involved.

The Jay Jordan IFLA/OCLC Early Career Development Fellowship Program: A Long Name for an Important Project

NANCY LENSENMAYER AND GEORGE NEEDHAM

The Jay Jordan IFLA/OCLC Early Career Development Fellowship Program, jointly sponsored by the American Theological Library Association, the International Federation of Library Associations and Institutions (IFLA) and OCLC, provides early career development and continuing education for library and information science professionals from countries with developing economies. The program's history, selection process, and curriculum are described in detail. Fellows comment on their experiences, new perspectives, lessons learned, and benefits gained from participation in the Fellowship program.

21st Century Library Systems

ANDREW PACE

Less than a decade into the 21st century, perhaps it is more fitting to describe library automation as approaching its 80th birthday, is a time to look back and carefully measure moving forward. Since the introduction of a punch card circulation system at the University of Texas in 1936, through the advent and perseverance of the MARC record, and following the ebb and flow of nearly 75 different library automation vendors, library automation has come a long way. For some, however, it has not come nearly far enough. If one were to stop the history of library automation in the mid-1990s and wish away the dominance of the Internet, libraries and patrons might have been quite content with the state-of–the-art as it existed 15 years ago. But wishing away the Internet is like envisioning a world without electricity and indoor plumbing; as such, that 1990s library automation summit is now a plateau from which many library technologists and futurists can see no launch pad to a next-generation of library software and services.

Next Generation Cataloging

KAREN CALHOUN AND RENEE REGISTER

During the past several years the Online Computer Library Center (OCLC) noted increasing concern from the library community regarding the future of cataloging. In response to this concern and to the rapidly changing metadata environment, OCLC is taking steps to further a paradigm shift toward early acquisition of metadata in WorldCat directly from the entities responsible for content purchased by libraries—chiefly the publisher supply chain. This shift in thinking requires the acknowledgement that metadata is dynamic and will change over time and relies upon the automated capture of metadata early in the publishing cycle as well as automated processes to help make the early metadata "good enough."

The DDC and OCLC

JOAN S. MITCHELL AND DIANE VIZINE-GOETZ

This article highlights key events in the relationship between OCLC Online Computer Library Center, Inc. and the Dewey Decimal Classification (DDC) system. The formal relationship started with OCLC's acquisition of Forest Press and the rights to the DDC from the Lake Placid Education Foundation in 1988, but OCLC's research interests in the DDC predated that acquisition and have remained strong during the relationship. Under OCLC's leadership, the DDC's value proposition has been enhanced by the continuous updating of the system itself, development of interoperable translations, mappings to other schemes, and new forms of representation of the underlying data. The amount of categorized content associated with the system in WorldCat and elsewhere has grown, as has worldwide use of the system. Emerging technologies are creating new opportunities for publishing, linking, and sharing DDC data.

The Revolution Continues: Resource Sharing and OCLC in the New Century

WILLIAM J. CROWE

The author explores the theory and practice of resource sharing in the OCLC cooperative. History of the OCLC Interlibrary Loan subsystem and subsequent developments through 2008 are reviewed, and prospects for the future are offered.

Virtual Reference Reflections

STEWART BODNER

When the Online Computer Library Center (OCLC) was incorporated as the Ohio College Library Center in July 1967, it was largely considered an enterprise whose primary task was investigating cataloging duplication in American libraries. Fred Kilgour, OCLC's founder, was the visionary behind a collaborative enterprise that would eventually reshape the library landscape for generations. The concept of a cataloging system using automation to share bibliographic information, thus allowing libraries to copy catalog records for their own purposes, seems obvious today. In hindsight, it is hard to imagine the effort it would take if every library across the globe were required to individually catalog their acquisitions. Yet Kilgour's vision went beyond the standard use of automation in cataloging applications. He believed automation can "provide not just information about where to find information, but the information itself, the text of the book or article, the map, the recording, each delivered directly to the user" (Mason, 1998, p. 57). Kilgour's audacious approach signaled a sea change in the way libraries operate. Traditionally, librarians acted as pointers to information. They provided search strategies for readers and sent them on their way. It was up to the reader to review the card catalog or the paper index, decipher the information in those sources, again consulting the librarian as interpreter. The reader then needed to find the monograph or periodical article by physically locating the material or by making a request, depending on the type of library they frequented. For the better part of the 20th century, this paradigm dictated the interactions between reference librarians and their patrons.

Digital Collections: History and Perspectives

GREG ZICK

The author reviews the history of early efforts by libraries to build digital collections, the development of CONTENTdm software at the University of Washington, and OCLC's current directions in helping libraries build and manage digital collections.

The RLG Partnership

JAMES MICHALKO

Created in 2006 with the coming together of RLG and OCLC, the RLG Partnership is a transnational research venue for libraries, archives and museums. In concert with OCLC Research, the RLG Partnership focuses on a work agenda that includes systemwide organization and interactions of libraries, archives and museums; research information management; mobilizing unique materials in collections; metadata support and management; and infrastructure to support metadata flow in the Web environment.

WebJunction: A Community for Library Staff

MARILYN GELL MASON

The author reviews the history, accomplishments and plans of WebJunction.

OCLC Research: Past, Present, and Future

NANCY ELKINGTON

From its modest beginnings in the mid 1970s as a small research and development unit of Online Computer Library Center, Inc. (OCLC), OCLC Research has evolved to become a significant research organization, a preeminent laboratory for the exploration of innovative uses of library data and information system technology, and a key agent of change, advancing the state of the art within OCLC and in the global library and information science community. OCLC Research is one of the world's leading centers devoted to exploration, innovation, and community building on behalf of libraries, archives, and museums and is dedicated to helping memory institutions more effectively serve users of information, information systems, and cultural heritage collections.

Advocacy and OCLC

CATHY DE ROSA

Promoting the evolution of library use, of libraries themselves, and of librarianship is one of OCLC's chartered objectives. The author discusses nonprofit business models and new approaches for advancing their missions through advocacy. OCLC's recent advocacy programs are described.

OCLC 1998–2008: Weaving Libraries into the Web

JAY JORDAN

The author briefly reviews OCLC's history from 1967 to 1998, then focuses on the accomplishments and activities of the OCLC cooperative from 1998 to 2008. Particular attention is given to OCLC's strategy of weaving libraries into the World Wide Web and the transformation of WorldCat from a bibliographic database into a globally networked information resource.

Chronology: Noteworthy Achievements of the Cooperative 1967–2008

PHIL SCHIEBER

This chronology lists programs, activities and accomplishments of OCLC and its members from its founding in 1967 as the Ohio College Library Center through 1998.

Introduction
OCLC 1998-2008: The Fourth Decade

JAY JORDAN

President and CEO, OCLC

1997 found the members of the OCLC cooperative in an expansive mood. More than 1,000 library leaders attended the OCLC President's Luncheon in San Francisco, where they celebrated OCLC's 30th anniversary.

There was much to celebrate. There were more than 25,000 libraries participating in the cooperative, including nearly 3,000 libraries in 62 countries outside the U.S. OCLC had just opened the OCLC Canada office in Montreal. The WorldCat database contained more than 37 million bibliographic records and 638 million holdings. WorldCat was among the most consulted databases in higher education, available to faculty, students and the general public through the OCLC FirstSearch service in libraries.

OCLC Users Council President Victoria Hannawalt told the President's Luncheon audience: "It was through partnerships and cooperation that OCLC was founded 30 years ago. Those principles have guided the membership through the emerging global, digital library of today, and charted a course into the 21st century."[1]

Moreover, to help libraries get ready for the 21st century, OCLC was in the midst of the Workstation Replacement Program, which would eventually provide a $5 million subsidy to member libraries to trade in 5,000 of their older, DOS-based workstations for state-of-the art machines using Windows 95, 98 or NT. OCLC was also replacing its old X.25 telecommunications network (installed in 1990) with a TCP/IP network that would deliver OCLC services over the Internet.

At the same time, OCLC and governments, businesses and organizations around the world were facing a critical deadline of December 31, 1999—the last day to make their computer systems Y2K compliant, which meant they could handle a four-digit identifier for the year. OCLC had started working on the problem in 1996 and would eventually modify, test and reinstall approximately 7.2 million lines of computer code.

Over the next 10 years, the global digital library would indeed emerge, but in a form that few could have predicted.

Against a backdrop of continuous technological change and the rapid growth of

---

1 "OCLC President's Luncheon celebrates membership," OCLC Newsletter, No. 228, July/August 1997, p. 6.

the Internet, the OCLC cooperative's WorldCat database continued to grow. Indeed, the persistence of WorldCat—its steady accumulation of the world's knowledge and the extension of its network effects and benefits to thousands of institutions and millions of people around the world—is the central theme of the past decade.

In 1998, Haworth Press published *OCLC 1967-1997: Thirty Years of Furthering Access to the World's Information* under the editorship of K. Wayne Smith, President and CEO of OCLC from 1989 to 1998. This new volume picks up where that one left off.

As the chapters in this book show, OCLC's chartered objectives of furthering access to the world's information and reducing the rate of rise of library costs continue to resonate among libraries and librarians as the OCLC cooperative enters its fifth decade.

Jay Jordan

Biographical Sketch of Frederick G. Kilgour
Librarian, Educator, Entrepreneur, 1914–2006

Excerpted from NextSpace, the OCLC Newsletter,
No. 3, October 2006.

The article traces the career of Frederick G. Kilgour (1914–2006), who is widely recognized as one of the leading figures in 20th-century librarianship. He founded the Ohio College Library Center (OCLC) and from 1967 to 1981 was its first president and chief executive officer, presiding over OCLC's rapid growth from an intrastate network to an international network. In 1971, under Kilgour's leadership, OCLC introduced an online shared cataloging system and an online union catalog (WorldCat) that is today the world's foremost bibliographic database. In 1978, he created the OCLC Office of Research, and in 1979, under his direction, OCLC launched its online interlibrary loan system. The author of 205 scholarly papers, Kilgour received numerous awards and honors over the course a career that took him from Harvard University Library, to the Office of Strategic Services in World War II, to Yale Medical Library, to OCLC, and finally, to the University of North Carolina at Chapel Hill, where he spent his final years on the faculty of the School of Information and Library Science as a Distinguished Research Professor.

Frederick G. Kilgour was a librarian and educator who created an international computer library network and database that changed the way people use libraries. Widely recognized as one of the leading figures in 20th-century librarianship, he was among the earliest proponents of adapting computer technology to library processes. At the dawn of library automation in the early 1970s, he founded the Online Computer Library Center (OCLC) and led the creation of a library network that today links thousands of libraries and other knowledge institutions around the world.

In 1971, he developed a database, the OCLC Online Union Catalog (WorldCat), that at this writing contains more than 137 million entries for books and other materials and more than 1.4 billion location listings for these materials in libraries around the world, and it is available on the World Wide Web. It is regarded as the world's largest computerized library catalog. It contains descriptions of library materials and their locations. More recently, the database provides access to the electronic full text of articles and books as well as images and sound recordings. It spans 4,000 years of recorded knowledge. Every 10 seconds a library adds a new record.

Kilgour had been an academic librarian and historian of science and technology at Harvard and Yale for 30 years when the Ohio College Association hired him in 1967 to establish the world's first computerized library network, the Ohio College Library Center, on the campus of The Ohio State University in Columbus. Under Kilgour's leadership, the nonprofit corporation introduced a shared cataloging system in 1971 for 54 Ohio academic libraries.

At that time, most libraries maintained card catalogs as guides to their collections, and librarians had to type individual cards for each item, a labor-intensive and expensive procedure. The shared cataloging system and database that Kilgour devised made it unnecessary for more than one library to originally catalog an item. A library could use the cataloging information already in the database and add items not already entered. Of equal importance, the shared catalog enabled interlibrary lending, sparing libraries the expense of adding material to their own collections. The network quickly grew beyond Ohio to all 50 states and then internationally.

Thanks to Kilgour, WorldCat connects libraries of all types and sizes, from giant research libraries to small public libraries around the world. It enables people to have access to library collections irrespective of where they are located. People can also access the database and library collections through the World Wide Web.

Frederick Gridley Kilgour was born in Springfield, MA on Jan. 6, 1914, to Edward Francis and Lillian Piper Kilgour. Upon graduating from Harvard College in 1935, he became assistant to the director of the Harvard University Library, where he began experimenting in automating library procedures, primarily the use of punched cards for a circulation system. At the same time he undertook graduate study under George Sarton, a pioneer in the new discipline of the history of science, and began publishing scholarly papers. He also built a collection of microfilmed foreign newspapers to give scholar's access to newspapers from abroad, an activity that quickly came to the attention of government officials in Washington, DC. In 1940, he married Eleanor Margaret Beach, a graduate of Mount Holyoke College, who had taken a job at the Harvard College Library, where they met. They had three daughters and a son.

From 1942 to 1945, Kilgour, with a commission as a lieutenant in the U. S. Naval Reserve, was Executive Secretary and Acting Chairman of the U.S. government's Interdepartmental Committee for the Acquisition of Foreign Publications (IDC), which developed a system for obtaining publications from enemy and enemy-occupied areas. This organization of 150 persons in outposts around the world microfilmed newspapers and other printed information items and sent them back to Washington, DC.

One example of the kind of intelligence gathered was the Japanese "News for Sailors" reports listing new mine fields that were sent from Washington, DC. directly to Pearl Harbor and U.S. submarines in the Western Pacific. Kilgour received the Legion of Merit for his intelligence work in 1945.

From 1946 to 1948, Kilgour served as Deputy Director in the Office of Intelligence Collection and Dissemination in the U.S. Department of State.

In 1948, he was named Librarian of the Yale Medical Library. At Yale he was also a lecturer in the history of science and technology and published many scholarly articles on those topics.

While running the Yale Medical Library, Kilgour began publishing studies and articles on library use and effectiveness. He asked his staff to collect empirical data, such as use of books and journals by categories, to guide selection and retention of titles. He viewed the library not as a mere depository of knowledge, but as "an instrument of education.

In 1961, he was one of the leaders in the development of a prototype computerized library catalog system for the medical libraries at Columbia, Harvard, and Yale Universities that was funded by the National Science Foundation. In 1965, Kilgour was also named Associate Librarian for Research and Development at Yale University, continuing experiments in library automation and promoting their potential benefits.

In his professional writings, Kilgour pointed out that the explosion of research information was placing new demands on libraries to furnish information completely and rapidly. He advocated the use of the computer to eliminate human repetitive tasks from library procedures He recognized nearly 40 years ago the potential of linking libraries in computer networks to create economies of scale and generate "network effects" that would increase the value of the network as more participants were added.

In 1967, the Ohio College Association (a group comprising the presidents of Ohio's colleges and universities) hired Kilgour to lead a nonprofit corporation, the Ohio College Library Center (OCLC), in the development of a computerized library system for the academic libraries in the state. In

1971, after 4 years of development, OCLC introduced its online shared cataloging system, which would achieve dramatic cost savings for libraries. For example, in the first year of system use, the Alden Library at Ohio University was able to increase the number of books it cataloged by a third, while it reducing its staff by 17 positions. Word of this new idea spread on campuses across the country, starting an online revolution in libraries that continues to this day.

Kilgour was president of OCLC from 1967 to 1980, presiding over its rapid growth from an intrastate network to an international network. In addition to creating the WorldCat database, he developed an online interlibrary loan system that last year libraries used to arrange nearly 10 million loans. Today, OCLC has a staff of 1,200 and offices in seven countries. Its mission remains the same: to further access to the world's information and reduce library costs.

Kilgour stepped down from management in 1981 but continued to serve on the OCLC Board of Trustees until 1995.

In 1990, he was named Distinguished Research Professor for the School of Information and Library Science at the University of North Carolina at Chapel Hill and served on the faculty until is retirement in 2004.

Kilgour was the author of 205 scholarly papers. He was the founder and first editor of the journal, *Information Technology and Libraries*. In 1999, Oxford University Press published his *Evolution of the Book*. His other works include: *Engineering in History; the Library of the Medical Institution of Yale College and its Catalogue of 1865;* and the *Library and Information Science CumIndex*.

He received numerous awards from library associations and five honorary doctorates.

In 1982, the American Library Association presented him with Honorary Life Membership. The citation read:

> In recognition of his successful pioneering efforts to master technology in the service of librarianship; the acuity of his vision that helped to introduce the most modern and powerful technologies into the practice of librarianship; the establishment and development of a practical vehicle for making the benefits of technology readily available to thousands of libraries; his long and distinguished career as a practicing librarian; his voluminous, scholarly and prophetic writings; and above all his fostering the means for ensuring the economic viability of libraries, the American Library Association hereby cites Frederick Gridley Kilgour as scholar, entrepreneur, innovator, and interpreter of technology steadfastly committed to the preservation of humanistic values.

In 1979, the American Society for Information Science and Technology gave him the Award of Merit. The citation read:

Presented to Frederick G. Kilgour, in recognition of his leadership in the field of library automation: As Executive Director of OCLC since 1967, he has succeeded in changing the conception of what is feasible in library automation and library networking. His major technological developments, superb planning and executive abilities, deep insight into bibliographic and information needs, and unfaltering leadership have transformed a state association of libraries in a national interlibrary bibliographic utility.

OCLC has proved the feasibility of nationwide sharing of catalog-record creation and has helped libraries to maintain and to enhance the quality and speed of service while achieving cost control—and even cost reduction—in the face of severely reduced funding. This achievement may be the single greatest contribution to national networking in the United States. His work will have a lasting impact on the field of information science.

Governing a Global Cooperative

LARRY P. ALFORD

University Libraries, Temple University, Philadelphia, PA, USA

ABSTRACT. *The governance of the Online Computer Library System (OCLC) is understood best by placing it in the context of the arrangements that are typical for non-profit corporations organized within the United States to meet a public purpose. There are some provisions for OCLC's governance structures that are specific to the laws of Ohio, where OCLC was founded and where its principal offices remain.*

OCLC's public purpose is stated in the Articles of Incorporation: "The purpose or purposes for which this corporation is formed are to establish, maintain and operate a computerized library network and to promote the evolution of library use, of libraries themselves, and of librarianship and to provide processes and products for the benefit of library users and libraries, including such objectives as increasing availability of library resources to individual library patrons and reduce the rate of rise of library per unit costs, all for the fundamental public purpose of furthering the access to and use of the ever expanding body of worldwide, scientific, literary, and educational knowledge and information."

OCLC leaders—its officers and its trustees—have been guided by this statement of purpose for more than 40 years. All decisions made by OCLC are always informed by this statement of public purpose.

OHIO COLLEGE LIBRARY CENTER

There have been four stages in the evolution of OCLC's governance structure. OCLC, founded as the Ohio College Library Center, was formed in 1967 and governed under arrangements devised by the presidents and library directors of the 54 colleges and universities in Ohio that had created OCLC (Kilgour, 1969).

As OCLC expanded in the United States well beyond the borders of Ohio, and even a bit outside the United States, there were increasing calls from librarians to broaden the representation of interests beyond Ohio. Responding to this groundswell of interest, in 1977 OCLC commissioned a report from Arthur D. Little Associates to examine its governance structure and suggest options for change (Arthur D. Little, Inc., 1978). That report, vetted by a body of prominent leaders in librarianship and education, was approved by the Ohio librarians and presidents who had overseen OCLC from the beginning. Among other things, this change led to an expansion of membership on the OCLC Board of Trustees, but with a commitment to retain a majority of librarians on the board, which remains the case to this day. These changes also called for the establishment of a Users Council, with representatives elected by libraries to advise OCLC on its strategic directions and the development of new products and services. That Council also was empowered to elect six members to the Board of Trustees and to vote on any changes proposed by the Board of Trustees to OCLC's basic governance structure and constituent documents.

To structure representation on the new Council, regional networks—and, later, some OCLC service centers in those areas without such networks—were designated as the "Members" of Users Council. Libraries in each network elected delegates, with the number representing the libraries in each region based on a complex algorithm that took into account the total number of participating libraries and the numbers of holdings recorded, the number of items cataloged, and other activity from the libraries in that network area on a rolling average.

BECOMING A GLOBAL COOPERATIVE

This second stage of governance lasted until 2000 and, overall, served OCLC and its member libraries very well, as OCLC moved from an Ohio-based cooperative to become a true global network. To illustrate: In 1978, OCLC had 1,600 members in 45 states in the United States. By 1999, OCLC had grown to serve almost 9,000 member libraries in 76 countries. As the world of information changed (consider that that World Wide Web has not even been imagined by librarians except perhaps Fred Kilgour!), it had become very clear by 1999–2000 that OCLC needed to seek ways expand its governance to offer representation to a much wider community across the world. A blue ribbon advisory council on governance, led by Nancy Eaton, a member and past chair of the OCLC Board of Trustees, was formed by the OCLC Board in 1999. It included OCLC Trustees, Users Council delegates, and leaders in the field from the United States and Europe, which was asked to review OCLC's governance structure and make recommendations.

That process led to the report, "OCLC strategic directions and governance: report of the Advisory Council" (OCLC Advisory Council, 2000), which, in turn, led to the third stage of OCLC governance. There were a number of important changes from the 1977 structure, chief among them reconceiving the Users Council as a "Members Council." to acknowledge both symbolically and substantively that OCLC is, at its core, a membership collaborative. The new council was to be expanded to ensure wider representation from libraries outside the United States by adding six delegate positions to be appointed from various countries or regions of the world, beyond the provisions of the algorithm that determined representation on the old Users Council. Most of the remaining governance structure was left intact, but with a firm recommendation from the ad hoc body that the OCLC Board not wait a quarter-century again to review OCLC governance.

PUBLIC PURPOSES

The latter recommendation led to the fourth stage to OCLC's governance, which is being implemented as this article was written, in late 2008. Much of the rest of this text will focus on the changes in OCLC governance that are evolving during this fourth stage.

Before discussing these changes, however, it is important to take note of several overarching points. First, for OCLC governance to remain vital, especially for it to remain connected to the membership, it must evolve as the environment changes. Even so, that evolution should proceed in accord with several fundamental principles of the cooperative, as has been the case from the earliest years of OCLC's life:

1. OCLC is a not-for-profit organization. That structure is important legally and operationally, but it is vitally important as well for its symbolic value. OCLC is not a commercial enterprise to make profit for its owners. Rather, it is an enterprise whose purpose is to foster the sharing of information through the libraries (and now allied institutions, such as museums and archives) of the world, to strengthen libraries, and to reduce the rate of rise of costs for the operation of those libraries. While the ways in which OCLC supports that purpose must continue to change over time, especially as the information landscape changes, this fundamental purpose has not changed.
2. This "public" purpose informs all decisions made by OCLC's management and by OCLC's Board.

3. Members must have strong representation in OCLC's governance in setting its strategic direction. The voice of the membership is currently heard through a Board of Trustees that includes a majority of people who work in leadership positions in libraries (and similar organizations, such as archives and museums) and others who are connected to education or related fields, including business, publishing, and information technology. This voice also is heard through a strong Members Council, to be changed in 2009-10 to become a "Global Council," with elected representatives from libraries and other cultural heritage organizations around the world. These representatives will continue to advise OCLC on its strategic directions and represent the voices of thousands of librarians and millions of library users both to OCLC management and to its Board.

4. Although OCLC is a not-for-profit entity, it also must operate in a business-like way if it is to have the financial strength to continue to serve its members. There is a well-worn quip that while OCLC is not for profit, it is also "not for loss." Not only must OCLC be able to meet the costs of its on-going operating obligations, it also must be able to invest on behalf of its members in such areas as technology innovation and in migrating its systems and services in new directions. Overall, it must invest in the future on behalf of its members by developing new, leading edge information services that will enable OCLC to meet its public purpose. Most succinctly, OCLC must be strong enough financially to enable it to help its member libraries grow stronger. This commitment is more important than ever as libraries face both opportunities and challenges in a rapidly evolving information landscape and many competing demands on the world's money and time.

PRO BONO

Since 1974, OCLC has engaged in and supported a host of activities that strengthen libraries. While there are too many initiatives to list here, one must note OCLC's hosting the cooperative Conversion of Serials (CONSER) Project, beginning in 1974. At the other end of the spectrum, in 1978, OCLC helped the Cambia County Library system reconstruct its card catalog after the disastrous Johnstown, PA flood of that year. Over the years, OCLC also has assisted the FBI in identifying the owners of stolen library materials, supported the development of the Dublin Core metadata mark up standard, and conducted and disseminated reports of environmental scans to help inform and strengthen library decision making. Libraries around the world are stronger because of this work by OCLC, work that does not generate revenue but that helps libraries and their users.

Forty years after OCLC's founding, the vision of its founders, and especially of Fred Kilgour, the wise man chosen by Ohio leaders to build the organization, continues to inform OCLC's strategic directions. From OCLC's very beginnings (indeed before OCLC's creation), Kilgour envisioned the creation of a cooperative database of bibliographic information and library holdings that would further scholarship by providing access to knowledge and promoting efficiencies in library operations. He envisioned OCLC as a truly global enterprise from the beginning.

KILGOUR'S VISION

Many librarians consider Kilgour's primary contribution as the creation and building of a database for shared cataloging records and the facilitation of resource sharing through online interlibrary loan. This is all true *and* important, but this is not the whole story, or perhaps even the most important aspect of the story. In a conversation between this author and Mr. Kilgour a few years before his death in 2006, OCLC's founding leader emphatically said that his original vision was not about sharing cataloging or even about sharing resources. Rather, he was committed to building a comprehensive database that would *promote learning* on a global level. Cataloging and interlibrary loan, as successful and transformative as they have been, were for him simply means to that greater purpose, as articulated in the statement of OCLC's public purpose.

Cooperation among libraries and librarians through the contribution of and sharing of intellectual resources always was core to Kilgour's vision for OCLC and has driven the OCLC enterprise from its inception. Thousands of librarians and others from around the world have—for more than 40 years—contributed their intellectual effort to build and improve the OCLC online union catalog, now known—aptly—as OCLC WorldCat. They have done that work as members of a cooperative expressly to help others seek information to support and encourage learning. OCLC has enabled that work by providing a continuously updated technological platform and by bringing together expert staff to preserve and enhance the original contributions of the members, to ensure the quality of those contributions, and to facilitate the equitable sharing of those contributions.

The extraordinary success of OCLC WorldCat is at its core the fulfillment of Fred Kilgour's vision. That success has been made possible both by the effort of countless librarians and by the dedication of a talented and committed body of OCLC staff to promote the sharing of intellectual effort and physical artifacts that contain information, and now virtual information, as well.

OCLC's success in sustaining its governance has been based on that willingness to share intellectual effort for the greater good of libraries and the users of libraries around the world. This idea has been transformative for libraries and librarians, but more importantly for the users of libraries. It is also at the heart of OCLC's governance structure.

In an earlier book, *OCLC 1967–1997: 30 Years of Furthering Access To the World's Information*, K. Wayne Smith, then President and CEO of OCLC, documented stage one and stage two of the evolution of OCLC's governance. This article has not focused on those stages except to discuss briefly the role of regional networks in OCLC's governance in the United States. Many of the regional networks were established in the 1970s in the early stages of OCLC governance. Conventional wisdom holds that the networks were established because OCLC lacked the infrastructure to train new users of OCLC services and to deal effectively with the hundreds—and later thousands—of libraries across the United States that wished to use OCLC's database for cataloging and, later, for interlibrary loan. Regional networks, which typically were non-profit corporations or entities of state government agencies, either existed in the early 1970s or were created for the purpose of both reselling "OCLC products and services" and providing the training support libraries needed to participate in the OCLC cooperative.

The whole picture is more complex. Mr. Kilgour, speaking in 1983, provided a very different view of the reason for the creation of the regional networks. He noted, "The Ohio membership ... would not approve operation outside Ohio except for extending the network into Pittsburgh ... so that the OCLC network would enjoy interstate long distance telephone charges ... A compromise involved three-year agreements with several library networks already in existence and with new networks incorporated for the prime purpose of signing agreements with OCLC. Because of Ohio's regionalistic position, it was intended that these networks would be operating independently by the end of the three years. Such was not to be. So there came into being the awkward system of independent regional networks using the OCLC system that has plagued OCLC, the networks, and participating libraries ever since" (Kilgour, 1985).

As a part of the fourth stage governance changes, the role of these U.S. regional networks in OCLC governance and, indeed, in the provision of OCLC products and services is being significantly changed. No longer will the networks be the "Members" of the new Global Council, electing delegates. No longer will networks "surcharge" libraries for provision of OCLC products and services. Rather, there will be uniform pricing throughout the United States with agreed upon standards for billing, training, and other services provided by the networks with reimbursement by OCLC. The member services that networks provided from these surcharges, some unrelated to OCLC products and services, may still be provided. However, leaders of libraries will have an opportunity to decide if they wish to avail their libraries of those network services by paying for them directly. Such a system provides for more transparency and allows libraries to decide what kinds of services they wish for the regional networks to provide.

A GLOBAL COUNCIL

This fourth stage of OCLC governance came about as a result of a study and report, Governance Study Committee: Final Report to the OCLC Board of Trustees (OCLC Governance Study Committee, 2007).

It was prepared by an OCLC Governance Committee appointed in 2007 by the OCLC Board of Trustees, mindful of the advice of the 1999–2000 advisory body. It was chaired by William Crowe, long-time trustee and former Board chair, and included current and former trustees, the then Members Council President, and the President-elect of the council, a Members Council delegate from Europe, and a retired executive director of a U.S. regional network. The committee's work was informed by the work of a consulting firm from the United Kingdom, itself a clear signal about the increasing globalization of OCLC and the issues: by 2008, OCLC was serving 11,674 member libraries in 112 countries, and for the first time OCLC WorldCat contained bibliographic records for more non-English than English language titles.

The 2007 report of this body was discussed extensively by both the Board of Trustees and the Members Council in early 2008. The final changes, ultimately approved by both bodies, called for a Board of Trustees with a more flexible size and composition but still with a majority of library and allied professionals. It also called for a transformation of the Members Council into a Global Council, with delegates elected from a number of newly forming "regional councils."

The concept of strong regional councils, coupled with a Global Council retaining the governance responsibilities of the predecessor bodies (e.g., Users Council, Members Council to advise OCLC, elect six trustees, ratify changes to the basic governance documents) is intended to create a strong connection to members around the world by ensuring representation in OCLC's governance at a global level. This new structure is being implemented with great excitement and optimism for the future. If it succeeds, the vision of the founders, not least of Fred Kilgour, to create a shared resource on a global scale to support learning—with libraries at the heart of that support—will continue to evolve. OCLC will bring together and focus the creativity of librarians, archivists, curators, and others working at the local level in a global cooperative enterprise.

REFERENCES

Arthur D. Little, Inc. (1978). *A new governance structure for OCLC: Principles and recommendations.* Metuchen, NJ: Scarecrow Press.
Kilgour, F. (1969). Initial System Design for the Ohio College Library Center: A Case History. In D. Carroll (Ed.), *Proceedings of the 1968 Clinic on Library*

Applications of Data Processing (pp. 79–88). Urbana, IL: University of Illinois, Graduate School of Library Science.

Kilgour, F. (1985) Resource sharing and information networks. *Experience and Expectation, 2,* 65–76.

OCLC Advisory Council. (2000). OCLC strategic directions and governance: Report of the Advisory Council. Dublin, OH: OCLC.

OCLC Governance Study Committee. (2007, November 12). Final report to the OCLC board of trustees. Dublin, Ohio. Retrieved September 16, 2009 from http://www.oclc.org/us/en/memberscouncil/documents/GovernanceStudyReport.pdf

A Brief History of the OCLC Members Council

GEORGE NEEDHAM

*Member and Cooperative Services, OCLC Online Computer Library Center, Inc.,
Dublin, OH, USA*

RICHARD VAN ORDEN

OCLC Members Council, Online Computer Library Center, Inc., Dublin, OH, USA

ABSTRACT. *On May 19, 2009, the Online Computer Library Center
(OCLC) Members Council held its 90th and final meeting. It was the
end of an era that began in 1977, when the Ohio College Library
Center changed its name to OCLC and adopted a new governance
structure that extended membership in the cooperative to libraries
outside Ohio. In the ensuing 30 years, libraries around the world
elected 450 delegates to attend three Council meetings each year at
OCLC.*

As Users Council, and later, as the Members Council, delegates were invested
with three main duties to:

1. Elect six members of the OCLC Board of Trustees on a regular basis.
2. Ratify proposed changes to the Articles of Incorporation and Code of
   Regulations of OCLC.
3. Provide the Board and OCLC management with advice, representing member interests and concerns.

Victoria Hanawalt served as President of the Users Council in 1996–1997.
She later chronicled the first 20 years of Council's history in an article,
"Users Council: an Institutionalized Role for Libraries in OCLC's Governance"
(Hannawalt, 1998). In looking back on the first 20 years she noted that the

Council had indeed provided a national forum for articulating member library interests to OCLC as well as a training ground for preparing individuals with library expertise to assume the responsibilities of governing the organization. She also looked to the future, noting that the Council's representation and mode of operation would need periodic attention in the decades to come. She asked how the growth of international membership would be accommodated in the composition of the Council and predicted virtual meetings someday. The first virtual Members Council was held in February of 2009.

Over the next decade, the Council addressed the issues and concerns that Ms. Hanawalt raised, as the rate of change affecting libraries and OCLC continued to accelerate. The demographics of the cooperative expanded dramatically. From 1998 to 2008, the number of institutions participating in OCLC increased from 30,000 to 69,840. The number of participating institutions outside the United States rose from 3,200 to 14,627. OCLC governing member libraries (those institutions that contributed to WorldCat and participated in the election of Council delegates) went from 1,700 to 11,871. The cumulative number of Council delegates elected from outside the United States now totals 30.

This article reviews the activities of the OCLC Members Council in its third and final decade, as libraries and OCLC moved toward becoming a truly global cooperative.

The 1998–1999 Users Council focused on the theme, "Digital Library Futures: Libraries, OCLC and New Models of Cooperation. In three meetings, delegates examined likely scenarios for further development of the digital library over the next 5 years. The Council's message to OCLC was to continue as a leader in working with libraries and others to advance the digital library in such areas as metadata standards. The January 1999 meeting was cancelled for the first and only time in Council's history because of severe winter weather in Dublin, Ohio.

Delegates also turned their attention to the rights and duties of OCLC members as new technological options, such as the World Wide Web, continued to surface in the library community. They reaffirmed the principles of cooperation adopted in 1994 that were intended to ensure the continuing viability of the WorldCat database and related services to the library and information community. They urged OCLC to provide increased support and options for libraries to help them contribute records and holdings to WorldCat and pressed for improved compliance with the principles through communication and education.

1999 GOVERNANCE STUDY

By the late 1990s, the need for change in the structure and composition of Users Council had become obvious to many of the varied stakeholders in the OCLC cooperative. Two key problems with the existing structure were apparent. First, the Council had almost no international representation at a time when OCLC was expanding its service centers for Europe, Asia, and Canada, as well as establishing a new base in Latin America. Second, OCLC's newest services were not counted in the algorithm for allocating Council delegates to regional service providers. Since the governance structure was adopted in 1977, the only activities that counted were contributing or enhancing cataloging records (original or copy cataloging and online or batch-load) or adding holdings to WorldCat and resource sharing through the Interlibrary Loan subsystem.

In November 1999, the Board of Trustees commissioned a study "to determine how OCLC can best organize its governance to achieve its global vision" (OCLC Web site, 1999). The Board also created a Strategic Directions and Advisory Council to steer the consulting firm of Arthur D. Little that was doing the study and to present recommendations for any changes to the Board. Noteworthy is that Arthur D. Little did OCLC's first governance study in 1977, which originally resulted in the creation of Users Council.

The 1999–2000 Users Council worked closely with the Advisory Council and the consultants. Delegates spent some 5 hours in sessions with the consultants. They provided thoughtful feedback and insights to a series of questions on OCLC's strategic directions and governance. What role options exist for OCLC in the digital age? How are libraries converging, diverging, or changing? What principal overall corporate strategic options should OCLC pursue? What changes, if any, should be made to OCLC's governance structure to enable it to become a global library cooperative? Users Council held an unprecedented meeting at the American Library Association (ALA) Annual Conference in Chicago in July 2000 to continue discussions regarding governance changes. In addition, members of the Advisory Council and OCLC staff participated in more than a dozen network and service center meetings to discuss the progress of the study and gather ideas from members.

In addition to governance discussions, the 1999–2000 Users Council looked at how OCLC and its regional networks could help libraries flourish in a global knowledge society. The Council's year-long theme was "The New World: OCLC, Libraries and Users in the 21st Century." Two well-known leaders in the worldwide library community, Christine Deschamps, President of IFLA, and Gary Strong, Director of the Queens Borough Public Library in New York, described the benefits and difficulties associated with participating globally while expanding library services locally. Delegates also discussed environmental trends affecting libraries and their users.

The 1999–2000 Users Council closed out its year on May 23, 2000, with a 2 hour satellite broadcast viewed by more than 5,000 persons in libraries around the world. Delegates met in a television studio to hear presentations on libraries, their users, and OCLC. A distinguished group of panelists answered questions phoned in by viewers.

USERS COUNCIL BECOMES MEMBERS COUNCIL

The 2000–2001 Users Council continued to work closely with the Board on proposed changes to OCLC's governance structure. There was another special meeting on governance held at the ALA Midwinter Meeting in January 2001 in Washington, DC. On May 21, 2001, by a vote of 60–0, Users Council delegates ratified amendments to OCLC's governance structure proposed by the Board of Trustees that changed the name of Users Council to Members Council and added six delegates from outside the United States to Members Council for 3-year terms. (There were three delegates from outside the United States on the 2000–2001 Council.)

In addition, the Board established a Standing Joint Committee on Membership, composed of representatives from the Board, Members Council, and U.S. regional networks and service centers, to recommend changes in the ways of valuing different types of contribution to the OCLC cooperative.

In their non-governance discussions, delegates focused on "The Library as Virtual Place." They explored virtual library models and concepts such as "library.org" and "the library as the portal of choice" which were then in use to describe collaborative activities of libraries to provide enhanced access to information resources.

In 2001–2002, Members Council welcomed new delegates from China, France, Japan, Mexico, the Netherlands, and South Africa. These "transitional" delegates, so named because they would help to transition OCLC from a national to a global cooperative, would have full voting rights, be eligible for election to Council office or the Board of Trustees, and serve 3-year terms on Members Council. In 2003 the transition period was extended for 3 more years, from 2004 to 2007. Two new transitional delegates would be elected then from each of three OCLC international service centers: OCLC Asia Pacific, OCLC PICA, and OCLC Latin America and the Caribbean. Canada already had an elected delegate to Council based on its usage of the OCLC system

INCREASED OPPORTUNITIES FOR PARTICIPATION

Delegates explored expanding the definition of OCLC membership in a global environment. They began to broadcast part of their meetings via the Web. In addition, Council passed the "Statement on Principles of Membership of the OCLC Collaborative," which served as a guide for the Ad Hoc Committee on Membership and the Board as they revised the definition of membership in the Code of Regulations.

In May 2002, the Council ratified amendments to the OCLC Code of Regulations proposed by the Board that provided more opportunities for participation in OCLC cooperative by more libraries and knowledge institutions around the world. There were now three levels of participation in OCLC: governing members, members, and participants. Depending on the extent of a library's engagement in contributing bibliographic records and interlibrary loan transactions to the cooperative (namely whether all or some holdings added to OCLC WorldCat and participating in the Interlibrary Loan Subsystem), the respective rights and responsibilities were different. Governing members elected delegates to Members Council, whereas member librarians could be elected to Council, but they could not participate in the vote to elect them.

TRACKING SIGNIFICANT ISSUES

The focus of the 2002–2003 Council was two-fold: "Libraries, Their Present and Future Global Environment: National, Regional, Local" and "OCLC Strategic Plans and Measurements for Success." Both were required for delegates to better understand and contribute to the future develop of OCLC. In tracking the progress of globalization, 2002 delegates intensified their focus on global issues in librarianship as well as national, regional, and local levels (OLCL Member's Council, 2002) Delegates' discussions contributed to the 2004 publication of *Pattern Recognition: The 2003 OCLC Environmental Scan* (DeRosa, Lorcan, & Wilson, 2004). A task force on staff development looked into the role of OCLC in assisting libraries in preparing their staff members for the changes in the library environment. The task force made several recommendations adopted by OCLC, including:

- Creation of a Web site that brings together the learning opportunities offered by OCLC and its regional networks (OCLC, 2005)
- Evaluation of the effective use of digital collections and user behavior in the realm of digitized information (OCLC Office of Research, 2004)
- Creation of a Web site that listed standards activities in which OCLC is engaged, to help promote such standards in the library community (Various Web sites)

Also in 2002–2003, Council adopted a process for improving the continuity of discussions with OCLC staff called the Significant Issues Reports, whereby each service group records any important issues that come up in its meetings which should receive further attention from OCLC management and/or the Council's own Executive Committee. The collected and de-duplicated list of issues is then forwarded to the appropriate units within OCLC for a response from management. These responses are then returned to the groups before the next Council meeting for further discussion or to make specific recommendations for action. Thus, Members Council and OCLC management are engaged in an ongoing circle of communication that keeps both groups better informed. (In 2007–2008, delegates sent 39 significant issues to OCLC management for responses, compared to 47 in 2006–2007, and 57 in 2005.)

From 2003–2004, delegates returned to the "WorldCat Principles of Co-operation" and added new language that addressed recent technological developments. A Committee on Communications for the Cooperative reviewed the various ways OCLC and the regional networks communicate with members. The committee reported on survey findings that indicated the top two ways members find out about what OCLC is doing are e-mails from the networks (favored by 61% of respondents) and the *OCLC Newsletter* (favored by 58%) (Ad Hoc Committee on Communication for the OCLC Member Council, 2004). These results led to changes in the *Newsletter*, making it more feature-oriented and colorful. It also led to revitalization of the weekly e-mail publication called *OCLC Abstracts* that focuses on new products and services from OCLC, services from the regional networks, lists new members, and highlights news from the information environment that affects libraries (OCLC Abstracts).

In 2004–2005, Council's theme was "Pattern Recognition: Moving Libraries Beyond Their Comfort Zones." Delegates provided OCLC with valuable advice and guidance as OCLC began the Open WorldCat Pilot, which studied the feasibility of making WorldCat records and library holdings available to the general public on the open Web via search engines such as Google and Yahoo! A task force was created to study how libraries and OCLC might shape future directions of electronic content.

In 2005–2006, delegates explored how to help make the OCLC cooperative more inclusive of libraries and cultural heritage centers worldwide and still develop revenue to sustain and further ongoing activities. Delegates also examined rural and small libraries to ensure that the cooperative "leaves no library behind" (Farrell, 2005). Members Council also finalized a report on electronic content that included recommendations for expanding access to electronic resources through OCLC products. Delegates held discussions on the role of networks and service centers in a rapidly changing global environment. This relationship would continue to be redefined and negotiated as services and products evolve along with the collaborative. It was noted that Members Council's role in these discussions would be to ensure all services are responsive to member libraries and that the underlying structure fulfills the needs of libraries (Farrell, 2005).

MEETING IN QUEBEC CITY

In 2006–2007, Ernie Ingles, Vice-Provost and Chief Librarian, University of Alberta, served as the first President of Members Council from outside the United States. In February 2007, the Council also met outside the United

States for the first time—in Quebec City, Quebec, Canada. Council monitored the progress of the RLG-OCLC integration, discussed relationships between libraries and other memory institutions, and provided input to the Governance Study. The Task Force on Integration of E-books presented a report on how libraries and OCLC can integrate e-books into library services and collections. Delegates also help evaluate OCLC products and services in the global marketplace. There were 13 delegates from outside the United States on the 2006–2007 Council (Ingles, 2006).

2007: ANOTHER GOVERNANCE STUDY

In April 2007, the Board of Trustees began another review of OCLC's governance structure. In announcing the study, OCLC Board Chair Lizabeth Wilson stated, "As OCLC becomes an increasingly global cooperative, it has also become clear that we need to adjust our governance to ensure representation and participation by our members around the world."

The 2007–2008 Members Council reviewed the work done by the Governance Study Committee of the Board of Trustees and provided input into their deliberations. At the recommendation of the Members Council Executive Committee, OCLC management established a Small Libraries Advisory Committee to work to improve access to information resources for small and rural libraries. Delegates also unanimously adopted a resolution presented by the Task Force on E-book Integration that urged OCLC to provide eContent to libraries worldwide.

On May 20, 2008, the Members Council ratified changes to OCLC's governance structure proposed by the Board of Trustees. These changes are discussed elsewhere in the volume and include the creation of regional councils that will send delegates to a Global Council. At this writing, Members Council delegates were working hard on the transformation to the new structure.

2008–2009: THE FINAL YEAR OF MEMBERS COUNCIL

"Embracing the Differences: Greater Understanding, Modeling, and Celebrating the Global Cooperative" was the theme of the 2000–2009 Members Council. Under the leadership of President Loretta Parham, Library Director and CEO, The Atlanta University Center, delegates convened for the last three meetings of the OCLC Members Council.

Throughout the year, the Members Council Executive Committee worked with the Transition Committee of the Board on implementing the new governance structure of regional councils and a global council.

In November, OCLC revised its nearly 20 year old record use policy; announcement of the changes generated controversy in the library community.

Members Council and the OCLC Board of Trustees jointly convened a Review Board of Shared Data Creation and Stewardship to get feedback from the membership and inform OCLC on the principles and best practices for sharing library data. A final report was scheduled to be submitted to the OCLC Board in May 2009. In the meantime, OCLC delayed implementation of the Policy until the third quarter of the 2009 calendar year.

The Council conducted a virtual meeting February 9–11, 2009, to discuss opportunities and challenges confronting the global information community, to learn more about collaborative services, and to continue the transition to a Global Council and Regional Councils. The virtual meeting was also an experiment in which delegates learned about virtual meeting technology and its applicability to the forthcoming Global Council and Regional Council meetings. Delegates evaluating the virtual meeting gave it high marks.

Delegates voted to ratify the Global Council Bylaws as approved by the OCLC Board of Trustees and also approved new Membership and Governance Protocols and referred them to the Board with the recommendation that the Board approve them.

Council discussed and passed two resolutions proposed by the Members Council Executive Committee. The first provided for the establishment of implementation committees that will organize three Regional Councils. These regional committees are chaired respectively by Chew Leng Beh, from the Asia Pacific region; Berndt Dugall, Direktor and Librarian, Universitat Frankfurt, from the Europe, the Middle East and Africa region; and Patrick Wilkinson, Director, University of Wisconsin-Oshkosh, from The Americas region.

A second resolution defined the process for transitioning to a Global Council Executive Committee, a group that includes the three regional committee chairs. Jan Ison, Executive director, Lincoln Trail Libraries system (ILLINET), current Members Council vice president/ president-elect, will serve as the first president of the new OCLC Global Council in 2009–2010.

The new Regional Councils and Global Council will serve as key discussion forums and major communications links among members, networks, and OCLC. The Regional Councils will send delegates to the Global Council, whose responsibilities are similar to those of the Members Council: elect six members of the Board of Trustees; ratify changes to the Articles of Incorporation; and provide OCLC with advice and counsel.

IMPACT OF MEMBERS COUNCIL

Throughout its history, Members Council frequently addressed the importance of membership and contribution to the cooperative. The "Statement on Principles of Membership of the OCLC Collaborative" adopted by Council in February 2002 includes such member commitments as:

- Share collections, metadata, best practices, and expertise without expectations of parity
- Promote internationally accepted standards to facilitate resource sharing and information exchange
- Participate in and work to enhance the governance structure of OCLC through Members Council and the Board of Trustees
- Promote responsible use of OCLC-derived records by approved users (OCLC Members Council, 2002)

Council also made recommendations that resulted in new OCLC services. For example, it urged OCLC to implement the ILL Fee Management (IFM) service, which simplifies transfer of small payments among libraries to reimburse each other for resource sharing. A long debate among the membership and within the OCLC staff had ensued about the advisability of OCLC facilitating libraries in charging one another for ILL. Council passed a resolution encouraging the organization to move forward with this service which saves libraries hundreds of thousands of dollars each year in staff costs. Delegates later made a similar recommendation for institutions exchanging digital documents among themselves. More recently in a discussion of the future of WorldCat, delegates were excited about and strongly suggested the concept of it becoming a local catalog. About three years later, OCLC WorldCat Local was introduced.

Under the new governance structure, the regional councils and OCLC Global Council will keep open the communication flow and have the potential to move the OCLC global community further towards a collaborative focused on collectively meeting user needs and beyond—even beyond a cooperative to a more productive, socially networked and engaged member environment of the fast-moving, but challenging 21st century world of information!

The Members Council frequently has been referred to as the voice of the OCLC membership. Over the past 30 years, its deliberations have contributed to OCLC's strategic directions and provided valuable feedback on operations and policies. Delegates have taken time from their busy schedules to participate in Members Council, and their contributions have benefitted institutions across the OCLC global cooperative. The more than 70,000 libraries in 112 countries who have contributed to OCLC owe them a deep debt of gratitude!

REFERENCES

Ad Hoc Committee on Communication for the Collaborative. (2004). *OCLC Members Council*. Final Report. Unpublished.
De Rosa, C., Dempsey, L., & Wilson, A. (2004). The 2003 OCLC Environmental Scan: Pattern Recognition. *A Report to the OCLC Membership*. Retrieved September 18, 2009 from http://www.oclc.org/membership/reports/escan/

Farrell, M. (2005–2006). Members Council Report. *OCLC Annual Report*, 40.

Hannawalt, V. (1998). Victor,"Users Council: An Institutionalized Role for Libraries in OCLC's Governance.," In *OCLC, 1967–1997, Thirty Years of Furthering Access to the World's Information* (pp. 11–18).: Haworth Press, New York: 1999.

Ingles, E. (2006–2007). Members Council Report. *OCLC Annual Report 2006/7002*, 36.

OCLC Members Council. (2002). Members Council 2002/2003 Annual Plan.

OCLC Members Council. (2002). *Statement on Principles of Membership of the OCLC Collaborative.*

OCLC Office of Research. (2004). *Sense-Making the Information Confluence: The Whys and Hows of College and University User Satisficing of Information Needs.* Retrieved from http://www.oclc.org/research/projects/imls/default.htm.

OCLC. (2004). *Online training from U.S. regional service providers.*

OCLC will be the leading global library cooperative, helping libraries serve people by providing economical access to knowledge through innovation and collaboration. (1999). *Mission, vision and quality policy statements.* Retrieved May 15, 2009 from http://www.oclc.org/about/mission/default.htm

Subscriptions to *OCLC Abstracts* are available at http://www.oclc.org/news/abstracts/subscribe.htm. Other OCLC publications may be viewed at http://www.oclc.org/news/publications/default.htm.

Various Web sites have promoted network and service center training.

RLG and OCLC: Combined for the Future

LIZABETH WILSON

University Libraries, University of Washington, Seattle, WA, USA

JAMES NEAL

Columbia University Libraries, Columbia University, New York, NY, USA

JAMES MICHALKO

Research Libraries Group, OCLC Online Computer Library System, Inc., San Mateo, CA, USA

JAY JORDAN

OCLC Online Computer Library Center, Inc., Dublin, OH, USA

On July 1, 2006, The Research Libraries Group, Inc. (RLG) and the Online Computer Library System (OCLC) combined their organizations and resources. RLG's products and services were integrated with OCLC's, and RLG's program initiatives went forward within an expanded OCLC Research division. This was a historic moment for libraries and research institutions consonant with the incredible changes in the information environment that had been underway during the previous decade. The expansion of WorldCat that resulted and the renewed attention given to research libraries by OCLC in the merger has positively impacted libraries around the globe.

The history of OCLC is well-known and restated elsewhere in this issue. Readers may not be as familiar with RLG. It was founded in 1974 with the express goal of reducing institutional costs of acquisitions, shared cataloging, preservation, resource sharing, and communications. Over time that goal was met in many ways and for many constituencies by blending managed collaboration and innovative service provision. This combination of an operational capacity with an institutional willingness to work jointly delivered a legacy of progress. Here are a few of the many things the RLG collaborative achieved together:

- Built a catalog of remarkable breadth and depth that met the essential management needs of librarians and archivists that grew to the point where it also met the research information needs of students and scholars.
- Built a trusted global community of institutions who borrow and loan materials so that researchers could do their work better.
- Took on the brittle paper challenge and collectively managed the preservation of thousands of at-risk volumes and saved them for the future.
- Helped the research library community gain deeper understandings of research collections and how collecting patterns could influence collaborative collection development.
- Fundamentally redefined the description and discovery of primary resources and changed the way users of original source materials sought and made use of the rare, the special, and the unique.
- Created communities of interest, professional associations, and interactions that transformed careers and informed a generation of library leaders.

RLG took research and scholarship as its starting point. Expanding access to research resources was the overarching goal that informed RLG's agenda for 32 years across huge shifts in technology, audiences, economics, expectations, and institutional roles. RLG's reason for existence was to help research institutions face and manage the transformational challenges.

The merger with OCLC was done in order to transform the organization so that it could most effectively continue to address those challenges. Combining the RLG ethos and experience with OCLC's capacities and practices established a renewed collective for research institutions.

WHY DID THE MERGER HAPPEN WHEN IT DID?

During 2005 both OCLC and RLG were engaged in comparable future planning efforts. Both organizations were feeling an urgent need to find innovative, cost-effective, and compelling ways to bring library collections into the heart of the online environment and into the hands of those who can benefit from them.

In April 2005, James Neal, Chair of the RLG Board of Directors, and Lizabeth Wilson, Chair of the OCLC Board of Trustees, had a conversation. Both organizations had been cooperating in several areas—preservation standards, CJK record exchange, and sharing of bibliographic information—for some time, but both believed that more could be done. Was there a way toward a deeper collaboration? Were the organizations ready to do something bold?

Those questions set in motion a year-long exploration of issues, and board negotiating groups from both organizations began high-level conversations. Their goal was to see if they shared a similar vision and commitment to serve the future needs of research institutions.

Those discussions were held off and on for more than a year under a strict confidentiality agreement. The motivation was the future of both organizations and the value that each was able to deliver, and ought to be delivering, to the research community. During these interactions it became clear that OCLC sought to renew and grow its support for research institutions, that RLG was constrained by resources and scope from doing all the things that would be needed and wanted by research institutions, and that the institutions served by both organizations would benefit from economies achieved through service integration.

Both boards recognized that maintaining two very large union catalogs in parallel had ceased serving the best interests of the community. Further, economies of scale could be achieved—in staffing as well as in the services arena—if the two organizations could find a way to work more closely.

Equally important, the RLG board and management acknowledged that RLG had reached the point in its evolution where it could be more effective at its historic strengths in combination with OCLC. The RLG Board was concerned that RLG in its current configuration and with its existing resource constraints might not be able to deliver the collective capacities needed by research institutions for the future.

RLG's Board concluded that its aspiration to deliver an exceptional agenda in support of research and learning in its growing membership of libraries, archives, and museums would be best realized if it were to focus on applied research, community building, and prototyping of systems and services and to do that in combination with OCLC.

The negotiations and agreement were accomplished over the course of the next 12 months by involving the presidents and chief executive officers of RLG, James Michalko, and OCLC, Jay Jordan, and a small cadre of senior leaders of both organizations from the onset.

On June 9, the RLG membership approved the proposal of the RLG and OCLC boards that the two organizations be combined. On July 1, 2006, the two organizations merged.

There were two key components to the proposed combination—the integration of RLG's programs into OCLC Research creating a new venue for research institution interests and the integration of RLG's online products and services with OCLC's service lines.

WHAT WAS CREATED?

By allying RLG's programmatic work with OCLC's research efforts the agreement created the leading venue for applied research, community building, and the prototyping of future systems and services in support of research and learning through libraries, archives, museums, and related cultural heritage institutions world wide.

This renewed group continues RLG's practices of identifying needs and working with the research-institution community to address them. It builds on the existing programmatic efforts and interest areas of RLG and the existing research agenda of OCLC Research. It has an agenda that is refined and focused with the input of the RLG Partnership. The current state of the RLG Partnership and its work is covered elsewhere in this issue.

WHAT WAS INTEGRATED?

RLG and OCLC provided their members and customers with a rich and complex set of services that had to be integrated in the most responsible way to preserve functionalities that are valued by research institutions while achieving economies desired by both organizations.

OCLC and RLG managers created transition teams and crafted detailed plans. The implementation started quickly and ensured the smoothest possible transition for both RLG and OCLC constituencies. These teams accomplished a complex set of activities in record time including:

- The RLG Union Catalog was integrated into WorldCat
- RLG's specialized databases—Hand Press Book and the Art Sales Catalog database (SCIPIO)—were integrated into OCLC's FirstSearch suite of databases
- ArchiveGrid was continued and expanded
- RedLightGreen features were incorporated into WorldCat.org
- RLG's resource sharing partnership—SHARES—was transitioned to a new support platform and continued

THE FUTURE REALIZED

More than two years after the merger, the integration of the organizations is complete. OCLC staff has been augmented by a rich talent pool of skilled practitioners. It has expanded its horizons in the museum and archive community. OCLC Research is providing new benefit to the library community, the OCLC cooperative, and the RLG Partnership. At the time of the merger Lizabeth Wilson and Jim Neal predicted, "In the years to come, we know that we will look back and say that this was a seminal event in the history of librarianship." Given what has been accomplished, the four authors of this article concur in that expectation.

NOTES

RLG Board

- James Neal, Vice President for Information Services, Columbia University
- David Cohen, former Vice President for Arts and Sciences and Dean of the Faculty, Columbia University
- David Ferriero, Andrew W. Mellon Director and Chief Executive, The Research Libraries at The New York Public Library
- Carol Mandel, Dean, Division of Libraries, New York University

OCLC Board

- Lizabeth Wilson, Dean of University Libraries, University of Washington
- Larry Alford, Vice Provost for Libraries and University Librarian, Temple University
- Edward W. Barry, President Emeritus, Oxford University Press
- William Crowe, Spencer Librarian, Kenneth Spencer Research Library, University of Kansas

OCLC in the Asia Pacific Region

ANTHONY W. FERGUSON
University of Hong Kong Libraries, Hong Kong, China

ANDREW WANG
OCLC Online Computer Library Center Inc., Dublin, OH, USA

This essay provides an overview of both the accomplishments and difficulties faced by OCLC as it has expanded in the vast Asia Pacific region. It describes the organizational changes as they evolved as this previously North American collaborative organization expanded westward and details initiatives pursued in each of the Asia Pacific countries where it has operated. Finally, it examines the five major challenges yet facing OCLC in the region: the lack of bibliographic name authority files, competing classification systems, competing MARC cataloging formats, the perceived high costs associated with participating OCLC programs and services, and the need for local vernacular products in addition to those developed largely for the North American and European markets.

BACKGROUND

Any discussion of OCLC in the Asia Pacific region has to begin with the realization that this part of the world is big in every way. As Table 1 suggests, it is geographically larger, has more people, and includes more countries than any of the other continents/regions where the Online Computer Library Center (OCLC) is operating. While on the surface, these figures suggest the growth outlook for an information services organization like OCLC is virtually unlimited, these three factors: size, population, and political complexity, however, pose enormous challenges for OCLC as it seeks to accomplish its goal of "connecting people to knowledge through library cooperation." The geographical distances between countries that must be visited by service

TABLE 1 Continents Compared: Size, Population, and Countries

	Sq. KM (Millions)	2005 Population (Millions)	No. Countries
Asia	**44.6**	**3,879**	**46**
Africa	30.1	8,77	53
North America	24.3	501	23
South America	17.9	379	12
Antarctica	13.2	0	0
Europe	9.9	727	46
Australia/Oceana	**7.7**	**32**	**14**

Worldatlas.com (2008).

representatives mean serious time and cost constraints. The large numbers of people translate into disparate kinds of needs that must be understood, let alone met for OCLC to succeed. Sixty countries mean the need to navigate through 60 different sets of cultural attitudes about the importance of information and libraries, scores of languages, and equally innumerable ways of doing business.

Another key factor that must be examined when discussing OCLC in the Asia Pacific region is the amount of resources available for libraries. A key reason for the success of OCLC in North America has been its ability to make good on the promise to help libraries save money—or at least reduce the rate in the rise of library costs. To succeed in Asia Pacific libraries, OCLC must also recognize that the librarians there also will want to experience cost savings. But this is no easy task. The differences in the levels of available wealth between North America and parts of Asia Pacific are enormous. The 2007 per capita GDP figure for the United States was $45,800 while the figure for China was $5,300, and for Bangladesh $1,300 per person (Central Intelligence Agency, 2008). If OCLC is going to help libraries in poorer countries save money, the range of services and products it offers not only have to be different but also much less expensive.

Irrespective of all of these problems, OCLC is gradually assuming a larger presence in the Asia Pacific region. Currently Asia Pacific has three representatives on Members Council: Beh Chew Leng, Senior Director, Library and Professional Services, National Library Board, Singapore; Jieh Hsiang, Professor of Computer Science, Director of the University Press and immediate past University Librarian, National Taiwan University Library; and Vic Elliot Director, Scholarly Information Services and University Librarian, the Australian National University. Anthony W. Ferguson, the University of Hong Kong Librarian, after having served on Members Council for 4 years, will shortly begin his term on the OCLC Board of Trustees. OCLC now is a truly global library cooperative.

ORGANIZATIONAL EXPANSION

In 1986, OCLC expanded its cataloging capabilities to support Chinese, Japanese, and Korean (CJK) scripts. This was a big step for OCLC if it was going to globalize its library information services. This enabled them to go beyond only providing information services in countries using the Roman alphabet.

OCLC was ready to move forward organizationally in that same year when Japan hosted the International Federation of Library Associations and Institutions (IFLA) annual meeting in Tokyo. At that time it made the strategic decision to open its OCLC Asia Pacific Office—still headquartered in Ohio—but with eyes focused westward. The goals for this new office were to extend OCLC's services, to support library cooperation at the country/regional level, and to weave these country/regional cooperatives into the OCLC global cooperative fabric.

Since that time, OCLC has made real progress. It is now serving more than 5,000 libraries in the region. In the fiscal year 2007–2008, which ended on June 30, 2008, OCLC provided library information services to institutions in the following 24 countries and territories in Asia and the Pacific region: Australia, Bangladesh, Brunei, China (Mainland), Fiji, Hong Kong, India, Indonesia, Japan, Korea, Laos, Macau, Malaysia, Maldives, New Zealand, Pakistan, Palau Islands, Papua New Guinea, Philippines, Singapore, Sri Lanka, Taiwan, Thailand, and Viet Nam.

On July 20, 2007, OCLC made another strategic decision when it established the OCLC Beijing Representative Office to better serve libraries in China. One year later it inherited through acquisition two additional offices in Australia in Melbourne and Perth. OCLC now has a total of three offices in the region, in addition to the Asia Pacific office in Ohio, all focused on improving the delivery of its services and programs.

MAJOR INITIATIVES

One of the main tactics employed by OCLC in the region has been to sign agreements with existing library cooperatives in order to market itself to hundreds of libraries all at the same time. The following selective overview of cooperative relationships entered into by OCLC's Asia Pacific Office reflects this method of operation during the past 22 years since its establishment. Where no such opportunities presented themselves, they have worked with individual libraries.

Australia

Through an agreement between the National Library of Australia and OCLC in 2007, the National Library began loading its national union catalog into

WorldCat. Consequently, all 1,072 libraries contributing to the Australian database became governing members and can participate in OCLC's global cooperative cataloging and resource sharing programs. This agreement builds upon OCLC's earlier cooperation since 1994 with the Council of Australian University Librarians (CAUL) to provide FirstSearch services to all university libraries.

China

Through a 2008 agreement between the National Library of China and OCLC, the National Library began using OCLC Connexion Service to catalog its collections on WorldCat and to load its Chinese records into WorldCat for global resource sharing. This development builds upon earlier OCLC efforts in China (e.g., cooperation with the China Academic Library and Information System (CALIS) universities in China to provide access to OCLC FirstSearch Service and NetLibrary eBooks). A total of four libraries in China are now governing members.

Hong Kong

As early as 1995, the Chinese University of Hong Kong had contracted with OCLC to bibliographically convert parts of its collections. Gradually, seven of the eight universities in Hong Kong, making up the Joint University Librarians Advisory Committee (JULAC), joined OCLC as governing members and both catalog all newly acquired titles on WorldCat and participate in its resource sharing activities. The year 2005 was a big year for Hong Kong and OCLC. In 2005, OCLC contracted with JULAC to share the latter's Hong Kong Chinese Authority Name (HKCAN) project with libraries worldwide and in the same year many of Hong Kong's academic libraries joined in on the Super eBook Consortium that purchased 42,085 English-language OCLC NetLibrary e-books. This mainly Taiwan-promoted consortium was led by a Hong Kong librarian who had formerly worked in Taiwan and included 42 libraries from there and six from Hong Kong.

Japan

In 2002 OCLC established a relationship with Japan's National Institute of Informatics (NII), a consortium of 703 government and private university libraries for interlibrary loan services and another in 2005 for access to the WorldCat database. Following this agreement, one of these member libraries at Waseda University decided to load its post 1995 holdings into WorldCat and have continued to the present (Niimoto, 2004). Subsequently, five more joined as OCLC governing member libraries in Japan.

Korea

In 1999, cooperative agreements were established with the Korea Education and Research Information Service (KERIS) to "provide online cataloging, interlibrary loan, and OCLC FirstSearch services to university students, faculty members, and researchers in Korea" (Korea Education and Research Information Service, 2008). Subsequently a collection of NetLibrary e-books was acquired for the use of students and faculty members at 70 university libraries. Only two libraries in Korea are governing members.

Malaysia

In 2002, the Sarawak State Library became the first library in Malaysia to join OCLC as a governing member, and the Kolej Universiti Sains Dan Teknologi followed a year later.

New Zealand

In 2007, OCLC signed an agreement with the National Library of New Zealand to load its union catalog into WorldCat and for all of its member libraries to participate in the global cooperative cataloging and resource sharing programs. Because their bibliographic records continue to be added to the WorldCat database, all 285 libraries also are considered governing members of OCLC. Additionally, since 1994 through cooperation with Council of New Zealand University Librarians (CONZUL), OCLC had provided FirstSearch service to all the university libraries of New Zealand.

Singapore

In 2000, the Singapore Integrated Library Automation Services (SILAS) entered into a cooperative agreement with OCLC, the first such agreement with OCLC in Asia and the Pacific region. Since SILAS loaded the national union catalog of Singapore into WorldCat for global resource sharing and cataloging purposes, all of the 97 participating libraries in Singapore became OCLC governing members. SILAS has also introduced OCLC's FirstSearch Service and WorldCat Collection Analysis Service to libraries in Singapore.

Taiwan

In 2006, OCLC entered into an agreement with 214 libraries to establish the Taiwan OCLC Governing Members Consortium. Previously, in 1999, OCLC forged a cooperative agreement with the Consortium on Core Electronic

Resources in Taiwan (CONCERT) to provide FirstSearch to its libraries. This was followed by an agreement in 2002 with the Taiwan eBook Network (TEBNET) to purchase e-books from OCLC NetLibrary, the first library consortium in Asia and the Pacific to establish such an agreement. Together, these agreements helped the libraries of Taiwan take an active part in OCLC's global cooperative resource sharing and cataloging initiatives.

Thailand

In 2008, Thammasat University became the first OCLC Governing Member in Thailand. This is a major step forward for OCLC in Southeast Asia. Earlier in Thailand in 2003, 30 private and public universities, the Thai University eBook Net, and in 2004 another group, the University Network of Thailand (UNINET) had purchased OCLC NetLibrary e-books

SUMMARY AND REMAINING CHALLENGES

Enormous progress has been made since 1986 when OCLC decided to establish its presence in the Asia Pacific region. It now has three offices focused on the needs of Asia Pacific's librarians and their readers, and there is representation from the region on its Members Council and Board of Trustees governing bodies. OCLC has made agreements with four national cataloging organizations to upload their records into WorldCat. In all, there are a total of 1,717 governing member libraries in OCLC from the region.

While all of this reflects the progress that has been made, OCLC has literally only touched the surface. Asia Pacific's huge territory, population and countries all translate into the need for information and huge numbers of libraries. While there are no comprehensive directories of libraries in the region, a review of online resources for just a few of the region's countries produces numbers similar to the following: Japan 47,287 libraries, Korea 11,754 libraries, and Malaysia 10,362 libraries. And these are small countries compared to India, Indonesia, and China where the numbers of libraries are much larger.

With so many libraries, what are the major challenges that must be faced by OCLC? The following is only a partial list:

1. Authority files. Shared cataloging assumes shared authority files. When that doesn't exist, the work is much more difficult.
2. Classification schemes. The Dewey versus LC classification disagreements, when both numbers are in most shared cataloging records, do not any longer amount to much in North America. In Asia Pacific, however, the

picture is much more complicated and this poses a huge challenge for an organization like OCLC, which thrives on homogeneity of need.

3. MARC formats. Contributing to and benefitting from the WorldCat bibliographic database assumes that everyone employs the same bibliographic record standards. There are multiple MARC formats just in the Chinese speaking countries and the idea that everyone do things following the same cataloging rules is seen as worthwhile but it is still novel idea to many librarians in the region.

4. Money. Libraries in North America are attracted to OCLC because it makes good on the promise to help save money. The prices of many OCLC services, however, are simply beyond comprehension for the librarians in all but the well developed countries of Asia/Pacific. Librarians in this part of the world do not see OCLC as a means of saving money. The costs of becoming a governing member are also seen as prohibitive: to join, a library needs to resolve the MARC format problem, agree to upload all its new cataloging, upload its converted back files, and subscribe to FirstSearch WorldCat—all of these actions take resources. Unless there is differential pricing and a rethinking of these requirements, OCLC's expansion will be restricted to just a small proportion of the region's libraries.

5. Useful content. While the value of databases published in North America and Europe for the use of academic researchers is not debated by anyone in Asia Pacific, for most readers these materials are difficult to use and are not written in the languages they use on a daily basis. For the librarians of the region, they also see these databases as enormously expensive. In recent years OCLC has made significant progress in this area, but the focus has been on marketing the vernacular databases of the region to Western libraries.

Each of these challenges is significant, but when you bring them all together they are truly formidable. Can they be overcome? If the only reason why they needed to be overcome was for the benefit of OCLC, their simultaneous resolution would not be likely. However, they are general problems that have to be resolved whether OCLC exists or not. Yet, OCLC, based upon its wide ranging experience with libraries and consortia in many parts of the world dealing with similar problems, can increase the speed and quality of actions taken to overcome these problems. But OCLC needs to help resolve these problems not just because it wants more markets for its services, nor just because these are libraries in need, OCLC needs to help solve these problems because of the richness of the recorded human experience produced by this part of the world and because of the geopolitical criticalness of the region. In fewer than 100 years, Asia Pacific has been the locale for three major wars and is where the world's fastest growing economies are located. If OCLC is

"The World's Libraries Connected," the libraries and materials found in this region must be part of this collaborative enterprise.

REFERENCES

Central Intelligence Agency (CIA). (2008). *World Factbook.* Retrieved October 2, 2008, from https://www.cia.gov/library/publications/the-world-factbook/geos/xx.html

Niimoto, K. *OCLC Members Council power point report.* (2004). Retrieved October 2, 2008, from http://www.authorstream.com/Presentation/Lindon-17551-niimoto-OCLC-Libraries-Japan-NIIthe-National-Institute-Informatics-Services-NII-GIF-Global-as-Entertainment-ppt-powerpoint/

Korea Education and Research Information Service Forms NetLibrary eBooks Consortium. (2008). Retrieved October 2, 2008, from http://www.oclc.org/asiapacific/zhcn/news/releases/20030128.htm

World Atlas.com. (2008). *The list.* Retrieved October 2, 2008, from http://www.worldatlas.com/geoquiz/thelist.htm

History and Activity of OCLC in Canada

DANIEL BOIVIN

Director, OCLC Online Computer Library Center, Inc., Brossard, Quebec, Canada

ABSTRACT. *Canada has always been an important and natural trading partner for the United States, and this was reflected within the library field when a Canadian library, the Alberta Alcoholism and Drug Abuse Commission (AADAC) became an Online Computer Library Center (OCLC) member in 1979. This was OCLC's first member library outside the United States.*

OCLC served Canadian libraries from its main offices in Ohio until 1990, when it signed a distributorship agreement with ISM Canada. The agreement allowed ISM Canada to resell and provide support for cataloging, interlibrary loan, and EPIC services only. This helped to grow OCLC membership during that period, resulting in Canada's sending its first delegate to the OCLC Users Council in 1996. Helen Hoffman, University Librarian from York University, was the first elected delegate to represent Canadian member libraries on Users Council.

By 1997, there were approximately 100 member libraries and roughly 250 participants in Canada, but ISM had announced that it was discontinuing its library division. Thus, in 1997 OCLC opened an "office" in Canada, with this article's author as its Director. Actually, the Director worked from his home until 2001, when OCLC rented its first office space in Chambly, a suburb of Montreal. By that time, the OCLC Canada staff had grown to three persons, including a support and implementation librarian and a sales and marketing specialist.

In 2000, OCLC acquired from ISM Canada a contract cataloguing operation based in Winnipeg, Manitoba—LTS, Library Technical Services. In 2008,

approximately 30 persons were employed there, working on contract cataloguing and digitization projects for Canadian libraries and institutions. At
this writing, the Universities of Alberta, Guelph, Manitoba and Saskatchewan
were using OCLC Canada LTS for outsourced cataloging on an ongoing basis.

In 2001 the first OCLC Canada Advisory Council meeting took place in
Ottawa. This Canadian Council was a first for OCLC outside United States.
The Council comprises seven library leaders from across the country and
representing various library types to advise OCLC on important Canadian
and local matters. Ten individuals have served on the OCLC Canada Advisory
Council since 2001.

Over the years, OCLC Canada has had five delegates on Users then
Members Council. Ernie Ingles, Vice Provost and Chief Librarian at the University of Alberta, was elected President of the 2006–2007 OCLC Members
Council. This was the first time that a non-U.S. delegate was elected President of the Council. During Mr. Ingles' tenure, the Members Council met
outside the United States for the first time. The February 2007 meeting took
place in Quebec City, Quebec, Canada during the famous Winter Carnival.

In 2003, OCLC Canada hired a translator to deliver uniform translations
in French across services. Here is a brief history of some of the key applications that were offered in French for the Canadian market over the years:

- FirstSearch interface in 1998–1999
- OCLC Canada Web site in 2004
- QuestionPoint interface in 2004
- NetLibrary search interface in 2004
- CONTENTdm client interface in 2004
- CatExpress interface in 2006
- Open WorldCat in 2006
- WorldCat.org in 2007
- VDX interface in 2008

In 2004, OCLC opened a digitization operation at its LTS office in Winnipeg.
Earlier, a survey of Canadian library directors and librarians had confirmed
that most libraries were not interested in shipping physical items, other than
microfilms, across the border to the United States. Since then, the operation
was contracted to work on large projects such as the "Peel's Bibliography of
the Canadian Prairies" at the University of Alberta and the "Manitobia: Life
and Times." built by various libraries in Manitoba.

Over the years, OCLC Canada began to participate in an increasing
number of events and conferences in various provincial library associations
and the national library association, Canadian Library Association (CLA). In
addition, OCLC Canada established three awards in support of the Canadian
library community: CLA/OCLC Canada Award for Resource Sharing Achievement, the OLITA (Ontario Library Information and Technology Association)

Technological Innovation Award, and the CLA/OCLC Canada Northern Exposure to Leadership Institute Bursaries.

Since 1997, Canadian libraries have become increasingly active in the OCLC cooperative. Highlights of that activity include:

- The Alberta Library acquired the SiteSearch software to create a universal barrier-free access for all Abertans to information and ideas, delivered in a dynamic model of cooperation extending beyond walls and beyond current levels of performance. In doing so, over 230 libraries representing 90% of library services and collections in Alberta were connected to create a virtual union catalog. (2001)
- The COOL consortium of Ontario libraries began using a collection of 4,700 NetLibrary eBooks. (2003)
- Windsor Public Library, Ontario, was named a grand prize winner in WebJunction's annual Awards Program for Technology Planning. (2004)
- OCLC Canada had over 1,000 library participants. (2005)
- OCLC published *Canadian Libraries: How they stack up*, a membership report with statistical comparisons. (2005)
- Vancouver Public Library fielded the 1 millionth question logged on QuestionPoint virtual reference service. The question was, "How can I get a library card." (2006)
- OCLC ran advocacy ads in *University Affairs* and *Canadian Public Administration* on behalf of libraries. (2006)
- The Toronto Public Library entered the 63 millionth bibliographic record in the WorldCat database. (2006)
- OCLC Canada started its Cooperative Purchasing Program by offering the Grove Art & Music databases to its participating libraries. (2006)
- The Province of British Columbia acquired QuestionPoint to establish its AskAway provincial virtual reference service. (2007)
- OCLC signed an agreement with Library and Archives Canada to load and offer access to the Canadian Subject Headings through OCLC Terminologies service. (2008)
- OCLC Canada presented the first OCLC Symposium in Canada during CLA (Canadian Library Association) on Social Networking and Web 2.0. (2008)
- Novanet, a group of university libraries in Nova Scotia, acquired WorldCat Local to improve their patrons' discovery experience. (2008)

Library participation from Canada has grown exponentially over the past 12 years. Growth has also been experienced in terms of Canadian content provided through the various e-content platforms at OCLC. At this writing, Canadian libraries have contributed more than 216.4 million holdings to WorldCat, and this number continues to increase daily. Similarly, eBook content from French and English Canadian publishers went from zero to over 2,200 titles. This number grows every month as new publishers are being signed and existing ones continue to submit their titles for libraries to buy.

Early in 2009, the OCLC Canada office has moved in a brand new facility within 10 kilometers of downtown Montreal, more precisely, in Brossard, Quebec. This new facility has a larger meeting room, more space for the existing staff and, of course, room to grow as OCLC Canada continues to support libraries in Canada that participate in the OCLC global cooperative.

REFERENCE

OCLC Canada Advisory Council. (2001). from (http://www.oclc.org/ca/en/membership/canadacouncil/default.htm).

OCLC in Europe, the Middle East and Africa, 1998–2008

JANET LEES

OCLC Online Computer Library Center, Inc., Europe, the Middle East, and Africa, Birmingham, UK

ABSTRACT. *This article is a continuation of the article of the same name by Christine Deschamps who described the evolution of OCLC in Europe 1981–1997. This article continues the story for the period 1998–2008 and covers the expansion of OCLC services to the Middle East and Africa. It also includes the organizational, governance and product portfolio developments for this period under the global leadership of Jay Jordan.*

HISTORICAL PERSPECTIVE 1981–1997

The initial start up of OCLC in Europe is well documented by Christine Deschamps in her article of the same name[1]. The first OCLC office outside of the United States was opened in 1981 in Birmingham and led by David Buckle, initially providing libraries in the United Kingdom with an online shared cataloguing service. A transatlantic cable, a dedicated telecommunications network, and proprietary terminals installed in the library's cataloguing department were necessary to provide the service together with a locally sourced software operation to process the weekly computer tapes and provide the microfiche (COM) catalogues that U.K. libraries required.

Over the next 15 years Buckle and his team introduced more OCLC services—ILL, retrospective conversion and the DDC printed products and,

The author would like to thank Dorien Hooman in the OCLC EMEA Leiden office for her advice and counsel in the preparation of this article, particularly to the section on the early history of PICA.

as telecommunications became more open, expanded operations to France, the Scandinavian countries, Germany, Spain, Italy, Greece, Slovenia, Turkey, and the newly emerging Eastern European countries including the Czech Republic, Hungary, and Poland. Many of the U.K. university libraries became OCLC members, and OCLC Europe developed a special relationship with CURL (Consortium of University Research Libraries). From the mid 1980s, OCLC Europe had negotiated a series of national agreements with the Ministry of Education in France to provide first a shared national cataloguing system and later a contract retrospective conversion services to French Universities that included a Ministry-funded OCLC support team, AUROC, based in Paris.

OCLC Europe remained based in Birmingham and operated outside the United Kingdom and France through a series of distributors who were able to provide local language support and most importantly telecommunications support and training to their library customers. In many cases these distributors were local vendors offering a range of library services who added OCLC to their service list. Their OCLC customers were mainly national and large research and university libraries who were attracted to the comprehensive coverage that the OCLC Online Union Catalog could provide. It is worth noting here that at this time the OCLC Online Union Catalog—later WorldCat—comprised some 37 million titles of which approximately 29 million (64%) were English. The additional coverage that these new OCLC European members received came at a price because most European library communities used national MARC (or MARC-like) formats, national cataloguing rules, and subject authorities so that use of OCLC bibliographic records often came with an unwelcome overhead of format conversion and additional editing.

By the time of Buckle's retirement in 1996, OCLC Europe was operating in more than 25 European countries, and the number of OCLC European members had reached 400. Buckle was succeeded by the author, then Janet Mitchell.

BEYOND EUROPE—AFRICA AND THE MIDDLE EAST

Before retiring however, Buckle together with Mitchell had accepted the OCLC Board of Trustees' challenge to think beyond Europe. In 1996, following the ending of Apartheid and associated trading sanctions, OCLC Europe had met with representatives of Sabinet Online, the South African national library organization and host of the South African Union Catalogue (SACAT). A series of presentations of OCLC services in Johannesburg, Durban, and Cape Town were successful enough to begin offering services through a distributor agreement with Sabinet Online. Given the lack of telecommunications bandwidth between South Africa and the United States, a new model was developed whereby South African libraries primarily catalogued in the SACAT, which in turn was used to batch update WorldCat. This was a new process for OCLC in Dublin and in the light of subsequent developments internationally, an important one.

Using the model of national presentations and taking advantage of emerging international telecommunications protocols and standard PC equipment, the OCLC Europe road show explored more new countries in the Middle East, including Bahrain, Kuwait, Qatar, Saudi Arabia, and United Arab Emirates. OCLC Europe staff also visited libraries in Israel. Many of these libraries had relationships with U.S. research libraries with Hebrew and Arabic collections sometimes as a consequence of the experience of expatriate U.S. library managers who were recruited to the many new universities being established in the region. Major libraries in the region became OCLC members and began using OCLC Cataloguing for their western collections. Non-roman script support became a major issue, but thanks to Jay Jordan's arrival as OCLC CEO in 1998 and his encouragement of a more international attitude in Dublin, the time was ripe for an experiment with Arabic script cataloguing involving libraries in the region together with U.S., U.K. and French OCLC-member libraries. This pilot scheme was probably the first multi national service development undertaken by OCLC and marked a turning point in product development. The resulting OCLC Arabic Cataloging Service was introduced in 2001.

In 1999, to reflect these developments OCLC Europe became OCLC Europe, the Middle East and Africa and in 2001 celebrated its 20th anniversary.

BEYOND CATALOGUING AND RESOURCE SHARING—SERVING THE EUROPEAN END USER

While cataloguing formats and rules still provided barriers to the adoption of cataloguing services in some countries, there were no such barriers to the adoption of a new generation of end-user services and electronic resources that OCLC began to introduce in the 1990s, beginning with FirstSearch. These subscription services became popular with library consortia forming across Europe and became the means of introducing OCLC to large numbers of libraries in different countries.

The first of a number of successful agreements for FirstSearch was made in Norway in 1996 with Riksbibliotekjenesten (Norway's National Office for Research and Documentation). Following a pilot with a number of U.K. academic libraries a national agreement for FirstSearch was made in the United Kingdom with CHEST (Combined Higher Education Software Team) and with a number of individual French university libraries through AUROC in 1998. This was followed by national agreements with MALMAD

(Israel) in 1999; and IZUM (Slovenia), HEAL Link (Greece), and UNAK (Turkey) in 2001. These national arrangements provided a good basis for long term relationships with these libraries and provided the platform for holding national user group meetings where OCLC's newest products such as Electronic Collections Online (ECO), Question Point, and later netLibrary and WorldCat.org could be showcased. Many of these national consortia used multiple OCLC end-user services that did not qualify them as OCLC members, and they therefore viewed OCLC in the same way as other vendors of electronic services they did business with.

CREATING A NEW EUROPEAN ORGANIZATION WITH PICA

While OCLC Europe was expanding across Europe it was doing so largely by working around the central European countries of the Netherlands and Germany that were served by PICA (Samenwerkende, 1969). In fact Frederick G. Kilgour, OCLC's founder, had visited PICA and met its Managing Director Look Costers many times, and had provided 750,000 bibliographic records to seed the PICA database. PICA had been started as the "Project for Integrated Cataloguing Automation" by the collaboration of the Dutch Royal Library and the Dutch Universities in 1969. In 1976 the PICA Bureau started offering centralized services similar to OCLC and establishing a Dutch national infrastructure. The PICA staff moved out of the Dutch Royal Library in the Hague to a new building in Leiden in 1989.

While OCLC focused on developing centralised services and exporting them overseas, PICA expanded by developing software tools and local systems. After saturating the Dutch market, PICA licensed its software and implemented a similar infrastructure as in the Netherlands to a number of Partners, first in Germany and later in France. The Partners were all regional library networks with union catalogues and were involved in jointly developing the PICA systems and services, and most importantly customizing them to reflect their national language, library standards, and processes. In order to build the infrastructure the PICA Central Bibliographic System (CBS) was used to host their regional union catalogue and to provide regional ILL services. Some Partners also licensed the PICA Local Bibliographic System (LBS) as the local system for their member libraries. In the Netherlands PICA itself used the CBS system with the Dutch Union Catalogue to provide cataloguing and interlibrary loan services to the Dutch market as well as selling the LBS local system and an end-user reference service called PiCarta.

PICA and OCLC Europe had an agreement dating from 1995 to link to OCLC in the United States via Z39.50 to provide greater data coverage. The synergies between the two organizations became very apparent, and as Jordan began to develop his global strategy he found a willing partner in

PICA. In 2000 OCLC acquired a 35% share in PICA. Significantly, the same year the implementation of the CBS system was successfully finalized with ABES, the consortium of French university libraries. PICA staff had worked with ABES staff to build a French academic union catalogue and migrate away from the OCLC cataloguing service the French university libraries had been using for some 15 years. The new CBS system was able to provide a French-language interface for both cataloguing and interlibrary loans, was Unicode compliant and perhaps most significantly, was managed by ABES staff in Montpellier, France rather than OCLC staff in Dublin, Ohio.

In 2002, OCLC EMEA operations in Birmingham were merged with PICA under a new Managing Director, Rein van Charldorp, to become OCLC PICA. This was a much larger organization of some 100 staff in Europe. However increased numbers were not the only benefit; for the first time OCLC had software development and technical operations staff in its European organization and a new strategy for growth.

Developing the European Organization—The Merger and Acquisition Strategy

The success of the merger of OCLC EMEA and PICA set a trend that van Charldorp was well qualified to continue. In 2003 OCLC PICA acquired LIBPAC, a U.K. software company that hosted LinkUK, a resource sharing service for U.K. Public Libraries. In 2005 followed the acquisition of Sisis, a local library system software development organization in Germany and FDI, a U.K. based library software company. In 2007, OCLC Inc. became the sole shareholder of OCLC PICA, which led to the disappearance of the name "PICA" in the company name, which is now referred to as OCLC EMEA. By the end of 2008, OCLC EMEA had 260 staff and offices in the United Kingdom (Sheffield and Birmingham), Netherlands (Leiden), France (Paris), Germany (Munich), and Australia (Melbourne and Perth).

The new organization had three immediate successes in 2003. First, the Baden-Wurtemberg library consortium (BSZ) in South West Germany became a new CBS Partner. Second, the Northwest Academic Libraries Consortium (NOWAL) in the United Kingdom acquired the largest netLibrary eBook collection outside the United States. Finally, OCLC began a major retrospective conversion project for the Dutch Royal Library. The wider portfolio of services, local staff, and the ability to customise services to meet national needs became a benchmark for widening the reach of OCLC across Europe and beyond as the National Library of Australia became a CBS Partner in 2004. FDI's VDX ILL service also had customers in Australia, the Netherlands, and the United States. In 2008, OCLC acquired Amlib, a Web-based library management system developed in Australia and implemented in more than 525 libraries worldwide, including Africa, Australia, and the United Kingdom.

The new development capabilities enabled OCLC PICA to provide a new ILL platform to UnityUK, another UK Public library ILL system in 2004 and then to merge the LinkUK service it had already acquired from LIBPAC to create by 2007 a de facto national Public Library ILL system in the United Kingdom for the first time. The OCLC QuestionPoint service was customised to create a 24/7 virtual reference service for Dutch Public libraries known as Al@din and again to produce Enquire for the Peoples Network in the United Kingdom.

ADDING THE EUROPEAN WORLD TO WORLDCAT

As already noted, OCLC WorldCat contained some 37.5 million bibliographic holdings in 1998 of which 64 percent described English language materials. OCLC had begun discussion with a number of national libraries to load national bibliographies into WorldCat to enrich the database. In 1995, OCLC began the loading of the National Library of the Czech Republic's file into WorldCat. A number of discussions with other national libraries, however, floundered on the inability of OCLC's cataloguing platform to accept non-Latin character sets, variant cataloguing rules, and languages of cataloguing.

OCLC's new Oracle Platform was implemented in 2003. It supported Unicode, Dublin Core, and the Functional Requirements for Bibliographic Records (FRBR) model. A research project to "FRBRize" a national file was made with the National Library of Finland, which loaded its file into World-Cat as part of the agreement in 2005. The way was now open to load more files, beginning with the Dutch national union catalogue, the German National Bibliography, and the South African Union Catalogue. As a result dataloading into WorldCat grew exponentially between 2005 and 2008, adding more than 200 million records including national files from Sweden, Poland, GBV (Germany), Hebis (Germany), Australia, Israel, and the catalogue of the Bavarian State Library. By mid-2008 OCLC was loading more than 250 million records per annum. WorldCat now contained more than 100 million unique records of which only 50% were English language titles. At the time of writing, agreements with Biblioteca Nacional Espana and the Danish Bibliographic Agency have been finalized and a letter of intent has been signed with the Bibliotheque nationale de France, and these files are waiting for loading into WorldCat.

A significant addition to the service is a technical innovation to use the SRU Update protocol for synchronizing national/regional files with WorldCat to avoid the delays inherent in batchloading. This process has been, at the time of writing, tested with the Dutch union catalogue file and will be implemented with other files over time.

BUILDING WEB-SCALE IN EUROPE

Being part of a global union catalogue was not the only motivation for many of these national groups to load their data into WorldCat. Many institutions had resisted the concept of "exporting" their data into what had been perceived as a U.S. database for more than 3 decades. However, the Web and more particularly organizations such as Google, Amazon, and Yahoo! had changed the perception of libraries and more importantly their users worldwide. Libraries had to create Web-scale and needed an organization that could provide a Web presence.

OCLC had begun a pilot in 2004 with Google and Yahoo! to load subsets of WorldCat in a project called Open WorldCat. The pilot was to demonstrate the ability for users to be able to begin their search on the Web and to be directed to holdings in their local library. In 2006 OCLC PICA began an Open WorldCat pilot with libraries in the United Kingdom and Netherlands that included the translation of the Open WorldCat interface into Dutch, French, and German and the implementation of U.K. and Dutch postal codes. The success of these pilots and the implementation of OCLC's own destination portal, WorldCat.org, were as much the drivers for national groups to load their data into WorldCat as the desire to become part of a global union catalogue and members of OCLC.

EMEA REPRESENTATION IN OCLC GOVERNANCE

In 1998, OCLC EMEA had only a single representative, Ian Mowat, Edinburgh University, on OCLC's Users Council whose overall size at that time was 60 delegates. Representing such a large region was very difficult for one individual, although Mowat did an excellent job in meeting key constituencies particularly during the 1999–2000 Governance Study. In 2001 as a result of the governance study, the Users Council became the Members Council, and OCLC added six international transitional delegates to seed the globalization effort. Two of these transitional delegates came from the EMEA region, and the EMEA delegation was enlarged to include Wim van Drimmlen, Royal Library of the Netherlands, and from South Africa, Hennie Viljoen from Stellenbosch University and later Norma Read, University of Cape Town. Mowat continued to be influential within Members Council and was elected to the Executive Committee in 2001 and to the Board of Trustees in 2002. Mowat, however, tragically died in a hill walking accident before he could take up his Trustee position.

The growth in take-up of OCLC services and particularly the increased data loading described above accelerated the increase in representation from EMEA to eight delegates by 2008. The delegation in the past few years has included representatives from Denmark, Finland, France, Germany, Netherlands, South Africa, and United Kingdom, thereby fulfilling the goal of the Governance Study to make Members Council much more international. While small in numbers, these EMEA delegates created a significant presence within the Members Council and became active in Members Council activities. Berndt Dugall from University of Frankfurt, Germany and Poul Erlandsen from the Danish National Library of Education, served on the Members Council Executive Committee in 2007 and 2008 respectively, while Ellen Tise of Stellenbosch University and Graham Jefcoate, University of Nijmegen, Netherlands, led the Members Council Global Discussion group in 2007 and 2008 respectively.

Christine Deschamps, France, had served as an OCLC EMEA Users Council Delegate from 1993 to 1996, when she became the first non-U.S. delegate to be elected by Users Council to serve on the OCLC Board of Trustees. Deschamps' influence and her international stature as IFLA President provided OCLC with a strong Trustee with a global voice during her term from 1996 to 2003. Her legacy includes the first meeting of the OCLC Board outside the United States in Paris in 2003.

Elisabeth Niggemann, Director of the Deutsche Nationalbibliothek, continued the European representation on the Board when she became a Board-appointed Trustee in 2004. Her stature as a National Librarian and her involvement in the activities of the Foundation Conference of European National Librarians (CENL) continued the work that Deschamps had pioneered. Niggemann, as the leader of an organization that was also a CBS partner, and active in many European and international forums, was influential in both the decision to load the DNB's national bibliography into WorldCat and the extension of the Virtual International Authority File (VIAF), a joint project of the Deutsche Nationalbibliothek, the U.S. Library of Congress, and OCLC to include the Bibliotheque nationale de France in 2007. The National Library of Sweden joined the project in 2008.

In November 2007, a further governance study recommended changes to both the OCLC Members Council and the Board of Trustees that further encourage and support the growth of OCLC's membership internationally. These recommendations were adopted by both the Board and Members Council in 2008. The forthcoming changes will provide a new structure of representation that include establishment of Regional Councils and a new Global Council. At the time of writing an EMEA Regional Council is being set up that will meet for the first time in the region in 2010 and will provide the opportunity for libraries across the region to become much more active participants in OCLC's governance and membership activities.

CONCLUSION

It would have been difficult to predict the scale of change that OCLC has achieved in EMEA in the past decade. From selling U.S. centric services to some 400 libraries in 1998, OCLC is today embedded in the European and South African library infrastructure and now touches more than 7, 000 libraries across the region with a global portfolio of services, many of which are developed and supported from its European offices. OCLC EMEA is poised to increase the dialogue with its many customers and users through the New Regional Council.

REFERENCES

Deschamps, C. (1998). OCLC in Europe. I *Journal of Library Administration, 25,* 141–157.
Samenwerkende bibliothecarissen en technische innovaties: PICA van 1969 to 2002/Anton Bossers. Leiden, OCLC PICA, 2005.

OCLC in Latin America and the Caribbean: A Chronology

LAWRENCE OLSZEWSKI

OCLC Online Computer Library Center, Inc., Dublin, OH, USA

ABSTRACT. *From one library in 1995 to 884 in 2008, the number of Online Computer Library Center (OCLC) libraries in Latin American and the Caribbean has grown significantly. They are presently active in 27 countries and territories. The following chronology highlights not only the significant achievements since 1997 that OCLC has made in providing products and services to the region but also the contributions the libraries in the region have made to OCLC in providing input and advice to the governance and product development.*

1998

The library system of the Universidade Estadual Paulista, São Paulo, becomes the second OCLC member in Brazil. Its 25 libraries have the second largest bibliographical collection in Brazil.

OCLC releases a Spanish language interface for the OCLC FirstSearch service.

1999

The library of the Universidad de San Andrés, Buenos Aires, becomes the first OCLC member in Argentina.

The Universidad Veracruzana Library, Xalapa, Mexico, becomes the 13th OCLC member library in the Latin American region.

Jesús Lau, then of the Universidad Autónoma de la Ciudad de Juárez, Mexico, serves on the OCLC Advisory Committee on College and University Libraries.

The Instituto Tecnológico y de Estudios Superiores de Monterrey (ITESM), Mexico, becomes a cataloging member of OCLC and also one of the first to participate in the CORC project. The Instituto consists of 27 specialized libraries in 29 campuses spread throughout the country.

Bermuda is the first country in Latin America and the Caribbean participating in the OCLC Interlibrary Loan service.

2000

OCLC publishes *Sistema de Clasificación Decimal Dewey* (SCDD 21), the Spanish translation of DDC 21.

The Daniel Cosío Villegas Library, El Colegio de México, Mexico City, joins OCLC as a cataloging member; it also begins using the OCLC Interlibrary Loan service and CORC. Founded in 1940, El Colegio de Mexico is known for its academic excellence.

The Instituto Tecnológico de Estudios Superiores de Monterrey (ITESM), Quéretaro Campus, Mexico, hosts the first meeting of OCLC catalogers in Mexico and establishes a Mexican OCLC cataloging users group.

The University of the West Indies, St. Augustine, Trinidad & Tobago, the Universidad Autónoma Ciudad Juárez, Mexico, and the Universidad de Chile, Santiago, become CORC participants.

The Universidad de Guadalajara, Mexico, joins OCLC as a cataloging member. Founded in 1792, it consists of six campuses located throughout the state of Jalisco.

Twelve representatives from 10 institutions in Argentina, Barbados, Brazil, Mexico, and Trinidad and Tobago attend the 18th Annual Research Libraries Directors Conference at OCLC.

In collaboration with two Argentine institutions, the Sistema de Información Universitaria (SIU), Buenos Aires, and the Universidad Nacional del Sur (UNS), Bahía Blanca, OCLC sponsors a seminar/workshop entitled "New Tools for Cataloging: Assessment of Cooperative Work" in Bahía Blanca, Argentina.

The Biblioteca Benjamín Franklin of the U.S. Embassy in Mexico City becomes a cataloging member of OCLC. Founded in 1942, it is the first official U.S. government library outside the United States.

The libraries of the Universidad Argentina de la Empresa (UADE), Buenos Aires, and the Universidad de Montemorelos, Mexico, become cataloging members of OCLC.

The libraries of the Universidad de Quintana Roo, Chetumal, Mexico and El Colegio de México, Mexico City, and the Universidad Católica de Valparaíso, Universidad de Santiago de Chile, the Universidad de los Lagos, Osorno, and the Universidad de la Frontera, Temuco, in Chile begin using OCLC FirstSearch.

2001

Álvaro Quijano Solís, Director of the Daniel Cosío Villegas Library, El Colegio de México, Mexico City, is the first delegate to Members Council elected from Latin America.

The Raúl Baillères Library of the Instituto Tecnológico Autónomo de México, Mexico City, joins OCLC as a cataloging member. Among its rare resources is a collection of historical documents from the 17th, 18th, and 19th centuries and the personal papers of several prominent Mexican thinkers.

Representatives from Argentina, Barbados, Brazil, Chile, Jamaica, Mexico, and Trinidad & Tobago attend the 19th Annual Research Libraries Directors Conference at OCLC.

The eight member libraries of the Red de Sistemas de Bibliotecas de las Universidades del Centro (RESIUC) in Mexico form the first consortium of cataloging libraries in Latin America.

The Universidad Anáhuac and Anáhuac del Sur, Mexico City, and the Universidad de Mayab, Mérida, Mexico join OCLC.

The first meeting of the Latin American OCLC Users Group meets at the 67th annual IFLA conference in Boston, attended by library directors and professionals from Argentina, Brazil, Chile, Colombia, Jamaica, Mexico, and Trinidad & Tobago.

The Sistema de Bibliotecas de la Pontificia Universidad Católica de Chile (SIBUC), Santiago, becomes a cataloging member of OCLC. It is one of the leading university libraries in the country, with over 1.5 million volumes.

2002

OCLC establishes an OCLC Mexico office in Mexico City, under the direction of José Antonio Yáñez de la Peña.

The Biblioteca General of the Pontificia Universidad Javeriana, Bogotá, Colombia, becomes an OCLC member. Founded in 1621, it is one of the oldest libraries in Latin America, with a notable collection of materials on Colombian and international law.

The Universidad de Quintana Roo, with campuses in Chetumal and Cozumel, Mexico, joins OCLC.

Eleven library directors and professionals from Brazil, Mexico, and Trinidad & Tobago attend the 20th annual Research Libraries Directors Conference at OCLC.

The Dirección General de Bibliotecas of the Universidad Nacional Autónoma de México (UNAM), Mexico City, becomes a cataloging member of OCLC.

The six members of the Anáhuac Library Consortium in Mexico begin offering First Search to its members.

The Universidad Autónoma de Nuevo León, San Nicolás de los Garza, Mexico, begins using OCLC FirstSearch.

The Universidad Anáhuac, Xalapa, Mexico, and the Universidad Icesi, Cali, Colombia, become cataloging members of OCLC.

The Academia Nacional de Estudios Políticos y Estratégicos de Chile (ANEPE), Santiago and the Universidad Pedagógica Nacional (UPN), in Mexico City, begin using OCLC FirstSearch.

2003

OCLC loads the CLASE and PERIÓDICA databases into the OCLC FirstSearch service. The bilingual indexes, produced by the National Autonomous University of Mexico (UNAM), are the first member-produced databases to be available on FirstSearch. CLASE (Citas Latinoamericanas en Ciencias Sociales y Humanidades) specializes in the social sciences and humanities; PERIÓDICA (Índice de Revistas Latinoamericanas en Ciencias) specializes in science and technology.

The Chilean Directorate of Library, Archives and Museums (DIBAM) and the 368 public libraries it manages become governing members and begin contributing their current cataloging to WorldCat.

Lic. Patricia Ríos Collantes, Instituto Tecnológico de Estudios Superiores de Monterrey, Sinaloa Campus, Mexico is appointed to the OCLC Collections and Technical Services Advisory Committee.

The South Southeast Network in Mexico begins using OCLC conversion services to create a union catalog for the 10 participating libraries in the region.

The Biblioteca Regional de Medicina (BIREME) Virtual Health Library, São Paulo, Brazil and the Unidad de Servicios Bibliotecarios y de Información (USBI) of the Universidad Veracruzana, Xalapa, Mexico, become the first two libraries in Latin America to subscribe to QuestionPoint.

Brazil, Chile, Colombia, Mexico, and Trinidad & Tobago are Latin America and Caribbean countries studied in OCLC's report *2003 Enviromental Scan: Pattern Recognition*.

The Universidad de Colima, Mexico, joins OCLC.

Five Mexican libraries begin using NetLibrary.

The 20 libraries of the Universidad Autónoma de Yucatán (UADY), Mérida, Mexico and the 31 of the Universidad Autónoma de Nayarit, Tepic, Mexico, join OCLC.

The Biblioteca Francisco Xavier Clavigero of the Univerisdad Iberoamericana, Mexico City, joins OCLC. The library has almost a quarter of a million volumes and a vast collection of electronic resources.

The Biblioteca Rafael Montejano y Aguinaga of El Colegio de San Luis, San Luis Potosí, Mexico, becomes an OCLC member. Founded in 1997, it is one of the newest university libraries in the country.

The 14 special libraries that comprise the Sistema de Información Académica of the Universidad Autónoma de Baja California (UABC), Mexicali, Mexico become members of OCLC.

Twenty-five libraries in the Universidad Autónoma de Nuevo León (UANL) system, San Nicolás de los Garza, Mexico begin using the OCLC Interlibrary Loan service.

2004

410,000 holdings—including 230,000 original records—from the National Library of Chile are added to WorldCat.

The Brazilian Institute for Scientific and Technical Information (IBICT), Brasília, begins using OCLC interlibrary loan to request documents from outside the country on behalf of more than 95 universities.

The Scientific Electronic Library Online (SciELO) Brazil and SciELO Chile files of scientific and medical e-journals are loaded into WorldCat.

Daniel Mattes, Director of the Library, Universidad Anáhuac del Norte, Mexico City, and Margaret Rouse-Jones, Campus Librarian, The University of the West Indies, St. Augustine, Trinidad & Tobago, are elected delegates to Members Council.

The Universidad de Monterrey, San Pedro García Garza, Mexico, begins using QuestionPoint.

The Sistema Bibliotecario of the Universidad Juárez Autónoma de Tabasco (UJAT), Villahermosa, Mexico, becomes an OCLC member. Among the nine libraries that make up the system is the Biblioteca José Martí, the oldest in the university (founded in 1944). It contains many rare and old books dealing with famous Tabasco citizens.

2005

Edwar Delgado, Albania School, Albania, Guajira Colombia and Gillian Wilson, United Theological College of the West Indies, Kingston, Jamaica, are selected as 2005 IFLA/OCLC Early Career Development Fellows.

The Biblioteca Acadêmico Luiz Viana Filho of the Brazilian Senate, Brasília, becomes an OCLC member, using cataloging, interlibrary loan, and QuestionPoint.

10,000 records from Chilean e-library of scientific and technical journals are added to WorldCat.

Antigua Public Library, St. Johns, Antigua & Barbuda, begins using OCLC FirstSearch, offering e-content access to its users for the first time.

The University of the West Indies, Kingston, Jamaica, becomes the second user of CONTENTdm in the Caribbean and adds NetLibrary to its services.

Tim Rapp is named Director of OCLC Latin America and the Caribbean.

The Universidad Autónoma de Ciudad Juárez, Mexico, begins using QuestionPoint.

BIBMEX, a catalog containing 1.1 million holdings of over 80 Mexican academic institutions, becomes available exclusively on the OCLC FirstSearch service.

Three Mexican libraries—the Universidad Autónoma de Tamaulipas, Ciudad Victoria; the Instituto Nacional de Ecología, SA, Mexico City; and the Universidad Autónoma de Campeche, Campeche—become cataloging members of OCLC

Records from the Latin American and Caribbean Literature on Health Sciences Database (LILACS) are loaded into WorldCat. LILACS is a cooperative product of the Latin American and Caribbean Centre on Health Sciences Information, coordinated by the Biblioteca Regional de Medicina (BIREME).

The National Library of Jamaica, Kingston, begins using CONTENTdm to digitize Jamaican heritage materials.

2006

Janete Estevão, of O Boticário Franchising S/A, São José dos Pinhais, Brazil, and Maria Cherrie, of the National Library and Information System Authority (NALIS), Port-of-Spain, Trinidad & Tobago, are selected as 2006 IFLA/OCLC Early Career Development Fellows.

The Biblioteca Regional de Medicina, São Paulo, Brazil, enters the 70 millionth record into WorldCat.

The International Conference on Dublin Core and Metadata Applications is held in Manzanillo, Mexico.

The University of Puerto Rico Medical Sciences Campus, San Juan begins using QuestionPoint.

The Caribbean Funnel, consisting of the libraries of the University of the West Indies in Kingston, Jamaica, St. Augustine, Trinidad & Tobago, and Cave Hill, Barbados; the National Library and Information System of Trinidad and Tobago (NALIS), Port-of-Spain; the College of Science, Technology and Applied Arts of Trinidad and Tobago (COSTAATT), Port-of-Spain, and the University of Guyana, Georgetown, is formed. Its partnership with OCLC has helped these institutions provide an infrastructure to create a regional authority file.

2007

The National Library of Mexico agrees to load its catalog into WorldCat

The Universidad Peruana de Ciencias Aplicadas (UPC), Lima, becomes the first Governing Member library in Peru.

Elisangela Alves Silva, Abrinq Foundation for the Rights of Children and
   Adolescents, São Paulo, Brazil, and Pauline Nicholas, The University of
   the West Indies, Kingston, Jamaica, are selected as 2007 IFLA/OCLC Early
   Career Development Fellows.
Five academic libraries in the Sistema Bibliotecario de la Educación Superior
   Universitaria Estatal de Costa Rica (SIBESE-CR) consortium in Costa Rica
   become cataloging members of OCLC.
More than 48,000 records from RedALyC, a research group from the Uni-
   versidad Autónoma del Estado de México, are loaded into WorldCat. The
   database consists of full-text articles from over 350 scholarly scientific e-
   journals from Latin America, the Caribbean, Spain, and Portugal.
Micaela Chávez, El Colegio de México, Mexico City, is elected a delegate to
   Members Council.
The National Library and Information System Authority (NALIS), Port-of-
   Spain, Trinidad & Tobago, becomes the first national library in the Ameri-
   cas offering QuestionPoint service to provide virtual reference services.
The National Library Service of Barbados, Bridgetown, creates the Barbados
   Group Catalog, combining more than 56,000 records from eight libraries.
The Fundación Global Democracia y Desarrollo (FUNGLODE), Santo
   Domingo, Dominican Republic, becomes a cataloging member of OCLC.
The Brazilian Institute for Scientific and Technical Information (IBICT),
   Brasília, loads its file of 34,000 records from the Digital Library of The-
   ses and Dissertations (BDTD) Metadata Base into WorldCat.

2008

The Pedro Henríquez Ureña National Library, Santo Domingo, Dominican
   Republic, joins OCLC.
More than 470,000 records from Embrapa, a database of scientific material
   related to agriculture and animal research from the Brazilian Agricultural
   Research Corporation, Brasília, are loaded into WorldCat.
The State of Jalisco Public Library system, Guadalajara, Mexico, begins using
   NetLibrary.
The Universidad Metropolitana, San Juan, Puerto Rico, the University of
   Puerto Rico—Arecibo & Humacao; and the University of the West
   Indies—Mona, Kingston, Jamaica, begin using QuestionPoint.
A comparative study of the use of QuestionPoint libraries outside the United
   States finds that the Universidad Veracruzana, Xalapa, Mexico, is the only
   institution of the 23 studied in which every question asked via the service
   was of the reference type.
The National Library Service, Bridgetown, Barbados, loads over 91,000 hold-
   ings into WorldCat.

REFERENCE

Lawrence Olszewski and Paula Rumbaugh. (2008). *"An International Comparison of Virtual Reference Services."* Accessed August 31, 2009. http://www.uv.mx/usbi_ver/alci08/docs/C6_Larry_Olszewski.pdf

The OCLC Network of Regional Service Providers: The Last 10 Years

BRENDA BAILEY-HAINER

BCR, Aurora, CO, USA

Developed in the early 1970s, the alliance between the Online Computer Library Center (OCLC) and its regional service providers is a strategic partnership that has survived for over 30 years. Originally created by OCLC to help it efficiently reach out to libraries in other states beyond its initial Ohio focus, this alliance is now starting to transform into a new structure. This new structure as well as other changes in the relationship between OCLC and its partners will have an impact upon all of the organizations involved.

It is difficult to talk about the last 10 years without touching briefly on the evolution of this strategic partnership. The structure that existed until July 2009 was the product of history and OCLC's evolution from an organization serving a single state to one providing services throughout the United States. Its form was the result of a combination of serendipity and deliberate action. In the late 1970s, some organizations like BCR and NELINET already existed and were willing and able to take on support for OCLC products and services. In other cases, new organizations were formed, such as SOLINET and SUNY/OCLC (now Nylink), specifically to serve as distributors to a particular constituency in a specific geographic area. A complex symbiotic relationship resulted. Revenue gained through the provision of OCLC services allowed these organizations, sometimes referred to as OCLC-affiliated regional service providers, to expand into more diverse services that benefited their member libraries in other ways. OCLC, in turn, through this dedicated service structure, was able to expand and penetrate the library market outside of Ohio at a much faster rate than it would have been able to on its own (Brunell, 1998).

This structure established through the agreements between OCLC and its regional service providers is in itself a "network." According to Mandell and Steelman, networks are "a spectrum of structures that involve two or more actors and may include participants from the public, private, and nonprofit sectors with varying degrees of interdependence to accomplish goals that otherwise could not be accomplished independently" (Mandell & Steelman, 2003).

The establishment of this OCLC service network was part of a larger national movement toward forming networks that took place in the greater business world in the 1970s and 1980s. Competition in many business sectors became more international, and the impact of technology implementation began to ripple through U.S. industries and companies, causing them to restructure. New firms created during this era often sought alliances with independent suppliers and/or distributors, just as OCLC did with its regional partners. This network model, more so than with other business models, depended on the various components of the network recognizing their interdependence. These partners were willing to share information, cooperate with each other, and customize their product or service—all for the purpose of maintaining their position within the network. Many components in networks expected a more proactive role by participants, namely, voluntary behavior that went beyond fulfilling any contractual obligations and that improved the final product or service (Miles & Snow, 1992).

The service network formed by OCLC and its regional partners fell very much into this network form. Both parties had a common goal of benefiting libraries and helping them thrive. Often activities that supported libraries were undertaken at a financial loss to an organization and the costs subsidized through other business ventures.

BENEFITS AND PITFALLS

While the network form had many benefits for the parties involved, it also had some inherent limitations and pitfalls despite the best intentions of all. This situation had the potential to result in a "stale" network organization: a core firm linked forward and backward to a limited number of carefully selected partners that changed little over time (Miles & Snow, 1992).

The OCLC network of regional service providers historically was based on a patchwork of a dozen or more organizations, both independent and internal to OCLC, which covered the entire geographic United States, with little territorial overlap. The organizations involved were very diverse, ranging from independent non-profits to units of state or federal government, and serving libraries in only a single state or multiple states. Figure 1 shows the regional providers and their designated geographic territories for providing

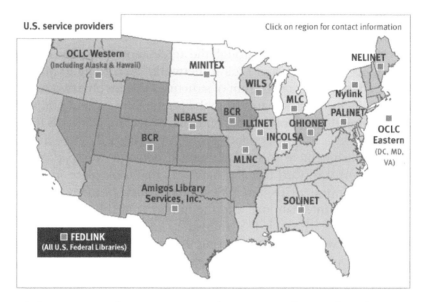

FIGURE 1 Map of OCLC U.S. Regional Service Providers as of March 2009.

OCLC services within the United States prior to July 2009. The precedent was set for utilizing OCLC internal units outside of Ohio with the establishment in 1976 of an OCLC unit in California, later called OCLC Western Service Center, to provide training, support, and marketing services in four western states not serviced by other entities. The October 2008 *Guide to Networks and Service Centers: An OCLC Members Council Directory* (OCLC, 2008), lists 15 independent organizations and two OCLC units that together make up the network of U.S. regional service providers (Table 1).

While this distribution network proved successful in the United States for many years, both the environment in which OCLC and the regional service partners operated and the organizations themselves changed significantly over time. OCLC grew from an entity focused on expanding nationally to one with international reach. The advent of the Internet and other services such as Amazon and Google has had an impact on the arena in which libraries and other information providers play. Increasingly, OCLC has entered into business partnerships with organizations outside of the traditional library industry, such as Google and Yahoo!, in order to both expand their customer base for WorldCat and to assist libraries with exposure through online channels that have become more familiar to the general population than direct access to library websites.

ENVIRONMENTAL FACTORS

Regardless of whether the particular organization pre-existed the creation of OCLC or was created specifically to provide its services, all of the regional

TABLE 1 OCLC Independent Regional Service Providers as of March 2009 (Guide to Networks and Service Centers: An OCLC Members Council Directory, 2008)[1]

Network	Type of organization	Year Founded
Amigos	Private nonprofit organization	1974
BCR	Private nonprofit organization	1935
FEDLINK	Government agency	1976
ILLINET	Government agency	1977
INCOLSA	Private nonprofit organization	1974
MLC	Private nonprofit organization	1974
MINITEX	Affiliated with Minnesota higher education	1968
MLNC	Private nonprofit organization	1981
NEBASE	Government agency	1976
NELINET	Private nonprofit organization	1964
Nylink	Not-for-profit organization, unit of Division of Academic Operations and Services in SUNY Central Administration	1974 (originally founded as The SUNY/ OCLC Network)
OHIONET	Private nonprofit organization	1977
PALINET	Private nonprofit organization	1936 (originally founded as Union Library Catalogue of the Philadelphia Metropolitan Area)
SOLINET	Private nonprofit organization	1973
WiLS	Private nonprofit organization	1972

service providers saw the need to increase their value to member libraries and began adding services beyond OCLC. By 2009, virtually all of them had expanded their products and services offerings to include an array of online databases, document delivery, library supplies, bibliographic services, hardware, and training and consulting services.

Other environmental factors have had an impact on the regional service partner framework, such as the consolidation of bibliographic utilities. In October 1998, WLN and OCLC announced their intentions to pursue a merger, which became effective on January 1, 1999. When this merger occurred, several state librarians from the Pacific Northwest whose states had been served by WLN sought to identify an organization that could provide products and services that complemented those offered to them by OCLC Pacific (later called the OCLC Western Service Center). In January 2001, five state library agencies joined seven other state libraries to become statewide members of BCR. Libraries within those new states for the most part continued to purchase their OCLC services directly from OCLC. Although BCR, which was founded in 1935, had throughout its history continuously provided a wide array of services to libraries, this new arrangement brought some tension to its relationship with OCLC.

Little else changed in the OCLC-affiliated regional network landscape with one notable exception. The membership of CAPCON, an independent regional partner that served the greater Washington, DC, area, approved the purchase of CAPCON by OCLC to form the OCLC CAPCON Services Center. This new organization, created in 2003, was later renamed the OCLC Eastern Service Center (History of OCLC Eastern Service Center).

In the late 1990s, a new contractual arrangement was created between OCLC and its partners, which was governed by the *Tiered Distribution Program Manual (TDP)*. TDP set up several levels of possible network involvement with different OCLC services, along with general guidelines for network service and financial incentives. It established a two-tiered structure in which some partners provided only training and support along with general marketing efforts, while others in addition hired staff designated as OCLC sales representatives. Compensation was dependent upon the tier level within which a partner operated. These efforts put a more institutionalized structure around the OCLC regional service network (Brunell, 1998).

Despite having placed more structure around the relationship, OCLC struggled with the challenge of equitably assessing the performance of such a diverse group of partners while at the same time the partners struggled with making OCLC understand the value of the local and unique touch that each brought to the constituents in their territories. This TDP structure stayed in place until 2005, when it was dismantled and a new partner distribution program governed by the *U.S. Network Partner Program Manual* was put in place (RONDAC Executive Committee, 2005). OCLC gradually reduced the level of compensation for its former sales partners, and this change had a significant financial impact on the partners involved.

ROLE IN GOVERNANCE

One complicating factor in the OCLC regional service provider relationship was the fact that the regional service providers played a role in OCLC's governance. These OCLC-affiliated networks and service centers were defined in the OCLC Code of Regulations as the Members of OCLC Members Council. In OCLC nomenclature *"networks"* were defined as "library service organizations that are independent from OCLC and which contract with OCLC to provide services to libraries and other organizations in their geographic region." Members Council Member status was reviewed annually to ensure that the Members Council Members and the libraries that contracted with them met the minimum requirements for usage of and contribution to the OCLC cooperative. Thus, the networks actually served as members of OCLC, with the libraries within each regional network electing representatives to serve as OCLC Members Council delegates. Each network was allocated a certain number of delegate slots based on an elaborate algorithm that was periodically reviewed to reflect OCLC's changing array of services and international expansion (OCLC Members Council Directory, 2008). As parties interested in the governance of the OCLC cooperative, network directors typically attended all Members Council meetings as non-voting guests, in addition to the voting delegates officially representing them.

Although purchase of OCLC products and services directly from OCLC without going through a network had always been available, few institutions took advantage of this option and historically OCLC encouraged libraries to use its regional partners instead. In 2007, some members of the Boston Library Consortium took steps to contract directly with OCLC for services and bypassed NELINET, the network in their geographic area. Because of the size of the libraries involved, this action reduced NELINET's contribution to the cooperative and resulted in BLC gaining a delegate seat on the OCLC Members Council. This action created the potential for other similar changes.

While the OCLC-network partnership arrangement served OCLC well in the late 1970s and early 1980s in the rapid adoption of OCLC services by libraries, clearly an outdated distribution structure created due to happenstance in the 1970s would no longer suffice for a growing international company. During fiscal year 2008, OCLC conducted two studies related to distribution channels. One was a more objective theoretical study conducted by Dr. Jay Barney and Dr. Jay Anand of Ohio State University (Barney & Anand, 2007), and the second by R2 Consulting LLC (RS Consulting LLC., 2007), a library consulting firm. Distribution models from other industries were examined, including such areas as insurance companies and Microsoft business partners. The Barney and Anand study looked at various models that might be applied to assess the costs and benefits of partnerships. They looked at the value of centralized versus localized service and pointed out some of the redundancies present in the current system, such as multiple organizations providing essentially the same training courses (Klitgaard & Treverton, 2004). The R2 study pointed out that it no longer may be practical to have a mutual expectation of exclusivity between OCLC and the networks. The regional service providers, often at the request of their members, had positioned themselves as neutral, one-stop providers to libraries looking for a variety of different services. Changing the distribution structure would free them up to do so. At the same time, R2 recognized OCLC's need to diversify their distribution network in any way they saw fit and to add new partners or easily shed partners that did not meet clearly stated standards (R2 Consulting LLC., 2007). This would eliminate the potential for the network to go "stale."

Governance was bound to shift along with OCLC's shift to a true global organization. At the same time that the distribution channel studies were being conducted, the OCLC Board of Trustees embarked on a governance study performed by an outside consulting firm. Several different models were proposed by the consultants, and the OCLC Board made recommendations that were discussed by the Members Council. In May 2008, the Members

Council approved changes in the governance structure that had been recommended by the Board of Trustees. These changes removed the network service partners from any role in governance of OCLC, including their role in helping to elect representatives from their regions (OCLC Press Release).

Discussions about proposed changes to the regional service provider model several times spilled over into the Members Council arena. Because of the interdependence of the service network model that had been originally established, any change to the overall structure had the potential to threaten the financial stability of the regional partners. Some Members Council delegates, feeling strong loyalty to the particular regional service partner they had been elected to represent, spoke up in open forums during meetings indicating their concern that a change instituted by OCLC could threaten the financial health of the regional networks and, by extension, other services these organizations provided that their member libraries valued. Members Council delegates from outside the United States, unused to this highly interdependent structure in place in the United States, were at times baffled by the level of emotions exhibited.

DISTRIBUTION CHANNEL STUDIES

After the release of the two distribution channel studies and the governance study, the regional service providers grappled with the conundrums they presented. Faced with the significant changes in their financial and programmatic operations that a new OCLC business partner model represented, how could a network service provider best serve their members' continuing interest in using OCLC products and services and at the same time preserve the network's own well-being? Most organizations concluded that there should be a continuing relationship with OCLC at some level and that this more limited role would allow them to re-direct some staff to develop other services.

During this time period, discussions between OCLC and the networks were sometimes difficult and emotionally charged. RONDAC (Regional OCLC Network Directors' Advisory Committee), which had been functioning as a regular forum for discussions between OCLC and the regional networks, was disbanded in October 2008. In the end, change prevailed, and OCLC embarked on instituting a new relationship with its business partners. In spring 2009, OCLC negotiated new contracts individually with any regional service providers interested in continuing to work with OCLC in a new form of business partnership that would allow libraries to continue to pay for OCLC services through their network. Part of the new model involved OCLC creating a centralized support center that opened July 1, 2009, essentially removing that responsibility and revenue generating opportunity from the regional partners.

It is not clear what will happen to the organizations that have served as OCLC regional service providers. At least one, NEBASE, ceased providing OCLC services at the end of June 2009. Part of the Nebraska Library Commission (NLC), NEBASE ceased to exist as a separately named entity, but the staff continues to offer other services through NLC, such as group database licensing. NEBASE members began using BCR for OCLC billing starting with July 2009 invoices.

At least three organizations have decided to merge. PALINET and SOLINET merged effective April 1, 2009 and formed a single organization called Lyrasis (SOLINET, 2009). NELINET members voted to join Lyrasis in June 2009. MLNC and MOBIUS (a Missouri-based academic consortium) briefly investigated the potential of a merger in late 2008, but the idea has since been dropped (MLNC, 2009). A different type of creative partnership related to OCLC billing was announced by INCOLSA and MLC, in which MLC provides OCLC billing services for INCOLSA libraries (MLC, 2009). MLC and INOLSA are now also exploring the potential of a merger. Other organizations will use the upcoming changes as an opportunity to redeploy staff to work on other projects and to create new centers of excellence. For example, the Collaborative Digitization Program, a multi-state cooperative of cultural heritage institutions, merged into BCR in April 2007, and has been used as the basis for forming a center of excellence in BCR's Digital and Preservation Services unit (BCR, 2009).

The confluence of these changes and the current economic downturn will no doubt have a significant impact on the vitality of the remaining regional partners. For the four organizations that pre-dated the creation of OCLC or its expansion beyond the borders of Ohio, (BCR, MINITEX, NELINET, and PALINET), this confluence may simply be the impetus for yet another shift in service offerings that have occurred over the years as the needs of libraries have evolved and these service organizations have evolved to meet them. For other organizations that were originally established specifically to provide OCLC products and services, they will have to make decisions about how they will evolve in this new environment.

OCLC has taken the first step in restructuring their overall distribution network by altering its relationship with the regional service providers to create new contracts for each individual business partner. While these new contracts allow the regional service providers to continue a business relationship with OCLC, the very fact of renegotiating the terms has upset the delicate financial balance that existed previously and will no doubt cause a ripple of change over the next several years. The success of this new model must be judged by those who come after. It does, however, mark the end of a significant era of OCLC's history as its dedicated exclusive partnership with regional service networks is dissolved.

REFERENCES

Barney, J., & Anand, J. (2007). *Report on the Effectiveness of the Current System for Distributing and Servicing OCLC Products.* Private report prepared for OCLC.

Brunell, D. (1998). The Strategic Alliance Between OCLC and Networks: Partnerships That Work. In *OCLC 1967–1997, Thirty Years of Furthering Access to the World's Information* (pp. 19–29). New York: Haworth Press.

OCLC. (2008). *Guide to Networks and Service Centers: An OCLC Members Council Directory.* (2008.) p. iii. Retrieved from http://www.oclc.org/us/en/memberscouncil/documents/networkdirectory.pdf

History of OCLC Eastern Service Center. (2009). Retrieved March 6, 2009, from http://www.oclc.org/eastern/about/history/default.htm

Klitgaard, R., & Treverton, G. (2004). Assessing Partnerships: New Forms of Collaboration. In J. Kamensky, & T. Burlin (Eds.), *Collaboration: Using Networks and Partnership* (pp. 21–59). Lanham, MD: Rowman & Littlefield Publishers.

Mandell, M., & Steelman, T. (2003). *Understanding What Can Be Accomplished through Different Interorganizational Relationships: The Importance of Typologies, Context and Management Strategies. Public Management Review, 5,* 197–224.

Miles, R., & Snow, C. (1992). Causes of failure in network organizations. *California Management Review, 34,* 53–72.

R2 Consulting LLC. (2007). *OCLC and Regional Networks: Distribution of OCLC Services.* Private report prepared by Rick Lugg and Matt Barnes for OCLC.

RONDAC Executive Committee. (2005). Internal Documents.

SOLINET. (2009). Merger announcement. Retrieved March 6, 2009, from http://www.mergerupdate.org/.

MLNC. (2009). Public notice regarding MLNC MOBIUS merger discussions. Retrieved March 6, 2009 from: http://pipeup.wordpress.com/2009/02/19/news-on-mlncmobius-merger-talks/

MLNC. (2009). Press release announcing INCOLSA and MLC billing partnership. Retrieved March 6, 2009 from: http://mlc.lib.mi.us/objects/rte/mediaupload/File/refdocs/incolsa_oclc_billing_press_release_2-09_v3.pdf

BCR. (2009). History of the Collaborative Digitization Program on the BCR website. Retrieved March 6, 2009 from: http://www.bcr.org/cdp/index.html

The Jay Jordan IFLA/OCLC Early Career Development Fellowship Program: A Long Name for an Important Project

NANCY LENSENMAYER and GEORGE NEEDHAM
OCLC Online Computer Library Center, Inc., Dublin, OH, USA

ABSTRACT. *The Jay Jordan IFLA/OCLC Early Career Development Fellowship Program, jointly sponsored by the American Theological Library Association, the International Federation of Library Associations and Institutions (IFLA) and OCLC, provides early career development and continuing education for library and information science professionals from countries with developing economies. The program's history, selection process, and curriculum are described in detail. Fellows comment on their experiences, new perspectives, lessons learned, and benefits gained from participation in the Fellowship program.*

HISTORY

On August 24, 1999, Jay Jordan, the President and CEO of the Online Computer Library Center (OCLC), and Christine Deschamps, the President of the International Federation of Library Associations and Institutions (IFLA) and a member of the OCLC Board of Trustees, announced the creation of the IFLA/OCLC Early Career Development Fellowship. The setting for the announcement, IFLA's General Conference in Bangkok, Thailand, was appropriate, because the fellowship was intended, in Christine Deschamps' words, to "allow librarians from developing countries to come to the United States, have good technical training, and visit a few North American libraries" (OCLC News Release, 1999).

The OCLC Institute, a relatively new division of OCLC under the direction of Dr. Martin Dillon, managed the program in its opening years. He planned to expose the Fellows to a variety of information technologies. "The program will be designed to provide as much background as possible on emerging technologies and their role in global cooperative librarianship," he said in announcing the program. "It will provide advanced, continuing education and exposure to a broad range of issues in information technologies and library operations" (OCLC News Release, 1999).

The application process opened in late 1999, and the first class of Fellows was selected in 2000. The American Library Association joined with IFLA and OCLC to sponsor one of the four fellowships. Additional support was provided by UNESCO and World Bank. The Fellows were named at the IFLA General Conference in Jerusalem in August 2000 (OCLC News Release, 2000), a pattern that has been followed in each subsequent year. One feature of the first year's program that was not continued was the selection of eight finalists, who were offered free registration at any other OCLC Institute educational event.

The Fellows, from India, Malaysia, South Africa, and Turkey, arrived at OCLC's headquarters in Ohio in May 2001 for their 4-week adventure (OCLC Web site). They were quickly immersed in a program of visits to libraries in Ohio and Washington, DC, tutorials on information technology, and discussions of library cooperation. Their visit also coincided with a meeting of the OCLC Members Council; however, subsequent classes had the opportunity to participate more fully in Council meetings.

The 2002 class included five librarians from India, Indonesia, Kenya, Malaysia, and South Africa (OCLC News Release, 2001). Late in 2002, the OCLC Institute was reorganized, and the Member Services division assumed responsibility for the program.

The 2003 class had been selected and plans were complete when the Severe Acute Respiratory Syndrome (SARS) epidemic emerged in Asia. As a result, the 2003 class was postponed, with the selected Fellows invited to participate in 2004. One student postponed participation until 2005, due to a scheduling conflict with her PhD program.

As a result, the group that convened in Dublin in April 2004 consisted of seven librarians, representing Ghana, India, Mauritius, Rwanda, South Korea, Sri Lanka, and Vietnam.

In late 2003, the Executive Director of the American Theological Library Association, Dennis Norlin, approached OCLC, offering to sponsor an additional Fellow from a theological or religious library. Several months later, an agreement was reached, and the 2005 class included the first of these librarians (ATLA News Release, 2004). 2005's class included the first librarians from the Western Hemisphere, Colombia and Jamaica (the theological librarian), along with representatives from China, Georgia, Malawi, Pakistan, and Turkey.

Another key partnership evolved in the early part of the decade with the Mortenson Center at the University of Illinois at Urbana Champaign (UIUC). Barbara Ford and Susan Schnuer of the Center provided tours of the UIUC Campus, sessions with the faculty of the Graduate School of Library and Information Science, and background on various programs in international librarianship. A side benefit of this partnership has been visits to the OCLC campus by the International Associates of the Mortenson Center.

For 2007, an additional week was added to the program. This week is spent at the OCLC office in Leiden, The Netherlands. This week includes visits to libraries in The Netherlands and Germany, as well as discussions of library cooperation and interaction from a European perspective.

By the time the 2008 program concluded, 38 Fellows representing 23 countries had participated. To celebrate Jay Jordan's 10th anniversary as President and CEO, the Board of Trustees renamed the program the Jay Jordan IFLA/OCLC Early Career Development Fellowship Program and added funding for an additional Fellow. The 2009 class was thus expanded to six Fellows.

SELECTION PROCESS

Promising library and information science professionals who are in early stages of career development and who meet program qualifications are encouraged to apply for the Fellowship. Program qualifications are reviewed and updated annually by the program's Selection Committee and are posted on the OCLC Web site (www.oclc.org).

Applicants must have a qualifying degree in library or information science. They must be in early stages of their career, having obtained their qualifying degree within the previous 5 years and having some library or information science experience, typically between 3 to 8 years. The program is targeted to professionals from developing countries, and applicants must be a legal national from a qualifying country and be working as a librarian or information science professional in that country. The list of Qualifying Countries is updated annually, reflecting changes in economies and human development as reported by World Bank, UNESCO and other organizations. Program presentations, seminars, and facilitated discussions are given in English, and it is essential that candidates read and speak English proficiently. Applicants must have a valid passport and be able to obtain visas permitting legal entry into the United States and into the European Union via The Netherlands.

Applicants complete and submit a formal application, including an essay describing why the applicant wants to participate in the program. The essay should demonstrate insight into the problems and opportunities facing libraries in the applicant's country, an awareness of the role of library cooperation, and evidence of personal commitment to professional development and service. Candidates also submit two letters of recommendation, providing evidence of the applicant's commitment to professional development and service, and assessing his/her promise as a developing professional.

A specially appointed Selection Committee, comprised of representatives from the sponsoring organizations, evaluates and scores the applications. Committee members select the Fellows. Award recipients are contacted via email to confirm their participation. Award recipients are announced at the IFLA General Conference and Council in August of each year. Names of award recipients are posted on the OCLC Web site after the announcement is made at the IFLA General Conference.

The award provides airfare from the recipient's home country to the United States and Europe program base locations, and return trip to the recipient's home country, transportation within the United States and Europe related to library visits, lodging and subsistence, including meals.

CURRICULUM

The curriculum focuses on four key areas: a) technology-based library services; b) library best practices; b) global library cooperation and networking; and d) professional development.

The technology-based library services component is designed to increase the Fellows' awareness of technological advances in cataloging, reference, resource sharing, and digitization and preservation. Fellows attend presentations by providers and users of technology-based services. Sessions include discussions about global issues and technology trends as well as demonstrations of specific automated library services and systems. Fellows observe, participate in facilitated discussions, conduct hands-on exercises, and complete electronic and written exercises.

The library best practices component helps increase the Fellows' awareness of best practices used in United States and European national, academic, public, school, and special libraries. The Fellows visit many libraries, participate in facilitated discussions, and complete electronic and written exercises summarizing experiences and identifying possible best practices that could be considered for implementation in libraries in the Fellows' home countries. Libraries visited vary from year to year, but typically include national libraries, such as the Library of Congress, Koninklijke Bibliotheek (Netherlands), and Deutsche Nationalbibliothek (Germany); academic libraries, such as The Ohio State University Libraries, University of Illinois Urbana Champaign, and University of Frankfurt (Germany); public libraries, such as Columbus (Ohio) Metropolitan Library, Chicago Public Library, Westerville (Ohio) Public library, and Amsterdam (Netherlands) Public Library; school libraries; and special libraries, such as the OCLC Library, Folger Shakespeare Library, and Newberry Library.

The global library cooperation and networking component demonstrates the value of global library cooperation and establishes contacts for continued communication among the Fellows and other library and information professionals. Fellows meet with librarians and other information professionals who work in a variety of library settings and professional library associations and organizations. Fellows meet additional international library colleagues while participating in an OCLC Members Council meeting, attending sessions sponsored by the Mortenson Center for International Library Programs and meeting with colleagues from sponsoring organizations ATLA, IFLA, and OCLC.

Professional development is an important component of the program. The curriculum includes scheduled blocks of individual professional development time, used for independent research, consultation, and creation of a professional development plan. Each Fellow creates a personal professional development plan, with specific short-and long-term goals that can be used to guide the Fellow's continued growth and contribution to libraries in the Fellow's home country. The plans, created under the supervision of the OCLC Program Director, Education and Professional Development, can be updated on an ongoing basis as the Fellows progress on their career paths.

These plans can have an important impact on the Fellows' future by helping them think about their futures in a different way. Elisangela Silva (Brazil, class of 2006), wrote, "This is a kind of 'prophetic paper' because . . . all things that I had planned are happening: when I returned to my country, in the same year I enrolled in the Master's Degree in Information Science at São Paulo University; moreover, I have been working on a development of a community libraries network. I learned more about planning and to think about daring goals. We can do it! We also can make the difference in our country: dream and make it come true!"

"The professional development plan that we were guided to develop has remained the guide for (my) career. I remember my aim was to become a University Librarian, a Lecturer and a Consultant. I am happy to report that 4 years after the program, I am now a Deputy Librarian (Associate Professor Status) and Agriculture University Librarian, a Lecturer in Records/Information Management, and a Consultant in the provision of Library and Information Services," wrote Mac Anthony Cobblah (Ghana, class of 2004).

IMPACT

Each Fellow experiences the program in his or her own way. For some, this is their first travel outside their home countries. Others are experienced travelers who have visited many countries. Some have diplomas or certificates in librarianship, others hold advanced degrees.

But for each Fellow, the program offers a variety of new experiences, new contacts, and new points of view about their chosen field.

The practical aspects of the curriculum were noted by Festus Ngetich (Kenya, class of 2006). "The fellowship was a wonderful opportunity for me. It exposed me to a host of experiences. I learned a lot about how Information and Communication Technologies have been applied to transform library operations and services as manifested through OCLC's technological products and services. I experienced the concept of library cooperation in its most pragmatic sense when we visited and learned from some of the United States' successful library cooperatives like OhioLINK. I also learned a lot about digitization and how it is helping institutions to create memories about their past events and undertakings which enables them to identify their strengths and weaknesses and strategize to seize emerging opportunities and avoid threats" (OCLC E-mails, 2008).

Pauline Nicholas (Jamaica, class of 2007) wrote, "The Jay Jordan IFLA/OCLC Early Career Development Fellowship was simply awesome and it was highly successful. It has inspired me to make a difference in my country in the areas of reference services, library cooperatives, and electronic books."

"Discussions with the decision-makers of major U.S. libraries and the sponsoring organizations influenced my approach towards problem-solving and the policy-formulation in my work with the National Library & Information System Authority (NALIS)," wrote Maria Cherrie (Trinidad & Tobago, class of 2006). "I also had the opportunity to share my fellowship experiences with colleagues at NALIS, and collaborate with OCLC for information literacy initiatives."

Roman V. Purici (Moldova, class of 2006) noted a common thread. "Every place we visited, whether a library or an OCLC partner organization, it was great to see dedicated people with a vision, and that vision was to offer great customer service to end users."

Networking is important to many of the Fellows. As Smita Chandra (India, class of 2001) wrote, "The time spent with experts from various fields and meetings with people who made an impact, respected and shared the same concerns, and had the distinct ability to make things happen, broadened my perspective and re-instated my confidence towards excellence in the field. The discussions with peers and experts at OCLC helped me re-evaluate my work, focus on realistic goals and draft a course of action for better contribution." Maria Cherrie agreed, saying, "The global discussions which began in Dublin, Ohio, among five Fellows, have grown into a stronger and wider network of past and future Fellows, supporting each other in our careers."

Several Fellows used the program as a springboard to further their formal education. Muhammad Rafiq (Pakistan, class of 2003) and Musa Olaka

(Rwanda, class of 2004) are among the Fellows working on doctorates. Mr. Olaka also helped to restore the archives of his civil war-ravaged country, re-iterating the importance of libraries and librarians in the communal memory of a nation.

For Ibrahim Ramjaun (Mauritius, class of 2003), the experience was more than professional. "By interacting with different OCLC staff and living side by side with other Fellows from different regions of the world, my intellectual and cultural horizons broadened within a short time span." Similarly, Hanan Erhif (Morocco, class of 2008) wrote, "My participation at this program changed my life. I feel more and more proud to be an information specialist and I am more motivated to develop libraries in my country."

Janete S. B. Estevão (Brazil, class of 2006) stressed the importance of mixing librarians from a variety of regions to accentuate the experience. "I could learn from multicultural colleagues we had the privilege to know, their difficulties and limitations, but also their stories of success and perseverance in promoting a more egalitarian society through access of information."

Elisangela Silva (Brazil, class of 2007) put her comments in the form of advice for the class of 2009. "Be prepared: you will learn a lot—much more that you all can imagine—and also, you will learn much of the other Fellows' culture, habits, everything! So, don't lose the chance to talk a lot with each other, ok? Don't lose the chance to ask simple or complicated questions, to taste foods, to see, and talk with people. Please, don't be shy about anything, and enjoy this great opportunity. At the end of the program you will have the feeling that you ate a delicious ice cream with the wisdom taste and certainly you will want more. I miss these days, or in Portuguese: *que saudades daqueles dias*!"

It is very important to note that this benefit is not one sided. OCLC staff members have made new friendships and met colleagues from around the world. Ishwar Laxminarayan, who is currently a library director in Michigan but who worked in OCLC's reference services in the early 2000s, wrote that the Fellows "added a unique international perspective to the just-concluded Reference Services Advisory Committee and Resource Sharing Advisory Committee meetings." Each Fellow is assigned an OCLC staff member as a mentor, and there are always significantly more volunteers than Fellows to be mentored. Other staffers take Fellows to dinner, to church, to the shopping mall, or into their homes to meet their families. One of the highlights of the program is the afternoon in which each Fellow presents an overview of libraries in his or her country, including the often considerable obstacles they face in offering library service to their countrymen and women.

Delegates to the Members Council also serve as hosts for the Fellows during the meeting, to help the Fellows understand the processes and issues with which the Council deals.

These interactions have resulted in some strong relationships. When a tsunami struck Sri Lanka in December 2004, Nayana Wijayasundara, a librarian from Colombo who had been a 2004 Fellow, was safe, but she acted as the locus of relief efforts organized by OCLC staff and by the Lexington (Kentucky) Public Library, the institution of her Members Council host, Kathleen Imhoff. OCLC staff also gathered funds for a school in Kenya that was lacking library books. Musa Olaka and Selenay Aytaç (Turkey, class of 2003) have returned to OCLC's campus after their Fellowships to speak to staff, Members Council delegates, and subsequent classes of Fellows.

The effects of the program can be long lasting. Purity (Mwagha) Muthoni (Kenya, class of 2002) offered this advice to future Fellows, "If you open your eyes, ears, and mind, and see it, hear it and think about it, it will be a life changing experience in your career that you will live not only to quote but also to act according to the learned principles as you go up the ladder in your career. We still do, 7 years down the line."

FUTURE

In the program's 1999 inaugural announcement, OCLC president and CEO Jay Jordan stated, "This career development program has the potential to positively affect individuals, their institutions, their countries and the global knowledge management practices of the future."

Ten years later, the program's potential is being realized daily. Thirty-eight remarkable Fellows from 26 countries are impacting the global library community. OCLC staff stay in close communication with the Fellows and provide ongoing support. The OCLC membership continues to benefit from the diverse viewpoints and experiences the Fellows bring to the program.

What began as a 4-week program, bringing four pioneering Fellows to Ohio, is now a 5-week program, bringing six Fellows annually to the United States and Europe. The Fellows are networking, becoming leaders in professional library associations, teaching in library schools, mentoring young professionals, pursuing master's and doctoral degrees, and working in national, academic, public, and special libraries. They are speaking at local, regional, national and international library conferences. The Fellows are providing input to global library organizations, investigating and implementing technology solutions, developing and implementing library best practices, sharing globally and continuing their own professional development.

REFERENCES

ATLA News Release. (2004, March 14). ATLA Seeks Theological Librarians for IFLA/OCLC Fellows Program. Retrieved August 29, 2008, from http://www.atla.com/news/press/press04.html#ifla_oclc

OCLC News Release. (2000, August 14). Four Librarians from India, Malaysia, South Africa and Turkey Named IFLA/OCLC Early Career Development Fellows. Retrieved August 29, 2008, from http://worldcat.org/arcviewer/1/OCC/2003/07/08/0000003707/viewer/file47.html

OCLC News Release. (2001, August 21). IFLA/OCLC Early Career Development Fellows named for 2002. Retrieved August 29, 2008, from http://worldcat.org/arcviewer/1/OCC/2006/07/19/0000023368/viewer/file30.html

OCLC News Release. (1999, August 24). OCLC to Sponsor New IFLA Early Career Development Fellowship. OCLC News Release. Retrieved August 29, 2008, from http://worldcat.org/arcviewer/1/OCC/2003/07/08/0000003706/viewer/file61.html

OCLC. (E-mails, August 5, 2008, and August 22, 2008).

OCLC.org. (2008). Photos. Retrieved August 29, 2008, from http://www.oclc.org/us/en/community/careerdevelopment/fellows/default.htm.

21st Century Library Systems

ANDREW PACE

Networked Library Services, OCLC Online Computer Library Center, Inc., Dublin, OH, USA

ABSTRACT. *Less than a decade into the 21st century, perhaps it is more fitting to describe library automation as approaching its 80th birthday, is a time to look back and carefully measure moving forward. Since the introduction of a punch card circulation system at the University of Texas in 1936, through the advent and perseverance of the MARC record, and following the ebb and flow of nearly 75 different library automation vendors, library automation has come a long way. For some, however, it has not come nearly far enough. If one were to stop the history of library automation in the mid-1990s and wish away the dominance of the Internet, libraries and patrons might have been quite content with the state-of-the-art as it existed 15 years ago. But wishing away the Internet is like envisioning a world without electricity and indoor plumbing; as such, that 1990s library automation summit is now a plateau from which many library technologists and futurists can see no launch pad to a next-generation of library software and services.*

"If you wish to make an apple pie *truly* from scratch, you must first invent the universe."—Carl Sagan

A SLOW START

The irony of the current stagnant situation for library systems is that libraries likely offered the public its first glimpse of computer use and database interaction. Long before ATM machines and the Web, many of the first public keyboards could be found attached to dumb terminals in libraries. These terminals were, in turn, connected to mainframes, and libraries supported workflows that either relied on data supplied from a central hub, or created stand-alone systems for local inventory control.

Those local inventory systems, built upon ordering, acquisition, and circulation of physical materials grew into the robustly functional integrated library systems (ILS) with which most libraries are now familiar. Because back office workflows were governed by electronic records and computerized inventory, libraries were able to leap forward in providing public access to those records. The displays seem quaint by today's standards, but were designed to transition patrons from card catalogs to their new electronic equivalent.

Unfortunately, libraries and their vendors were not prepared for the exponentially rising expectations that the advent of the Web would usher in. Mired in transitioning character-based telnet systems to rapidly selling graphical user interface (GUI) systems, most vendors were ill-prepared to make another transition to the Web just a few short years later. First-generation Web-based online catalogs reflected the nascent state of Web development and lacked much of the functionality that had been available in online systems for over a decade. Faced with few alternatives, libraries suffered the pain of first generation GUI systems and took a wait-and-see approach to more sophisticated patron interfaces. Unfortunately, this strategy resulted in a wait-and-wait scenario for both end-user experience and back-office operations.

PLUGGING THE GAPS

While libraries seemingly accepted the fate that the basic functions provided by an integrated library system would not change radically, the nature of their collections and associated workflow were themselves changing rapidly. Web-based content, licensed resources, born-digital documents, and institutionally significant digital collections emerged rapidly to overtake the effort required to maintain print collections, especially in academic libraries. Traditional integrated systems proved inadequate for managing these assets despite numerous noble efforts to fit square pegs into round holes—eSerials checkin, Cooperative Online Resource Cataloging (CORC), e-reserves scanning stations, etc.

The inadequacy of the ILS was compounded by a desire among vendors and libraries alike to build new solutions with new technologies. Electronic Resource Management (ERM), Digital Asset Management (DAM), and Institutional Repository (IR) systems would be built with 21st century technologies to aid in these new library workflows. Paradoxically, as industry expert Marhsall Breeding points out, "[The process of evaluating library workflow] may be confounded by the fact that many libraries have adapted their work-flows to match the limitations of their automation systems" (Breeding, 2007). This begs the question whether vendors have done a short-term service to libraries in the midst of a major sea-change, while doing a longer-term disservice to the efficiency of libraries.

Certainly, if automation experts were starting from scratch, they would endeavor to logically combine resource management in libraries under an umbrella of software that makes distinctions between resource format without unnecessarily bifurcating workflow into separate systems. A current list of essential products, of course, makes this challenge more daunting than it might seem at first glance. Many libraries might delineate a suite of services (in addition to the ILS) similar to the list provided by Mark Andrews (Andrews, 2007):

- OpenURL Link Resolver
- Federated search tool
- Digital archive, institutional repository, and portfolio products
- Electronic Resource Management (ERM)
- Compact and robotic storage systems for archived print materials
- Next-generation portal and discovery tools (for all of the above)
- A management interface (for all of the above) to determine usage and user satisfaction and allow for *ad hoc* reporting and statistical analysis

It's difficult to picture a library workflow, let alone a single integrated product that can handle so much. Nevertheless, there are some technical strategies, discussed below, that might make the tactical deployment of solutions adequately functional, faster to deploy and upgrade, and less expensive for libraries.

BUSINESS DISTRACTIONS

Before the demand for products capable of managing a new myriad of library content, vendors sought merely the state-of-the-art for managing print collections. "The hallmark of [first generation library] systems," writes Andrews, "was the struggle for 'functional completion' in an 'integrated library system'" (Andrews, 2007). By the late 1990s, the library software business had created several commodity-like applications. One vendor's offerings had become less and less distinguished from another, leading one pundit to liken the choice between ILSes to a choice between cars on a rental lot (Pace, 2004). Nevertheless, this plateau of innovation had yet to cause considerable churn within the market. Concomitant with the market saturation for integrated systems was the firm establishment of strong and loyal relationships between libraries and their vendors. In fact, an apparent paucity of new product penetration

TABLE 1 Mergers & Acquisitions, 2000–2008

TLC acquires CARL (2000)
Auto-Graphics acquires Maxcess Library Systems (2001)
Sirsi acquires DRA (2001)
Scott Cheatham acquires EOS (2001)
Jerry Kline acquires remaining shares of Innovative Interfaces (2001)
OCLC acquires netLibrary (2001)
Geac acquires Extensity (2002)
ProQuest acquires Serials Solutions (2004)
ISACSOFT acquires Bibliomondo (2004)
Bowker acquires Syndetic Solutions (2004)
Sirsi acquires Docutek (2005)
Sirsi acquires Dynix (2005)
OCLC PICA acquires Fretwell-Downing (2005)
OCLC PICA acquires Sisis (2005)
Golden Gate Capital acquires Geac (2005)
OCLC acquires Openly Informatics (2006)
Follet acquires Sagebrush (2006)
Geac becomes Extensity (2006)
Fransisco Partners acquires Ex Libris (2006)
Infor acquires Extensity (Geac) (2006)
Fransisco Partners acquires Endeavor Information Systems (2006)
Cambridge Information Group acquires Proquest (2006)
OCLC acquires DiMeMa (CONTENTdm) (2006)
Vista Partners buys out SirsiDynix (2006)
Bowker acquires MediaLab (AquaBrowser) (2007)
Liblime acquires Katipo's Koha division (2007)
OCLC acquires remaining shares of OCLC Pica (2007)
Ronald Brisebois acquires ISACSoft (2008)
LibLime acquires Care Affiliates (2008)
Leeds Equity acquires Ex Libris (2008)

made many vendors appear less like software companies and more like relationship management companies.

Customer relations and management would get a lot trickier in the early part of the 21st century. As indicated in Table 1, 2000–2008 activities in the library automation space have been largely driven by mergers and acquisitions, with over 30 major activities in less than 10 years. It's no wonder that a combination of business consolidation, stunted innovation, and rapid Web application development outside the library automation space would lead to disenchantment and restlessness among libraries.

TURNING TIDES

It's also no coincidence that the first half of this decade in which blogs became so prevalent was marked more by a clamoring and complaining about the state of library automation than by the actual development of in-novative software. Twenty-first century library system development is now

driven by restless customers, motivated not only by a few tireless advocates, but also by the publicly visible fruits of system development within
libraries.

Open Source Software (OSS) efforts such as the Open Archive Initiative (OAI), DSpace, and Koha—just to name a few, as an exhaustive
list would overwhelm the reader—challenged commercial proprietary systems, not only for market share but often in terms of sophistication and
functionality. Experimentation with new so-called bolt-on catalog interfaces
such as RLG's RedLightGreen and Casey Bisson's blog-powered WPOPAC
led to production efforts from several individual libraries and vendors, including, North Carolina State University Libraries, OCLC, and AquaBrowser
(Antelman, Lynema, & Pace, 2006).

Challenged by relative new-comers and outsiders of the library automation space—Endeca, MediaLab, WordPress, and FAST—vendors adroitly answered the call for improved public interfaces. In fact, it is fair for vendors
to decry at least some of the impatient clamoring of library IT specialists, as
many of the increasingly expensive incremental changes made to legacy ILS
systems were demanded by the libraries paying relatively small maintenance
fees. One might argue that vendors were squandering the money of their
customers doing exactly what was asked of them.

NEXT GENERATION AS A ZERO-SUM GAME

Despite the nimble reaction of many ILS vendors to fill some of the service
gaps created by the inadequacy of the ILS to meet 21st century needs, the
overall market for integrated library systems has not grown substantially over
the last 5 years. With annual revenues estimated at $570 million, sales of new
ILSes dipped 15% in 2008. These losses were partly offset by new end-user
product offerings, but do little to indicate incentives to radically change or
improve underlying systems.

> Several factors limited opportunities to sell traditional library automation
> systems this year. The higher-end market of public and academic libraries
> has saturated; fewer libraries have legacy systems in immediate need of
> replacement. Recent migrations from legacy systems have largely run
> to completion ... [L]ibraries considering ILS replacements are holding
> off, hoping better options will emerge soon, especially on the open
> source front. Libraries feel a sense of urgency to acquire next-generation
> interfaces that will allow them to cast aside library catalogs that work
> more like the Web of 1998 than 2008 and gain tools to manage ever-
> growing collections of electronic content (Breeding, 2008)

It's clear that to counter the impact of a zero-sum future for the ILS, the next generation of functional offerings must be technically compelling while providing all the functionality with which libraries are accustomed.

OPTIMISTIC FORECASTS

Two of the last three endeavors to create an ILS from scratch in the last decade have been business, if not also functional, failures. DRA's Taos system was killed after the company's acquisition by Sirsi, and Dynix's Horizon 8.0 was declared dead-on-almost-arrival after a merger with the same company. While some might tie these failed attempts at a next-generation management system to a common corporate ownership, some might have predicted lackluster outcomes of the somewhat overly optimistic picture created by the newly architected systems.

A more optimistic spin might say that the second mouse gets the cheese. The third (and thus far successful) venture alluded to above is the open source ILS venture, Evergreen, now supported by Equinox, Inc. By releasing their software as open source, the Evergreen team created a new compelling reason to consider switching systems. Though it combines the functionality sought after in a new patron front-end, the system actually falls short on the full functionality of other proprietary ILS systems. Nevertheless, it is the positioning of the open source code as something new, and embraced by forward-thinking customers, that has lured customers away from more traditional solutions.

Fortunately for libraries, the freshness of the open source solution is not the only 21st century innovation to look forward to; nor is it mutually exclusive of another burgeoning trend that is likely to have an impact on a next generation of service offerings.

THE CLOUD GENERATION

Neil Howe and William Strauss are experts in evaluating the trends of generations. They write, "to anticipate what 40-year-olds will be like 20 years from now, don't look at today's 40-year-olds, look at today's 20-year olds" (Howe & Stauss, 2007). It is worthwhile, therefore, to evaluate the platforms on which younger generations are computing. This is not to suggest that Facebook, Flickr, and Wikipedia will form the basis for a next-generation library management system. It is these very services, however, that should serve as a model for 21st century data storage, software on demand, and cloud computing capabilities.

The cloud is a metaphor for the Internet (based on how it is depicted in computer network diagrams) and is an abstraction for the complex infrastructure it conceals. It is a style of computing where IT-related capabilities are provided "as a service," allowing users to access technology-enabled services from the Internet ("in the cloud") without knowledge of, expertise with, or control over the technology infrastructure that supports them (Wikipedia, 2008).

The Gartner Group predicts that massively scalable service solutions provided by cloud computing will be as influential as E-business (Gartner, 2008). Fast-paced improvement to IT infrastructure and the continued industrialization of IT services over the last decade has laid the groundwork for Web-based software services. Popular examples include Google-Docs, QuickenWeb, or Salesforce.com. According to Daryl Plummer, Managing Vice President and Gartner Fellow, "this is due, in part to the commoditization and standardization of technologies, in part to virtualization and the rise of service-oriented software architectures, and most importantly, to the dramatic growth in popularity of the Internet" (Gartner, 2008).

If one accepts the premise that the ILS has reached commodity status, it stands to reason that the services provided by locally installed and maintained software can and should be provided by a networked service. Of course, a higher level of trust and reliability must be achieved, and it remains to be seen whether existing vendors can put the same trust and reliability into software services that many online publishers have established with online scholarly and popular content.

Nevertheless, if this generation's 20-year-olds are the next generation's library administrators, it might be worth taking a look at the increased

TABLE 2 Cloud Computing Activities by Different Age Cohorts *Internet users in each age group who do the following online activitiess (%)*

	18–29	30–49	50–64	65+
Use webmail services such as Hotmail, Gmail, or Yahoo! mail	77%	58%	44%	27%
Store personal photos	50	34	26	19
Use online applications such as Google Documents or Adobe Photoshop Express	39	28	25	19
Store personal videos	14	6	5	2
Pay to store computer files online	9	4	5	3
Back up hard drive to an online site	7	5	5	4
Have done at least <u>one</u> activity	87%	71%	59%	46%
Have done at least <u>two</u> activities	59	39	31	21

Source: Pew Internet & American Life Project April-May 2008 Survey. N = 1,553 Internet users. Margin of error is ± 3%.

level of trust placed in cloud computing and data storage by younger generations. A look at usage levels according to age groups shows rising levels of trust for storing personal data on the Internet (Horrigan, 2008).

While the Pew study does not specifically address business data storage, it is easy to make extrapolations about the level of trust in those areas, and several online businesses are banking on the future for cloud computing that Gartner, Pew, and others have predicted.

WEB AS PLATFORM

One such company banking on software-as-a-service (SaaS) and cloud computing is Bungee Labs, creators of Bungee Connect, an end-to-end environment that allows developers to build desktop-like applications from multiple Web services and databases and then instantly deploy them on Bungee's multi-tenant grid infrastructure. Services of this type are either extensions of or have been emulated by much more recognizable companies like Amazon and Google.

If such platforms—Bungee's Dave Mitchell goes so far as to call the model Platform-as-a-Service (PaaS)—were extended to library software usage, libraries might foresee a day when large capital expenditures for hardware and software could be replaced by subscription-based services. Mitchell writes:

> On the SaaS side of things, there have been some notable successes in the areas of [Customer Relationship Management] CRM-as-a-service, computing-as-a-service and storage-as-a-service. These are just a few examples of data, functionality and hardware as services over the network. These individual offerings represent the next logical evolution of software and computing in the cloud (Mitchell, 2008)

Technical Advantages of the PaaS Model

- Develop, test, deploy, host, and maintain on the same integrated environment
- Dramatically reduce costs of development while supporting a robust software life cycle.
- User experience without compromise: avoiding downloads, plugins, and Internet hiccups
- Built-in scalability, reliability, and security
- Multi-tenanc—the ability for an application to automatically partition state and data to service an arbitrary number of users

- Must support Web-scale use
- Built-in integration with Web services and databases
- Deep application instrumentation—see exactly how and when users are using the application (Mitchell, 2008)

It's at least time that libraries and vendors turned some of their attention from richer end-user experiences to the back-office workflows that support them. As Breeding contends, "We can't let the current focus on front-end interfaces make us complacent about the software systems that we use to automate routine library functions" (Breeding, 2007). The timing seems right to make such an effort at the creation of next-generation systems with the cloud in mind. There could come a day very soon that libraries would simply plug into the wall to receive all the required power of software services, rather than running locally deployed systems like home generators with all the associated expense, cyclical upgrades, and hardware maintenance.

The economic advantages to a service-based future for library automation should not be under-estimated. Despite a surge of online content being available to patrons, libraries will continue back-office operations for all types of materials. The more these workflows are industrialized and served by network-level applications, the more time and effort libraries can assign to other intellectual endeavors. Far too much time is spent getting systems to work at the expense of more fruitful activity.

In varied lists of technical demands made of library automation vendors, the library is poised to become part of the Web 2.0 culture, acknowledging and even supporting many Web service models. Most punditry, however, still calls for hardware independence and access to proprietary APIs; demands fall short by merely asking that local systems avail themselves of other Web services rather than establishing themselves as services in their own right. Moreover, integration with other business process systems—course management, financial services, and human resource systems—will require new thinking on a next-generation of integration. Acknowledgement that library management system will never attain dominance as college, university, community, and corporate business process systems should encourage libraries to seek integration through Web-based services—a loftier goal than mere "interoperability"—so that library workflows can be managed in conjunction with other services.

THE FUTURE IS INEVITABLE

When it comes to library automation, lamenting the past is nearly as easy as predicting the future is difficult. One thing seems fairly certain, however—that the library automation landscape requires dramatic change in order to ensure its future. The landscape metaphor itself is too pessimistic, though, as shifting ground often leaves only destruction as its aftermath. Libraries require a sea-change—a dramatic departure from the status quo of library automation, solutions that will scale like typical Web solutions, technologies that will ensure our future. To date, the swelling seas of library automation have been caused by the rising tide of discontent in libraries. Going into the future, libraries, service providers, and technology experts have an unparalleled opportunity to create the swelling seas on which all boats will rise.

REFERENCES

Andrews, M. (2007). OPAC changing markets, changing relationships: how libraries and vendors respond to the 'next generation' challenge. *Library Hi Tech*, *25*, 562–578.

Antelman, K., Lynema, E., & Pace, A. (2006). Toward a twenty-first century library catalog. *Information Technology and Libraries, September*, 128–39.

Bahr, E. (2007). Dreaming of a better ILS. *Computers in Libraries*, *27*, 10–14.

Breeding, M. (2007). It's time to break the mold of the original ILS. *Computers in Libraries*, 39–41.

Breeding, M. (2008). Automation systems marketplace 2008: Opportunity out of turmoil. *Library Journal*. Retrieved September 30, 2008, from http://www.libraryjournal.com/article/CA6542440.html

Fons, T., & Jewell, T. (2007). Envisioning the future of ERM systems. *The Serials Librarian*, *52*, 151–166.

Gartner Says Cloud Computing Will Be As Influential As E-business. (June 26, 2008). Press release. Retrieved September 30, 2008, from http://www.gartner.com/it/page.jsp?id=707508.

Henderson, M. (2008). Heresy and misconduct: evolution of library automation. *ILA Reporter*, *26*, 4–7.

Horrigan, J. (2008). Use of cloud computing applications and services. *Pew Internet and American Life Project*, 1–9.

Howe, N., & Strauss, W. (2007). The Next 20 years: How customer and workforce attitudes will evolve. *Harvard Business Review, July-August*, 41–52.

Mitchell, D. (2008). Defining platform-as-a-service, or PaaS. Bungee Connect Developer Network. Retrieved September 30, 2008, from http://blogs.bungeeconnect.com/2008/02/18/defining-platform-as-a-service-or-paas/

Pace, A. (2004). Dismantling integrated library systems. *Library Journal, February 1, 2004*. Retrieved September 30, 2008, from http://libraryjournal.com/article/CA374953.html

Wikipedia. Retrieved September 30, 2008, from http://en.wikipedia.org/wiki/Cloud_computing.

Wolven, R. (2008). In search of a new model. *netConnect, January 2008*. Retrieved September 30, 2008, from http://www.libraryjournal.com/index.asp?layout=articlePrint&articleID=CA6514921

Next Generation Cataloging

KAREN CALHOUN

WorldCat and Metadata Services, OCLC Online Computer Library Center, Inc., Dublin, OH, USA

RENEE REGISTER

Cataloging and Metadata Services, OCLC Online Computer Library Center, Inc., Dublin, OH, USA

During the past several years the Online Computer Library Center (OCLC) noted increasing concern from the library community regarding the future of cataloging. In response to this concern and to the rapidly changing metadata environment, OCLC is taking steps to further a paradigm shift toward early acquisition of metadata in WorldCat directly from the entities responsible for content purchased by libraries—chiefly the publisher supply chain. This shift in thinking requires the acknowledgement that metadata is dynamic and will change over time and relies upon the automated capture of metadata early in the publishing cycle as well as automated processes to help make the early metadata "good enough."

The explosion of content, the expectation of rapid metadata exposure in the Web environment, user expectation of "get it (or reserve it) now," economic concerns regarding the cost of metadata creation, and the decrease in cataloging staff make the development of more efficient, cost-effective methods for metadata creation and maintenance imperative.

LC WORKING GROUP ON THE FUTURE OF BIBLIOGRAPHIC CONTROL

In November 2006, Deanna Marcum, Associate Librarian for Library Services at the Library of Congress, convened a "Working Group on the Future of Bibliographic Control" to explore the current metadata environment and make recommendations on the future of bibliographic control in our evolving environment. The Working Group published its final report, titled "On the Record", in January 2008 (Library of Congress, 2008). One of the first recommendations contained in "On the Record" is to "Make more use of bibliographic data earlier in the supply chain." This recommendation was welcomed by OCLC since a pilot program called "Next Generation Cataloging and Metadata Services" had been in the planning stages during 2007 and was kicked off in January 2008. This pilot was designed to explore greater use of publisher supply chain metadata in record creation for libraries and to explore the use of library data to enrich publisher supply chain metadata.

The publisher supply chain responded positively to the OCLC pilot concept. The importance of Web-based discovery and buying tools has resulted in a strong movement in the publishing industry toward exchange of metadata in electronic format, the development of standards to support metadata exchange and growing consensus on the importance of consistent application of best practices in metadata creation. The increasing evolution and adoption of the ONIX format (http://www.editeur.org/onix.html)for the capture and electronic exchange of title information in the marketplace provides an opportunity for the library community to break down traditional silos between library and publisher supply chain metadata.

However, the publisher supply chain also struggles with the explosion of content and the cost of metadata creation and maintenance. Publishers and vendors who serve the library market as well as the retail market must also contend with metadata needs specific to the library community such as library-defined classification schema and terminologies, need for metadata in MARC format, and rules for description that differ from standard practice in the non-library metadata arena.

NEXT GENERATION CATALOGING PILOT

OCLC's Next Generation Cataloging pilot is designed to increase the level of interoperability between publisher supply chain and library data and add value to metadata for both through leveraging the strengths of each community. The organization of knowledge is a core competency for libraries. We excel in metadata consistency, the creation and application of classification schema and terminologies, the establishment and application of authority controlled fields. The publishing community often struggles with these aspects of metadata creation and maintenance resulting in users' failure to retrieve data that should meet their needs (loss of sales) and decreased consistency and granularity of data valuable in data mining and reporting for business intelligence.

Less than consistent and robust publisher supply chain metadata has implications for libraries as well, as this data drives our selection and acquisitions decisions and processes. For example, library vendors use this metadata to drive extraction of title information for approval lists, standing orders, opening day collections, etc.

Publishers have knowledge of forthcoming, new, and existing titles in their lists. They excel in the earliest knowledge of what will be published, close relationships with and knowledge of authors and other contributors, creation of descriptive text about the content they publish, metadata relating to publishing history of titles, metadata relating to the physical item, metadata relating to sales terms and rights, first knowledge of changes to publication dates, title changes, etc., and knowledge of reviews, awards, etc. relating to published titles.

Adding such metadata directly into WorldCat records will greatly enhance the search experience for users of library metadata—both inside and outside the library since library management also relies on metadata for business intelligence in the form of collection and circulation analysis.

OCLC is committed to pursuing development in this area as we are convinced there is a strong value proposition here for libraries, the publisher supply chain, and for OCLC's growth as an organization positioned to provide cost-effective metadata and services for libraries and cultural heritage institutions of all types.

The value proposition for libraries can be characterized as follows:

- Provides comprehensive and reliable upstream metadata in OCLC WorldCat for use in selection, acquisition, circulation, and technical services.
- Provides early MARC record availability to the library market through OCLC cataloging subscription services.
- Provides a mechanism for automatic receipt of record enhancements throughout the publishing cycle.
- Provides enhanced data and efficiencies in data creation or enhancement through use of OCLC tools such as FRBR, XISBN, and metadata creation and extraction.
- Reduces cost, labor, and duplication of effort in library cataloging and streamlining library technical processes from selection to circulation.

The value proposition for the publisher supply chain can be expressed as follows:

- Reduces cost, labor, and duplication of effort in the creation, organization, enhancement, and distribution of metadata.
- Allows global visibility for available and forthcoming titles through WorldCat.
- Provides a streamlined method for data delivery to publishers and their supply-chain partners.
- Allows publishers and vendors to promise early MARC record availability to the library market.
- Enhances metadata for use in business-to-business, customer-facing, and marketing tools used by publishers and vendors.
- Provides enhanced data through data mapping from library schema to publishing industry terminology (e.g., Dewey to BISAC and BIC).

PROCESS

The Next Generation Cataloging process works as follows. OCLC receives files of title metadata in ONIX format from publisher supply chain partners. This is the same metadata that is routinely produced for internal and external functions relating to marketing, buying, and selling content.

OCLC crosswalks the ONIX metadata to MARC format and attempts to match to an existing WorldCat record. If an exact match is found, the WorldCat record is enriched with appropriate data from the ONIX record. Examples of WorldCat record enrichment from ONIX include: contributor biographical information, descriptions, annotations, and publishing industry BISAC subject headings.

If an exact match is found, the FRBR work set for the record is retrieved, and the matching record is enriched using appropriate data mined from the work set. The WorldCat record enrichment from FRBR work set could include additional subject headings and classification.

Where possible, new data is created from mapping between existing data elements (e.g., DDC to BISAC Subject Headings and BISAC Subject Headings to DDC). For example, f the matching record contains a Dewey of 616.07543, the BISAC Subject Code MED098000—Medical/Ultrasonography will be derived from mapping and added to the ONIX record. If the incoming ONIX has a BISAC code but the matching record has no Dewey, the inverse will occur, and the Dewey will be added to the MARC record.

Enriched records are crosswalked back to ONIX, and the resulting ONIX file is returned to supply chain partners. Here are some examples of publisher metadata enrichment: authority controlled contributor names, contributor birth and death dates, Dewey call numbers, more granular BISAC subject headings derived from Dewey, LC call numbers, LCSH, NLM, and other subject schema, annotations and notes.

If no exact match is found a new record built from ONIX mapping to MARC is added to WorldCat. WorldCat attempts to FRBRize the new record, adding it to an existing work set when FRBR algorithms determine that data elements contained in the new record make it appropriate to do so. If the new record becomes part of an existing FRBR work set, records in the work set are used to enrich the newly created record. Enrichment occurs in such fields as DDC and LC Classification, authority controlled contributor names, LCSH, etc. As possible, new data is also created from mapping between existing data elements—DDC to BISAC Subject Headings and BISAC Subject Headings to DDC.

RESULTS

A Symposium for Publishers and Libraries hosted at OCLC in early 2009 confirmed the value of these services for metadata creation and enrichment in support of both communities. OCLC is preparing to put the services outlined above into production simultaneous with pilot completion and publication of pilot results. Once final MARC and ONIX output files representing the full scope the service are delivered to library and publisher pilot partners, OCLC will compile case studies and pilot partner evaluations of the metadata created during the pilot.

OCLC is working with LC and NLM to test the viability of these processes for their cataloging work flows, particularly in the area of CIP record creation. We believe this project is very much in line with the direction suggested by the LC Working Group on the Future of Bibliographic Control and will support the urgent need for more efficient and cost-effective methods of metadata creation, maintenance, and distribution.

OCLC is also maintains a close relationship with standards communities to ensure the services we build are in keeping with the direction supported by these organizations. We commissioned a study in coordination with NISO (http://www.niso.org/home) to examine current metadata work flows for library and publisher supply chain metadata creation, maintenance, and delivery. We are in frequent communication with Editeur (http://www. editeur.org/), who develop and maintain the ONIX standard internationally, and with the Book Industry Study Group (BISG) (http://bisg.org/),

who support the ONIX standard in North America, maintain the BISAC Subject Codes and perform intensive research on publishers supply chain practices, work flows, and economics.

CONCLUSION

OCLC is committed to supporting evolving metadata needs and the future of cataloging by implementing the practices outlined in this article. We will routinely ingest, enhance and create metadata in WorldCat through these processes and routinely output enhanced metadata in both MARC and ONIX formats, with mechanisms for ongoing delivery of enhancements to libraries and publishers.

In support of the idea of collaborative growth and enhancement of metadata across the life cycle of titles, and in response to requests from the cataloging community, OCLC is introducing the Expert Community Experiment, in which OCLC libraries with full-level cataloging authorizations will be able to improve and upgrade many more WorldCat master bibliographic records. We hope that the experiment will result in more corrections and additions to master bibliographic records and more timely actions to correct record problems.

The experiment also allows OCLC to test a "social cataloging" model involving the existing community of cataloging experts who have built WorldCat record-by-record over the past four decades.

We also plan to enhance the Next Generation Cataloging model so that we can routinely receive publisher updates to metadata across the title life cycle, including title changes, changes in publication date, and the addition of evaluative content and post-publication review and award information to WorldCat records as it is created by the publisher.

As a clearer picture of what the future of cataloging might bring emerges, OCLC will remain actively engaged in the community and committed to developing products and services that support a 21st century vision of metadata creation, enrichment, maintenance, and distribution.

REFERENCE

The Library of Congress. On the Record: Report of The Library of Congress Working Group on the Future of Bibliographic Control. Retrieved from http://www.loc.gov/bibliographic-future/news/lcwg-ontherecord-jan08-final.pdf (January 9, 2008 Washington, DC).

The DDC and OCLC

JOAN S. MITCHELL

OCLC Online Computer Library Center, Inc., Dublin, OH, USA

DIANE VIZINE-GOETZ

OCLC Online Computer Library Center, Inc., Dublin, OH, USA

ABSTRACT. *This article highlights key events in the relationship between OCLC Online Computer Library Center, Inc. and the Dewey Decimal Classification (DDC) system. The formal relationship started with OCLC's acquisition of Forest Press and the rights to the DDC from the Lake Placid Education Foundation in 1988, but OCLC's research interests in the DDC predated that acquisition and have remained strong during the relationship. Under OCLC's leadership, the DDC's value proposition has been enhanced by the continuous updating of the system itself, development of interoperable translations, mappings to other schemes, and new forms of representation of the underlying data. The amount of categorized content associated with the system in WorldCat and elsewhere has grown, as has worldwide use of the system. Emerging technologies are creating new opportunities for publishing, linking, and sharing DDC data.*

INTRODUCTION

OCLC acquired the Dewey Decimal Classification (DDC) system and Forest Press from the Lake Placid Education Foundation in 1988. The promise of

The authors thank Julianne Beall (Library of Congress), plus the following OCLC colleagues for their advice and assistance in preparing this article: Mary Bray, Terry Butterworth, Robin Cornette, Libbie Crawford, Tam Dalrymple, Rebecca Green, Larry Olszewski, Michael Panzer, Phil Schieber, and MaryAnn Semigel. All opinions expressed and any omissions or errors remain the responsibility of the authors. Connexion, DDC, Dewey, Dewey Decimal Classification, WebDewey, and WorldCat are registered trademarks of OCLC Online Computer Library Center, Inc.

OCLC's direct involvement in the DDC is presaged in the publisher's foreword to DDC 20:

> The year 1988 witnessed two events which will have a profound effect on the future of the Dewey Decimal Classification and other general classification systems. Curiously, both events took place on the same day. On July 29, a computer tape containing substantially all the text of DDC 20 was delivered to a firm in Massachusetts to begin production of this edition. ... On the same date, Forest Press and the Dewey Decimal Classification became a part of the OCLC Online Computer Center. ... Joining the DDC with the talents and resources of OCLC will allow the development of the computer products and services which are needed by DDC users (Paulson, 1989, p. xi).

While the relationship between the DDC and OCLC predated the acquisition in terms of research projects and inclusion of DDC numbers in WorldCat records, the system has flourished along a number of dimensions under OCLC's leadership. In addition to publishing numerous works based wholly or partly on the DDC, OCLC developed the first electronic version of a general classification system and made it available by subscription. International use of the system and the number of DDC translations have grown, as have mappings of the DDC to other terminologies. OCLC has played a prominent role in classification research in general, one that has resulted in new models of representation, prototypes of new services, and emerging uses of classification in the Web environment. This article highlights important events in the DDC–OCLC relationship, and concludes with prospects for future contributions (Mitchell, & Vizine-Goetz, 2006, Mitchell Vizine-Goetz, in press).

Acquisition of the Forest Press and the DDC

The 1988 library literature contains several reports announcing OCLC's acquisition of the rights to the DDC and the assets of Forest Press (the DDC's publisher) from the Lake Placid Education Foundation for a reported $3.8 million.

> The foundation was broke (revenues from DDC went back into DDC products and development, including contract payments to the Library of Congress); ... it needed a buyer who could carry DDC into the computerized environment of the 21st century. OCLC, which had worked with Forest Press in earlier cooperative activities, was that buyer (Plotnik, 1988a, p. 736).

In another report, the focus of OCLC on the electronic promise of the DDC is clearly stated: "OCLC will explore publishing electronic versions of the DDC, as well as continuing the ongoing revision and publication in print form … " (OCLC 1988, p. 443). In yet another report, then OCLC President Roland Brown commented, "The synergy between the legacy of Melvil Dewey and the mission of OCLC is powerful" (Plotnik, 1988b, p. 641).

In a 1999 interview following his retirement as Executive Director of Forest Press, Peter Paulson noted the sale to OCLC first among the most important occurrences during his leadership:

> First and most important, the sale of Forest Press and DDC to OCLC in 1988. This move brought us the skills and resources we needed, and OCLC has turned out to be a very good home for us (Intner, 1999, pp. 2-3).

MANAGEMENT OF THE DDC

When Forest Press was first acquired by OCLC, Peter Paulson remained executive director and the Forest Press office remained physically in Albany, NY. The Dewey Editorial Office continued at the Library of Congress (LC), where it had been located since 1923. OCLC took over annual payments to the Library of Congress to fund the Dewey editorial staff positions and operations—in 1988, all of these positions were filled by LC employees.

In late 1991, the editor of the DDC, John P. Comaromi, died suddenly. There was a hiring freeze at the Library of Congress during the period candidates were being considered for the position to succeed Dr. Comaromi. OCLC and LC agreed to convert the editor-in-chief position from an LC employee fully funded by OCLC to an OCLC employee physically located in the Dewey Editorial Office at the Library of Congress. Joan S. Mitchell was hired under these circumstances as editor in April 1993.

When Forest Press first joined OCLC, it was organizationally under a group devoted to electronic publications and information. The following year, it moved under the cataloging area, where it has remained nearly continuously until the present day. Peter Paulson retired at the end of 1998; upon his retirement, Joan Mitchell also took on the business operations of Forest Press and served simultaneously as editor-in-chief and executive director from 1999 through early 2003.[1] In mid-1999, the physical assets of Forest Press were moved from Albany, NY, to OCLC headquarters in Dublin, OH. Also in 1999, the editorial team was expanded by one member. Giles Martin, an Australian, was the first non-U.S.-citizen to be hired on the Dewey team, and the first editor to be based at OCLC headquarters in Dublin. In 2009, Michael Panzer became the first former member of a Dewey translation team to be appointed assistant editor.[2] In addition to the aforementioned, current editorial team members include Assistant Editors Julianne Beall (an

LC employee) and Rebecca Green (an OCLC employee), both based in the Dewey Editorial Office at LC, plus a part-time editorial assistant.

One other important piece in the management of the DDC is the 10-member international advisory board, the Decimal Classification Editorial Policy Committee (EPC). EPC is a joint committee of OCLC and the American Library Association (ALA), and advises the DDC editors and OCLC on DDC content and strategic directions. The committee has existed in its present form since the early 1950s—prior to 1988, it was a Forest Press-ALA joint committee. The committee plays an important role in bringing a global viewpoint to the development of the DDC—current members are from Australia, Canada, South Africa, the United Kingdom, and the United States. Representatives of DDC translations serve as corresponding members of EPC and receive proposals at the same time as EPC members for consideration and comment.

PUBLICATIONS

Prior to joining OCLC, the Forest Press publications list was focused primarily on the full and abridged print editions of the DDC plus separate publications associated with them, Dewey-related conference proceedings, and a few Dewey-related texts. After Forest Press became part of OCLC, the publications list expanded to a wide variety of Dewey publications in print and electronic form, plus DDC-related products such as bookmarks and posters. A majority of the print publications and all of the electronic publications were developed and produced in cooperation with marketing and research staff at OCLC.

In recent years, OCLC has chosen to license the production of DDC-related products to library vendors and has focused internal DDC publication efforts on the full and abridged editions of the DDC in print and electronic versions. OCLC also licenses the underlying DDC databases associated with the full and abridged editions as XML data files. The electronic editions and data files are discussed further in the Electronic Editions section of the article.

ELECTRONIC EDITIONS

An important relationship between OCLC and the DDC started several years prior to the acquisition of Forest Press with the Dewey Decimal Classification Online Project. The history and results of the study are available in full in the study report (Markey, & Demeyer, 1986); a short summary follows.

In the early 1980s, the OCLC Office of Research became interested in how classification could assist library catalog users in performing subject searches in an online environment. The Office of Research learned that

DDC 19 had been produced by computerized photocomposition—this led OCLC to inquire about the availability of the tapes for research purposes. Also in 1984, Inforonics Inc. was retained by Forest Press to develop an online database management system to support Dewey editorial operations. In January 1984, the DDC Online Project was initiated by the OCLC Office of Research with the support of the Council on Library Resources, Forest Press, and OCLC. In the study, led by OCLC Research Scientist Karen Markey, researchers built two catalogs, one of which (the Dewey Online Catalog) included subject-rich data from DDC captions, notes, and Relative Index terms linked through the DDC class number to MARC records drawn from participating libraries' collections. This groundbreaking study, along with OCLC's eventual acquisition of the rights to the DDC, no doubt prompted OCLC's continued interest and experimentation in the creation and use of DDC data in electronic form.

OCLC gained access to all of the Dewey schedules and tables in 1989 after the publication of DDC 20, the first edition produced using an on-line Editorial Support System (ESS). The ESS database was used by the OCLC Office of Research to prototype the Electronic Dewey software. In November 1992, catalogers at eight libraries began testing the prototype CD-ROM version of the DDC. The eight libraries were: National Library of Australia, Carnegie Mellon University Library, Columbus (OH) Metropolitan Library, Columbus (OH) City Schools, University of Illinois Library at Urbana-Champaign, Library of Congress (Decimal Classification Division), Stockton-San Joaquin County (CA) Public Library, and the New York State Library. Electronic Dewey was released the following year making Dewey the first library classification scheme available to users in electronic form. The system ran on a personal computer and enabled keyword searching of the schedules, tables, Relative Index, and Manual of DDC 20 on CD-ROM.

In summer 1996, OCLC Forest Press published DDC 21 and released a new version of the Dewey software. For the first time, a new edition of the classification was published in two formats: the traditional four-volume print format and an electronic version on CD-ROM (Dewey for Windows[3]). The publication of Dewey for Windows followed several years of close collaboration between the OCLC Office of Research and the Dewey editorial team; the groups continue to work together today on a range of research and development projects.

The year 2000 marked another milestone in the evolution of the Dewey software, the debut of a Web-based product. WebDewey, a Web-based version of DDC 21, was released by OCLC as part of the Cooperative Online Resources Catalog (CORC) service. The CORC release included features to apply authority control to Dewey numbers and to generate DDC numbers for Web resources automatically. Two years later WebDewey and Abridged WebDewey, the latter a Web-based version of Abridged 13, became available in the OCLC Connexion cataloging service.

The DDC is also available in multiple XML representations. The XML files are used in OCLC products and services and distributed to translation partners and other licensed users. As part of an update of the Editorial Support System, the proprietary representations are being converted to ones based on the MARC 21 formats for Classification and Authority data. The MARC 21 versions will be available as XML files.

TRANSLATIONS

The Dewey Decimal Classification is used in over 200,000 libraries in 138 countries—a reach into the global community that extends past OCLC's other services. An important feature of the DDC, its language-independent representation of concepts, makes it ideally suited as a global knowledge organization system. Since OCLC acquired the DDC in 1988, authorized translations of the full and abridged editions of the DDC have been published in the following languages: Arabic, French, German, Greek, Hebrew, Icelandic, Italian, Norwegian, Russian, Spanish, Turkish, and Vietnamese. Updated versions of the top three levels of the DDC are available in Arabic, Chinese, Czech, French, German, Hebrew, Italian, Norwegian, Portuguese, Russian, Spanish, Swedish, and Vietnamese. Plans are currently under way for a new Indonesian abridged translation and the first Swedish translation of the DDC (the latter currently envisioned as a mixed Swedish-English version of the full edition of the DDC). Currently, only the German translation is available in a Web version, but Web versions of the DDC are currently under exploration for the French, Greek, Italian, Norwegian, and Swedish translations.

Translations of the DDC start with an agreement between OCLC and a recognized bibliographic agency in the country/language group. For example, under an agreement with OCLC, Deutsche Nationalbibliothek leads efforts on the German translation with the cooperation of bibliographic agencies in Germany, Austria, and Switzerland. Current translations are localized and interoperable with reference to the English-language edition on which the translation is based—localized in terms of terminology and examples appropriate to the country/language group, and interoperable in terms of authorized expansions or contractions of provisions in the base edition. A common example of the latter is an expansion of the geographic table in a translation. The Vietnamese translation of Abridged Edition 14 contains an extended geographic table for Vietnam in which the explicit provisions for the areas of Vietnam are at a deeper level than those found in the current abridged and full English-language editions of the DDC—in other words, the English-language version is a logical abridgment of the version found in the Vietnamese translation (Beall, 2003).

MAPPINGS

Mappings between Dewey and thesauri, subject heading lists, and other classification schemes enrich the vocabulary associated with DDC numbers and enable the use of the DDC as a switching system. Mappings to new concepts in other systems also help to keep the classification up-to-date.

The electronic versions of DDC contain selected mappings between Dewey numbers and three subject headings systems—Library of Congress Subject Headings (LCSH), Medical Subject Headings (MeSH), and H.W. Wilson's *Sears List of Subject Headings*. The Dewey editors consult LCSH and MeSH as sources of terminology for the DDC and map terminology from both systems to the classification. Dewey for Windows was the first electronic edition to include intellectually mapped LCSH; MeSH mappings were introduced in WebDewey with the release of DDC 22 in 2003. Mappings between abridged Dewey numbers and Sears headings are created at H.W. Wilson under an agreement with OCLC and are included in Abridged WebDewey and in various products offered by H.W. Wilson.

In 2008, the Dewey editors began mapping DDC numbers to the BISAC (Book Industry Standards and Communications) subject headings. The work is part of OCLC's Next Generation Cataloging project which is piloting automated techniques for enriching publisher and vendor metadata (How the Pilot Works, n.d., para. 3). The mappings are used to add Dewey numbers to publisher records and BISAC subject headings to bibliographic records.

Subject heading-DDC number pairs statistically derived from WorldCat are also included in OCLC products and services. The OCLC publications *Subject Headings for Children* and *People, Places & Things* are lists of LC subject headings with corresponding DDC numbers. Both include statistical mappings as do all of the electronic versions of the DDC, beginning with Electronic Dewey. Statistical mappings supplement the mappings provided by the Dewey editors.

Several Dewey translation partners have projects under way to map Dewey numbers to local subject heading systems. Headings from Schlagwortnormdatei (SWD), the German subject heading authority file, are being mapped to Dewey numbers in the Criss-Cross project to date, 61,500 SWD headings have been mapped to the DDC ("Mapping of German" Subject Headings n.d.). At the Italian National Central Library in Florence, work is under way to map Dewey numbers to Nuovo Soggettario, the Italian subject heading list (*Nuovo Soggettario*, 2006; Paradisi, 2006).

In addition to mappings between Dewey numbers and subject headings, several concordances have been developed between Dewey and other classification systems. The Library of Congress's Classification Web system includes statistical correlations among LCSH, Library of Congress Classification (LCC), and DDC based on the co-occurrence of the three in Library of

Congress bibliographic records. The National Library of Sweden maintains a mapping between SAB, the Swedish classification system, and the DDC (Svanberg, 2008). The Czech National Library has built a concordance between UDC and DDC for the purposes of collection assessment (Balíková 2007).

RESEARCH

For many years, the OCLC Office of Research has focused its DDC-related efforts in three main areas: prototyping classification tools for catalogers, developing automated classification software, and applying and refining statistical mapping techniques. Several of the outcomes of this work are discussed in the Electronic Editions and Mappings sections of this paper. While OCLC remains interested in these areas, recent projects are taking DDC research in new directions.

One of these is the DeweyBrowser prototype (Vizine-Goetz, 2006). The DeweyBrowser is an end user system that incorporates many features of next generation library catalogs, including tag clouds and multi-faceted searching and navigation. The clouds provide a visual representation of the number of titles in each of the top three levels of the DDC (known collectively as the DDC Summaries). In the prototype, users can navigate the Summaries in English, French, German, Norwegian, Spanish, and Swedish. The Summaries provide an ideal browsing structure for multilingual environments.

In another project, OCLC researchers have developed an experimental classification service that provides access to classification information from more than 36 million WorldCat records ("Overview," n.d., para 1). The OCLC FRBR Work-Set algorithm is used to group bibliographic records to provide a work-level summary of the DDC numbers, Library of Congress Classification numbers, and National Library of Medicine Classification numbers assigned to a work. The beta service is accessible through a human interface and as Web service. The Web service supports machine-to-machine interaction. Two additional Web services are being developed to deliver DDC data. One will offer a history of changes for a DDC class (Panzer, 2009); the other will provide a generic view of a DDC class across all editions/versions and languages.

Finally, OCLC is investigating the issues involved in transforming the DDC into a Web information resource, including the design of Uniform Resource Identifiers (URIs) and the modeling of DDC in Simple Knowledge Organization System (SKOS) Panzer, 2008; Panzer, 2008 August). Emerging data models and new technologies (e.g., SKOS and linked data) will provide new opportunities for publishing, linking, and sharing DDC data in the years to come.

CONCLUSION

As we look back over the 20 years since OCLC acquired the rights to the DDC in 1988, we reflect on how OCLC has impacted Dewey's value proposition. The basic system features—well-defined categories and well-developed hierarchies, all interconnected by a rich network of relationships—have been enhanced by interoperable translations, mappings to other schemes, and new forms of representation of the underlying data. The amount of categorized content associated with the system in WorldCat and elsewhere has grown, as has worldwide use of the system. Dewey's language-independent representation of concepts makes it ideally suited to a myriad of uses in the current and future information environment. Its ongoing success as a knowledge organization tool will depend on the aggressive leadership that OCLC, in cooperation with the worldwide community of Dewey users, is willing to provide along a number of dimensions—updating and development of the system itself, availability of the system for experimentation and use, association of the system with content, mappings to other schemes, translations, and innovative research.

NOTES

1. At the request of Joan Mitchell, she returned to serving solely as editor-in-chief in early 2003. Dewey business operations were taken over by a business director in the OCLC cataloging area, and they have remained separate from the editorial operations since that period, mirroring the Forest Press/Dewey Editorial Office organization that had been in place for many years.

2. In the mid 2000s, Michael Panzer headed the technical team based at Cologne University of Applied Sciences that first translated Dewey into German. Michael Panzer succeeds long-time Assistant Editor and LC employee Winton E. Matthews Jr., but is based at OCLC headquarters in Dublin.

3. A Microsoft Windows®-based version of the software.

REFERENCES

Balíková, M. (2007). UDC in Czechia. In *Proceedings of the International Seminar "Information Access for the Global Community, The Hague, June 4–5, 2007, Extensions and Corrections to the UDC, 29* (pp. 191–227.) Retrieved February 27, 2009, from http://dlist.sir.arizona.edu/2379/01/MBalikova_UDC_Seminar2007.pdf

Beall, J. (2003, August). *Approaches to expansions: Case studies from the German and Vietnamese translations.* A paper presented at the World Library and Information Congress (69th IFLA General Conference and Council), Berlin. Retrieved March 1, 2009, from http://www.ifla.org/IV/ifla69/papers/123e-Beall.pdf

How the pilot works. (n.d.). Information retrieved February 27, 2009 from http://www.oclc.org/partnerships/material/nexgen/nextgencataloging.htm

Intner, S. (1999). Stream of consciousness: An interview with Dewey's Peter Paulson. *Technicalities, 19,* 2–3.

Mapping of German Subject Headings to the Dewey Decimal Classification. (n.d.). Information retrieved February 27, 2009 from http://linux2.fbi.fh-koeln.de/crisscross/swd-ddc-mapping_en.html

Markey, K., & Demeyer, A. (1986). *Dewey Decimal Classification Online Project: Evaluation of a Library Schedule and Index Integrated into the Subject Searching Capabilities of an Online Catalog.* OCLC/OPR/RR-86/1. Dublin, OH: OCLC Online Computer Library Center.

Mitchell, J. S., & Vizine-Goetz, D. (2006). *Moving beyond the Presentation Layer: Content and Context in the Dewey Decimal Classification (DDC) System.* Binghamton, NY: Haworth Press. Co-published simultaneously in *Cataloging & Classification Quarterly, 42,* 2006.

Mitchell, J. S., & Vizine-Goetz, D. (in press). Dewey Decimal Classification. In M. J. Bates & M. Maack (Eds.), *Encyclopedia of Library and Information Science* (2nd ed., pp.) New York: Taylor & Francis.

Nuovo Soggettario: Guida al Sistema Italiano di Indicizzazione per Soggetto: Prototipo del Thesaurus (2006) (pp. 175–177). Milano: Editrice Bibliografica.

OCLC acquires Forest Press, publisher of Dewey Decimal Classification. (1988, December). *Information Technology and Libraries,* 443.

Overview. (n.d.). Information retrieved February 27, 2009 from http://www.oclc.org/research/researchworks/classify/

Panzer, M. (2008). Cool URIs for the DDC: Towards Web-scale accessibility of a large classification system. In J. Greenburg & W. Klas (Eds.), *Metadata for Semantic and Social Applications: Proceedings of the International Conference on Dublin Core and Metadata Applications, Berlin, September 22–26, 2008* (pp. 183–190). Göttingen: Dublin Core Metadata Initiative and Universitätsverlag Göttingen.

Panzer, M. (2008, August). *DDC, SKOS, and linked data on the Web.* Presentation at OCLC/ISKO-NA Preconference to the 10th International ISKO Conference, Universite' de Montréal, Canada. Retrieved February 27, 2009, from http://www.oclc.org/us/en/news/events/presentations/2008/ISKO20080805-deweyskos-panzer.ppt

Panzer, M. (2009, January). *More than lists of changes: tracing the history of DDC concepts.* Presentation at Dewey Breakfast/Update, ALA Midwinter Meeting, Denver, CO. Retrieved March 2, 2009, from http://www.oclc.org/us/en/dewey/news/conferences/more_than_lists.ppt

Paradisi, F. (2006, August). *Linking DDC numbers to the new 'Soggettario Italiano.'* Presentation at Dewey Translators Meeting, World Library and Information Congress (72nd IFLA General Conference and Council), Seoul, Korea. Retrieved February 25, 2009, from http://www.oclc.org/dewey/news/conferences/ddc_and_soggetario_ifla_2006.ppt

Paulson, P. (1989). Publisher's Foreword. In M. Dewey, J. P. Comaromi, J. Beall, W. E. Matthews, Jr., & G. R. New (Eds.), *Dewey Decimal Classification and Relative Index,* vol. 1 (p. xi).

Plotnik, A. (1988a). Would Dewey have done it? *American Libraries, 19,* 736.

Plotnik, A. (1988b). OCLC pays $3.8 million for Dewey Classification. *American Libraries, 19,* 641.

Svanberg, M. (2008). Mapping Two Classification Schemes—DDC and SAB. In *New Perspectives on Subject Indexing and Classification: International Symposium in Honour of Magda Heiner-Freiling* (pp. 41–51). Leipzig, Frankfurt am Main, Berlin: Deutsche Nationalbibliothek.

Vizine-Goetz, D. (2006). DeweyBrowser. In J. S. Mitchell & D. Vizine-Goetz (Eds.), *Moving beyond the Presentation Layer: Content and Context in the Dewey Decimal Classification (DDC) System* (pp. 213–220). Binghamton, NY: Haworth Press. Co-published simultaneously in *Cataloging & Classification Quarterly, 42,* 2006, 213–220.

The Revolution Continues: Resource Sharing and OCLC in the New Century

WILLIAM J. CROWE

University of Kansas, Lawrence, KS, USA

ABSTRACT. *The author explores the theory and practice of resource sharing in the OCLC cooperative. History of the OCLC Interlibrary Loan subsystem and subsequent developments through 2008 are reviewed, and prospects for the future are offered.*

The dream of achieving "universal bibliography" has been central to the work of librarians and scholars for centuries. Indeed, reaching what had been thought to be a bibliographic Shangri-La was the ultimate goal of the visionary Frederick G. Kilgour and the other pioneers of the mid-20th century who created the OCLC (Online Computer Library Center) Online Union Catalog that we now know as OCLC WorldCat.

This quest always has been animated by librarians' desire to enable learners (read: searchers) to discover *and obtain access* to information beyond what may be available locally, however "locally" is defined. Indeed, it is *this* imperative—to help people not only to learn about but also to obtain access to information—that has been the driving force for libraries to cooperate among themselves.

OCLC, as the world's largest library cooperative, thus always has had as its fundamental reason for being the offering of help—through libraries—for people to discover and gain access to information to do their work (which may be to produce new knowledge), to help them make informed decisions in their everyday lives, or simply to promote delight in discovery and learning.

OCLC's work has always been about more than promoting efficiency in each library's work processes to contain the rate of rise of library costs, as vitally important as that role always must be. As OCLC's statement of its public purpose makes plain, OCLC is about enabling libraries, working collaboratively, to do three important things: help people discover *any* information of potential use, reveal its whereabouts, and provide means to help the searcher obtain that information when and where needed.

THE ORIGINS OF OCLC'S WORK IN RESOURCE SHARING

Kate Nevins (1998) recounted the early history of OCLC's efforts to achieve improvements in resource sharing. She aptly described OCLC's work as supporting a revolution. Her review of OCLC's achievements shows how OCLC moved remarkably quickly to build on its successes. By 1979, only 8 years after the successful launch of cooperative online cataloging, OCLC had developed, tested, and launched its second service—the Interlibrary Loan Subsystem.

The story of the effects of the OCLC Interlibrary Loan Service on libraries, librarians, and library users is told in compelling terms in a compilation of essays published to celebrate the 20th anniversary of the service: *What the OCLC Interlibrary Loan Service Means to Me* (1999). The words used by many of the contributors are powerful, often very personal, as, for example, the closing passage of the entry by Liz McCumsey of the Del Norte County Library, Crescent City, California. She wrote, "The best of OCLC Interlibrary Loan service is the proof that I'm working in a library without walls, spread through space and time, and I'm not alone" (McCumsey, 1999, p. 150).

Thirty years have passed since the appearance of the Interlibrary Loan Subsystem and the subsequent rapid proliferation of derivative ventures introduced by OCLC, library consortia, and many individual libraries. The published literature is replete with examples of these early efforts to build on it, as two generations of library leaders worked to improve the speed of transmitting requests for loan of items for their users, devised means to control the costs of those processes, and, overall, promote efficiencies in what had always been among the most labor-intensive and cumbersome of library services. Many millions of dollars were saved and the work of many library users markedly eased thanks to OCLC's efforts to promote library resource sharing.

The Nevins article ends with a description of OCLC's first systematic efforts to expand resource sharing internationally and an overview of the movement toward "End User Borrowing." She describes efforts under way in the late 1990s to help library users initiate and manage their own loan requests, unmediated by library staff; to better integrate OCLC services with local online library systems and with campus or community electronic mail systems; and, last, to draw in third-party suppliers of information content to expand the options available for supply of that content.

THE SECOND STAGE OF DEVELOPMENTS

OCLC's efforts in the last decade have yielded many advances. Perhaps the most familiar of these efforts was the introduction of the OCLC ILLiad Resource Sharing Management software, in 2000. This software, developed by interlibrary loan staff at Virginia Polytechnic Institute and State University, has been expanded and enhanced by Atlas Systems, Inc., as the primary developer in collaboration with OCLC staff.

OCLC ILLiad is now in use by 1,032 libraries in all 50 United States and in Canada, Egypt, Greece, Hong Kong, and Qatar. It provides a fully integrated interface to both OCLC WorldCat and the OCLC Interlibrary Loan Subsystem and offers the capability for end users to submit requests for electronic documents and receive them at their desktops. Library staff have access to a rich array of management data in real time and can reach out to services beyond those offered by OCLC. For example, ILLiad enables library staff to send, receive, and track requests on the U.S. National Library of Medicine's DOCLINE service.

In a like development overseas, OCLC promoted "UnityUK," a Web-based resource-sharing and interlibrary loan service, in partnership with the Combined Regions (see www.combinedregions.com). UnityUK is the United Kingdom's first and only national network for resource sharing, bringing together various union catalogs, including COPAC (the academic and national library catalog) and the catalog of the National Library for the Blind, to offer a unified search service. To illustrate the rapidity of change in this area, plans to integrate UnityUK with WorldCat Resource Sharing were not to be implemented, based on later market research. UnityUK is used by 153 library services (141 public libraries) in the United Kingdom: 128 in England, 7 in Scotland, and 12 in Wales (Birch, 2008).

Because OCLC is the source of indispensable bibliographic and library holdings information and provides direct access to much digital content, as well as to the knowledge and experience of expert staff at OCLC and in member libraries, OCLC continues to be at the center of a proliferation of experiments in resource sharing. Increasingly, OCLC helps many libraries test methods and processes that can help them meet the needs of people who may never visit a library building and whose expectations for access to information are shaped increasingly by the proliferation of E-commerce and E-learning.

These efforts are consistent with OCLC's commitment always to think and act afresh, alert to current and prospective changes in the environments in which libraries function. Those environments are marked by rapid changes in communications technology, globalization of much of commerce and many aspects of culture and education, a proliferation of forms of electronic/digital information, and rapid changes in how many people seek and use information in their everyday lives. The core question remains: Where and how can OCLC best help its member libraries?

Consider Mark Dahl's comments (from his blog, http://synthesize-specialize-mobilize.blogspot.com/):

> OCLC is in a position to be a sort of EBay for libraries. EBay is valuable precisely because of its wide user base. It is the dominant player in online auctions because it offers the widest possible marketplace for buyers and sellers. That same comprehensiveness and global scope also has value when building a search system for books and doing resource sharing.

The model for OCLC's current and future work to promote "resource sharing," then, must be with this worldview in mind. Indeed, the many studies of interlibrary loan and document delivery undertaken in the last two decades, in particular those sponsored by the Association of Research Libraries, most recently in 2004 (Jackson, 2004), drew not only from OCLC's incomparable store of data on patterns of lending and borrowing, but also on the expertise of OCLC researchers (Prabha & O'Neill, 2001). These studies have proliferated, often highlighting the effects in individual libraries and in library consortia of OCLC systems and services. An excellent recent example is a study of the effects of OCLC union listing on rates of use of interlibrary loan by library users (Madarash-Hill & Hill, 2008).

Even as OCLC moves into new directions, however, it continues its commitment to improve means of offering traditional interlibrary, or library to library, sharing of library-owned information content, through the OCLC WorldCat Delivery Network. These services are being enhanced in several key areas, notably strengthening the "policy directory" to ease understanding of the terms under which resource-sharing transactions may be made (especially important in a global context); developing and adhering to accepted and emerging relevant international standards; experimenting with digitization of requested content; and, in general, making continuous improvements in such services as OCLC's Interlibrary Loan Fee Management service.

LOOKING TO THE FUTURE

It remains OCLC's challenge to help libraries meet the changing expectations of the new generation of seekers: to ensure that "resource sharing" is seen as a means to support libraries in offering a service that—transparent to the searcher—will enable "scoping" of any seeker's request for information to be fulfilled with a straightforward one-stop (or "few clicks") process. In early 2009, OCLC launched the WorldCat Navigator service (http://www.oclc.org/services/resourcesharing/default.htm), which is intended to do just this: move resource sharing to a new level of cooperative services.

This new offering supports a familiar interface for the local user and manages the user's search/request. It selects a supplying source from the local library's own holdings, physical or digital, or, through a series of choices based on a profile established by the user's home library, reaches out to consortial and licensed resources to which that user may have access. The service sequence is made complete with a user-managed "circulation" of the desired content, fully integrated with the local library's own policies and processes, up to and including "home delivery" of the physical or virtual information content.

More than 9,100 libraries now participate in the OCLC resource-sharing network that began in 1979 with the implementation of the interlibrary loan subsystem. They are now arranging 10 million interlibrary loan transactions a year on OCLC. The impetus for continuing change in resource sharing is inherent in OCLC's decades-old commitment to achieve universal bibliography—construed broadly, learning from current research and emerging good practice and offering improved and new services to help libraries. Change at OCLC also is always driven by the innovative ideas generated by the OCLC staff and contact with staff of member institutions, as well as from the expressed interests of representatives of the membership in advisory bodies, whether in the newly forming OCLC Regional Councils, the OCLC Global Council, or the OCLC Board of Trustees. With the strength of the cooperative—now globally focused more than ever before—OCLC is well on its way to the next stage of promoting the fullest possible access to the world's information.

The revolution continues.

REFERENCES

Birch, K. (2008). UnityUK celebrates its second birthday: A paradigm shift for UK public libraries. *Interlending & Document Supply, 36*(1), 11–14.

Jackson, M. E. (2004). *Assessing ILL/DD services: New cost-effective alternatives.* Washington, DC: Association of Research Libraries.

Madarash-Hill, C., & Hill, J. B. (2008). Recent developments in union listing and interlibrary loan: Retrieval at a university library. *Journal of Interlibrary Loan, Document Delivery & Information Supply, 18*(3), 325–333.

McCumsey, L. (1999). *What the OCLC interlibrary loan service means to me.* Dublin, OH: OCLC Online Computer Library Center.

Nevins, K. (1998). An ongoing revolution: Resource sharing and OCLC. In K. W. Smith (Ed.), *OCLC 1967–1997: Thirty years of furthering access to the world's information* (pp. 65–71). New York: The Haworth Press.

Prabha, C. G., & O'Neill, E. T. (2001). Interlibrary borrowing initiated by patrons: Some characteristics of books requested via OhioLINK. *Journal of Library Administration, 34*(3/4), 329–338.

Virtual Reference Reflections

STEWART BODNER

The New York Public Library, New York, NY, USA

ABSTRACT. *When the Online Computer Library Center (OCLC) was incorporated as the Ohio College Library Center in July 1967, it was largely considered an enterprise whose primary task was investigating cataloging duplication in American libraries. Fred Kilgour, OCLC's founder, was the visionary behind a collaborative enterprise that would eventually reshape the library landscape for generations. The concept of a cataloging system using automation to share bibliographic information, thus allowing libraries to copy catalog records for their own purposes, seems obvious today. In hindsight, it is hard to imagine the effort it would take if every library across the globe were required to individually catalog their acquisitions. Yet Kilgour's vision went beyond the standard use of automation in cataloging applications. He believed automation can "provide not just information about where to find information, but the information itself, the text of the book or article, the map, the recording, each delivered directly to the user" (Mason, 1998, p. 57).*

Kilgour's audacious approach signaled a sea change in the way libraries operate. Traditionally, librarians acted as pointers to information. They provided search strategies for readers and sent them on their way. It was up to the reader to review the card catalog or the paper index, decipher the information in those sources, again consulting the librarian as interpreter. The reader then needed to find the monograph or periodical article by physically locating the material or by making a request, depending on the type of library they frequented. For the better part of the 20th century, this paradigm dictated the interactions between reference librarians and their patrons.

IMPLICATIONS

Those in the profession who witnessed the massive changes that technology brought now understand the implications of automating content. In 1975, as a graduate student in library school, I was able to catch a glimpse of the future. I was part of a small study working on a research project for which I had no content knowledge. I was assigned to work with a chemist using "new" technology that involved using, of all things, a computer. At the time, computers were a novelty in libraries so this was a significant undertaking for someone with experience in libraries but little experience with computers. Developers at the Lockheed Corporation, proponents of a product called "Dialog," wanted to test the ability of scientists to use "databases" on their own first and with library staff after to conduct research. In addition, the folks at Lockheed wanted to see if individuals without library backgrounds could effectively handle the search mechanisms.

The chemist with whom I was paired was working on derivatives of nicotinamide, a scientific term totally alien to me. However, he had great difficulty in performing the search on his own. When we worked together, however, we were able to refine the search to his particular need by using the basic reference interview and applying the interview to the Dialog idiom. In this manner, the researcher's needs were met, proving a library axiom—that a librarian or an information professional assisting a researcher will always improve on that person's search more readily than if the research had been conducted without assistance.

This brings us to the crux of the potential for virtual reference. In 2002, print, film, magnetic, and optical storage media produced 5 exabytes of new information, equivalent in size to the information contained in 37,000 new libraries the size of the Library of Congress book collections (How Much Information?, 2003). With the vast amount of digital material being published, and mindful of Fred Kilgour's vision of delivering quality content to individuals, a constant remains. Researchers will continue to require assistance from formation professionals. However, this assistance did not and does not come cheaply.

The implication of the 1975 study, namely, the ability to use a computer to quickly sort through vast amounts of data to produce impressive, high quality results, came at a very high price. To many in the information industry, Dialog searches were unaffordable. One sure way to curl the shorts of a library administrator was to conduct a Dialog search that always showed the "metered" cost at the end of a page of results. This search methodology was a long way from the type of "virtual reference" librarians would begin practicing in the late 1990s.

CHILLING EFFECT

The meter had quite a chilling effect on librarians since the cost to conduct a search was so high. Moreover, there was no way to directly deliver search results and content except at the particular terminal where you were sitting. In the early 1980s, with the rise of primitive search engines—some of which were known as gophers, and sported evocative names like Archie, Veronica, and Jughead—there developed the opportunity to deliver content over the Internet. Of course, one needed to be versed in DOS (disk operating system) commands and understand binary functions to make effective use of the gopher clients. Yet a visionary might detect the possibility of one day delivering, at the very least, books and articles, or more to the point, text, to a number of terminals belonging to a network.

While gophers were developing, the creation of the CD-ROM took libraries by storm. Publishers began providing databases on compact discs that had similar and, in many cases, more relevant data than those found in Dialog. However, these compact disc products also had weaknesses. They were not up to date and entailed administrative costs—that is, receiving, loading, and in many cases returning discs. Nevertheless, the CD-ROM solved the onerous metering issue; one could conduct a number of searches for a subscription fee. For about a decade, CD-ROMs were an enormous success in libraries, but they proved a temporary expedient. There needed to be a way to create up-to-date information and a way to deliver this information without filling multiple and expanding CD-ROM towers.

WORLD WIDE WEB

At the beginning of the 1990s, the World Wide Web was developing as a new method to deliver content to information seekers. Viola and Mosaic were the first and most popular of the new Web browsers. They were a bit cumbersome to use, but they played significant roles as prototypes for Netscape, the Web browser that would change the reference librarian's landscape forever. In preparing us for Netscape, a major improvement over both Viola and Mosaic, information professionals began to create the future in a virtual environment. Reflecting on this stage of information dissemination, I am reminded of an anecdote involving Thomas Edison. When Edison improved a Western Union derivative of the stock ticker, the inventor was asked how much he thought the improvements were worth. Edison surmised that he could get along with $3,000. When he was offered a staggering $40,000

Edison confessed, "This caused me to come as near as fainting as I ever got" (Clark, 1977, p. 30). Edison's near-fainting spell was caused by his inability to calculate the value of his improvements. Well, any thinking librarian who was beta testing Netscape in 1996–97 was probably close to fainting, since the implications of Web browsing cut right to the heart of the library profession. The establishment of Netscape and the rise of Google are as profound in history as Gutenberg's invention of moveable type for printing books.

Yet virtual reference was on the minds of larger numbers of librarians as early as 1995. An event sponsored by Nylink, then the SUNY (State University of New York)/OCLC Network, attracted over 200 librarians from all over the United States and as far away as Norway. One participant, Barbara Richards of Carnegie Mellon University, stated, "It is going to take a lot of work and a lot of dollars to get our libraries to a virtual certainty" (Wilson Library Bulletin, 1995, p. 17). Since 1995, libraries have been feeding the virtual world on unprecedented levels. The trajectory of rapid information dissemination in the forms of text, images, sound, and video has been astounding. Netscape and eventually Google created unsurpassed opportunities. Indeed, the establishment of Netscape enabled Fred Kilgour to advance his visions concerning both the widespread practice of virtual reference and collaboration in delivering content. Fred Kilgour's legacy as the founder of OCLC is best exemplified by the enduring nature of the collaborative. OCLC's success derives in large part from its long-range thinking with respect to providing new avenues and frontiers for the creation of library services. The Research Department at OCLC has produced significant findings and given the library profession valuable tools for facing evolving trends. One of these was the movement away from library online public access catalogs (OPACs).

In late 1998 at a meeting of the OCLC Reference Services Advisory Committee, Thom Hickey was discussing the vagaries of OPACs and posited the view that, in the future, the results of our bibliographic searches would look like Netscape results. This observation sent tremors throughout the meeting room since the concept of bibliographic records looking like Netscape results would move our cataloged information into the realm of the Internet. Hickey's prescient views spurred a discussion on how this information could be conveyed over the World Wide Web. The long-term possibility of sending a digitized version of a book over the Internet ether was no longer implausible sci-fi fantasy.

LIBRARY OF CONGRESS

Librarians are resourceful people. It did not take long for an ambitious project to take shape under the auspices of the Library of Congress. The project was known as the Collaborative Digital and Reference Service (CDRS); its goals were lofty and achievable in the age of automation. Of primary importance was the creation of a collaborative network of librarians across the globe able to pose and answer questions to a system on a 24/7 basis. The service would operate at two levels for member libraries. "It will support local libraries that set up their own live online reference arrangements (sometimes called 'Ask a' services) by tapping their own internal staff or reference librarians from a regional consortia. At the second level, questions would go to a Global Reference Network, an international group of libraries led by the Library of Congress' own service" (Quint, 2002, p. 50).

CDRS was an ambitious project that brought major libraries together to work collaboratively on reference. Each member library submitted a detailed profile that identified subject strengths, language ability, and the time frame in which a given question might be answered. A question submitted at an odd hour might be routed to a library conceivably halfway around the world with the response forthcoming in a timely fashion. Roy Tennant theorized in 1999, "Imagine, if you will, an American University student needing reference assistance at 3 a.m. Why can't a librarian in Perth, Australia, provide some essential front-line help? Meanwhile, librarians in the American university could in turn help students in Perth in the middle of the night" (Tennant, 1999, p. 30).

Speaking on the effectiveness of the system, Diane Kresh related her experience with CDRS. A question regarding U.S. constitutional government was posed to the system at an off hour, but was quickly answered by an academic library in Hong Kong boasting a strong collection in U.S. constitutional history. The library in Hong Kong was most appropriate in terms of subject coverage and availability, thus underscoring the effectiveness and resiliency of a system sensitive to collection strengths and temporal constraints.

GLOBAL KNOWLEDGE BASE

One of the novel features of the CDRS was the development of a Global Knowledge Base. This was largely an attempt to capture the intellectual output of librarians by storing answers to questions in a database that could receive automatic inquiries. Obviously, this would provide the system with the ability to answer questions by taking repeat queries and providing answers or portions of answers without the librarian making the effort to search for them. Something as mundane as finding the titles of the Harry Potter series could be furnished automatically without involving a reference librarian. The foresight in this part of the operation can be discerned in Wikipedia, where individuals provide information on a variety of topics. The use of the knowledge base would work in the same way. Librarians furnish answers to a large database that can be shared by others. At the time, this was a novel approach to reference, but the concept of providing answers to a global knowledge base or keeping local information in a local database saved time for those involved in reference work. The major issue confronting this fledgling system was traffic. Since librarians were the only intermediaries to provide questions to the system, it was only a matter of time before the system would need a new approach to drive business to this new enterprise.

Although a product allowing a user to search libraries' local records and determine item availability was almost a decade away, OCLC started to look at collaborative ways to conduct reference as early as 2001. A standing-room-only audience gathered in the Library of Congress' (LC) renowned Coolidge Auditorium on the afternoon of January 12, 2001, to hear an expert panel of presenters. The symposium, cosponsored by LC and OCLC, was entitled "Building the Virtual Reference Desk in a 24/7 World." Jay Jordan, president of OCLC, Winston Tabb, LC's associate librarian for library services, Diane Kresh, LC's director of public services, R. David Lankes, director of the virtual reference desk and assistant at Syracuse University's School of Information Studies, Susan McGlamery, reference coordinator of the Metropolitan Cooperative Library System, Nancy O'Neill, principal librarian at the Santa Monica Library, and Cornell University's Paul Constantine, head of reference services at the Olin Kroch Uris Libraries, participated in a key meeting to highlight developments in virtual reference (Saunders, 2001).

Two key elements of this symposium were: (a) the findings of Diane Kresh with respect to the final test of a CDRS pilot project to check the viability of a question-and-answer Web form, assigning and tracking transactions, measuring response time in a 24/7 environment, defining the scope of requests for automatic routing, and defining best practices; and (b) the announcement that the Library of Congress and OCLC had agreed to design and deliver a new reference service based on the CDRS pilot project (Saunders, 2001). Outlining OCLC's role in this new venture, Chip Nilges and Frank Hermes detailed the mission of OCLC as an organization "that supports emerging networks, partners with commercial service providers, delivers low-cost alternatives for local use, develops supporting services, and supports cooperative efforts to deliver services in the public Web space." In throwing its weight behind the development of the CDRS pilot, OCLC clearly understood that it would have a major influence in the future development of a virtual reference service appealing to a wide number of its members. The issue was how to take the lessons learned from the CDRS experience and hone the service to appeal to a wider potential audience (Saunders, 2001).

Leveraging the skill of the members and other interested parties outside of LC and OCLC would prove critical to the success of any virtual endeavor of this kind. In order for this type of activity to have a chance for success, a product had to be developed that would meet the needs of librarians working in the trenches. Methodology to develop this new product would have to include a group of stakeholders committed to marketing this new service. As Machiavelli noted, "There is nothing more difficult to undertake than to carryout a new order of things (Machiavelli, 1999). Success would depend on developing both a quality service and a strong marketing plan.

QUESTION POINT

Building on cooperative values already exhibited in cataloging, acquisitions, and resource sharing, OCLC's evolving challenges were outlined by Jeff Penka. The service must be based on supporting an efficient, patron-focused digital reference service, based on library values that include Michael Gorman's eight central values of librarianship: stewardship, service, intellectual freedom, rationalism, literacy and learning, equity of access to recorded knowledge and information, privacy, and democracy (Penka, 2003).

In order to develop a system that embraced these values, the newly envisioned QuestionPoint needed to push the virtual reference service as far as possible by building on three strong foundations: developing a powerful technical infrastructure employing the Internet and innovative information management applications, collective expertise of reference members' reference staffs, and finally, the great long-standing tradition of libraries helping each other to do the best job for their patrons (O'Leary, May/June, 2003).

OCLC worked to unveil this new product, and in 2002 the introduction of QuestionPoint was announced. The new service would provide for:

- Filing, tracking, and managing Web-delivered questions from patrons
- Linking tools for insertion on local library Web sites for customizable, locally branded access to the QuestionPoint service
- Web-based question submission forms, E-mail interaction, and live chat service
- Automatic routing of questions using a request manager to other library staff locally, to other libraries in consortia or cooperatives, and/or to libraries in the Global Reference Network
- Identification of appropriate library strengths for such routing through matching metadata on questions with automated profiles of library resources, expertise, availability of staff, etc.
- Integration of QuestionPoint services with alternative service providers and the resources that local libraries use
- Construction and sharing of a global knowledge base of asked and answered reference questions with full, maintained sources (Quint, 2002)

The goals that OCLC set for itself were daunting, but its documentation clearly indicates that they have achieved a large portion of them. In the overview of OCLC services, OCLC provides the following in these broad areas: Reference Management Service, the 24/7 Reference Cooperative, the Global Reference

Network, Policy Pages, the Base Management Environment, and the Service Unit Profile.

The Reference Management Service allows libraries to communicate with patrons in a virtual environment while providing tools to manage the reference service. QuestionPoint allows libraries to interact with patrons at their point of need. One can receive questions through a Web form and answer them through E-mail as well as receive and answer questions through chat and a cobrowsing feature. One can also record and follow up on questions received through E-mail, by telephone, by fax, or at the reference desk. Collaboration is available through libraries and local, statewide, and regional groups or across the globe through the Global Reference Network. The system allows one to create a local knowledge base where questions and answers can be stored to be used again through the Global Knowledgebase. Finally the system provides the user with account management information, customization of services, in-depth statistical reports, and patron surveys.

24/7 REFERENCE COOPERATIVE

One of the key components of QuestionPoint (QP) is the 24/7 Reference Cooperative. When the Metropolitan Cooperative Library System could not financially support the 24/7 Reference service, OCLC saw an opportunity to acquire this unique entity. Using the infrastructure that OCLC could provide, 24/7 could be marketed on a large scale. Forming a QuestionPoint 24/7 transition team that included QP and 24/7 members helped inform the decision-making process as both services began to explore the possibilities that collaboration offered. The 24/7 Reference Cooperative is a subset of QuestionPoint libraries providing round-the-clock reference coverage. Libraries that participate in the Cooperative contribute effort and time to meet the demands of a 24/7 service. Libraries contribute based on a service formula in order to allow complete 24/7 coverage for their patrons. In addition, the Cooperative provides subject experts to handle difficult queries.

An essential element of the Cooperative is the development of policy pages where libraries provide information regarding general and specific practices and policies. This allows members of the Cooperative the ability to answer questions in an expeditious manner. While a member library is serving in chat mode, the library providing service can review policy pages and provide accurate answers concerning matters as simple as how to return a book, verification of a personal identification number, and explanations with regard to loan and fine procedures. Leveraging the labor of your staff to provide 24/7 is one of the significant achieved goals of the virtual reference concept.

Another key element to QuestionPoint is the Global Reference Network (GRN). The brainchild of the Library of Congress, the GRN is a service that relays questions and answers to libraries based on, as discussed before, detailed profiles of expertise. The GRN creates and maintains a global knowledgebase of high quality questions and answers and provides automatic service similar in manner to a Wiki. The Base Management Environment, an additional feature of QuestionPoint, allows members access to an entire suite of tools in the Reference Management Service, including E-mail management, question forms, chat forms, walk-up phone reference tracking and followup, chat reference and followup, scripted messages, a local knowledgebase, and access to the Global Reference Network. A group administrator uses reports and statistics to monitor and manage each group.

Finally, QuestionPoint offers the Service Unit Profile to allow a library to create and identify a specific work unit. In this way, a library or work unit has access to its own questions, chat transcripts, reports and statistics, policy information, librarian accounts, scripted messages, E-mail messages, question forms, and chat forms.

OCLC understood early on that the need to market the service effectively was essential to success. Developing a quality product that would find endorsement among librarians and users was critical. The OCLC developers together with members, including the QuestionPoint transition team and a group of users, ensured that the product would be fine tuned with a critical eye. OCLC compiled every suggestion in a list and, where possible, utilized the information to provide enhancements. This created a number of stakeholders within the system and generated interest and attachment to the system. It was to OCLC's credit that they allowed for this type of input from members; the amount of potential customization is remarkable.

The transition team met on a regular basis, at least once a month, to critically review technological developments and brainstorm on enhancements. Those meetings produced remarkable evaluations that sharpened the product to meet the needs of users. Today, the QuestionPoint Users Council, a mix of global users and OCLC staff formed in spring 2007, offers feedback to the QuestionPoint Product Team regarding strategic directions for QuestionPoint, especially as they relate to the environment of library virtual reference services. They advise the QP team regarding software and new features, act as a liaison to the membership including assisting the QP Team to communicate more effectively with the QP community, run user group meetings at conferences, and assist the QP team at virtual user group meetings.

INTERNATIONAL

The successful transition of QuestionPoint and the 24/7 Reference service was a critical moment in the development of quality virtual reference. Today, the system is supported all over the globe. QuestionPoint is available in 24 countries and answers are provided in 26 languages. There are large national or regional services in Australia, Europe (the Netherlands, France, Germany, the United Kingdom), North America (Canada, the United States, Mexico, the Caribbean), and South Africa.

Some of these groups have initiated creative services such as the one at Zentral-und Landesbibliothek Berlin. Known as Infopoint, the service is the brainchild of librarian Paul Ulrich and answers questions in 14 languages: English, German, French, Turkish, Polish, Chinese, Czech, Estonian, Greek, Latvian, Romanian, Russian, Swedish, and Finnish, with more planned for the future. The flexibility of software applications developed by OCLC allows this operation to flourish and clearly reflects QuestionPoint's global reach. The significant investment that OCLC has made in QuestionPoint cannot be overestimated. QP is firmly established all over the world. It is doubtful that virtual reference would be as successful if OCLC did not recognize the need to support this endeavor.

The establishment of virtual reference has spawned a great deal of interest within the profession. The work of Buff Hirko, especially in developing best practices, Joe Janes in challenging the profession to adapt technology, and David Lankes in examining question-and-answer transactions, as well as the work of Marie Radford and Lynn Connaway in transcript analysis have led to dramatic improvements in virtual reference services.

The building blocks that led to the creation of QuestionPoint are relatively new. Enhancements such as the newly introduced Qwidget, a widget -type device that allows the service to be used on a variety of Web pages, catalogs, etc., attest to OCLC's consistent commitment to innovation. The extent to which QuestionPoint adapts to Google, WorldCat, Facebook, and other social networking tools, the iPhone and derivatives of handheld devices will ultimately determine future patterns of service and open up the possibilities for expanding user and affinity groups. With the ubiquitous possibilities that QuestionPoint offers, the ability to connect from just about anywhere, virtual reference appears to have a sound future.

CHARTERED OBJECTIVES

As OCLC continually reinvents itself, it is important to review its original 1967 mission:

- Maintain and operate a computerized library network
- Promote the evolution of libraries, library use, and librarianship
- Provide services for library users and libraries
- Increase availability of library resources to library patrons
- Reduce library costs
- Further ease of access to and use the ever-expanding body of worldwide scientific, literary, and educational knowledge and information (Mason, 1998, p. 62)

On every level, OCLC has delivered on its 1967 mission with respect to virtual reference. Yet OCLC could not accomplish this without a strong membership contribution, particularly librarians who toil day in and day out and night in and night out, sharing their knowledge with the global community. They are the conscientious conduits that daily fulfill Fred Kilgour's and OCLC's proud founding vision.

REFERENCES

Clark, R. (1977). *Edison, the man who made the future.* New York: G. P. Putnam's Sons.

How Much Information? 2003, Executive Summary (p. 1). Retrieved March, 2005 from http://www2.sims.berkeley.edu/research/projects/how-much-info-2003/

Machiavelli, N. *The Prince* New York, New American Library, Signet Classic, 1999, p. 49.

Mason, M. G. (1998). Reference revolutions. In *OCLC 1967–1997: Thirty years of furthering access to the world's information* (p. 57). New York: Haworth Press.

O'Leary, M. QuestionPoint fortifies libraries in Internet age. *Online*, May/June, 2003 27(3) p. 70.

Penka, J. T. (2003, February). The technological challenges of digital reference. *D-Lib Magazine* (9)2. Retrieved December, 2008 from http://www.dlib.org/dlib/february03/penka/02penka.html

Quint, B. (2002). QuestionPoint marks a new era in virtual reference. *Information Today* (July/August), (19)7 p. 50.

Saunders, L. (2001). Building the virtual reference desk. *Information Today* (March), (18)3 p. 25.

Tennant, R. (1999). Of human and humane assistance. *Library Journal* (June 15), (124)11 p. 30.

Librarians meet to turn online services into "virtual certainty." *Wilson Library Bulletin* (June 15 1999). 69 p. 17.

Digital Collections: History and Perspectives

GREG ZICK

Global Engineering, OCLC Online Computer Library Center, Inc., Dublin, OH, USA

ABSTRACT. *The author reviews the history of early efforts by libraries to build digital collections, the development of CONTENTdm software at the University of Washington, and OCLC's current directions in helping libraries build and manage digital collections.*

INTRODUCTION

Today, the result of a search in WorldCat often includes the full digital file of a large selection of primary source material. This primary source material in digital form is accessible through your browser. The available digital content is rich and diverse—from peer-reviewed images of cells for the study of cell biology to multiple fully transcribed and searchable handwritten diaries from the U.S. Civil War held in collections of multiple libraries. Since it is in digital form, the primary source material can be reviewed, read, researched, retrieved, and included as part of a rich resource for scholarly research and learning for all ages. The breadth and depth of digital collections available is extensive. Other examples are:

Amelia Earhart search and rescue report (1937) from the George Putman collection of Amelia Earhart papers, Purdue University
http://earchives.lib.purdue.edu/cdm4/document.php?CISOROOT=/earhart&CISOPTR=3011&REC=3
Senator Joe McCarthy: Audio Excerpts, 1950–1954—An audio recording of McCarthy defending his methods at a veterans' gathering in Rhinelander, Wisconsin, in 1952 at the Marquette University Raynor Memorial Library

http://digitalmarquette.cdmhost.com/cdm4/item_viewer.php?CISOROOT
    =/p128701coll0&CISOPTR=3&CISOBOX=1&REC=18

Journal of the First Voyage of Columbus—American Journeys: Eyewitness
    Accounts of Early American Exploration and Settlement, Wisconsin Histor-
    ical Society
    http://content.wisconsinhistory.org/cdm4/document.php?CISOROOT=/aj
        &CISOPTR=4213

Letter from Maya Angelou to Alex Haley—The Voyages of Alex Haley:
    Notebooks and Memoirs of an African-American Writer, Broward County
    Library
    http://digilab.browardlibrary.org/cdm4/document.php?CISOROOT=/alex
        haley&CISOPTR=2342&REC=10

Absence of radius and ulna in mice lacking hoxa-11 and hoxd-11 (a peer-
    reviewed article published in the journal *Nature* that was coauthored by
    geneticist Mario Capecchi, who was a joint recipient of the Nobel Prize in
    Medicine for 2007 for this line of genetics research)—USpace Institutional
    Repository, University of Utah
    http://content.lib.utah.edu/cdm4/document.php?CISOROOT=/ir-main&
        CISOPTR=520&REC=2

Jane Eyre: Historical image character portrait of Katharine Hepburn in the
    title role (1936–1937)—Theater Photography from the Theresa Helburn
    Collection, Bryn Mawr College
    http://triptych.brynmawr.edu/cdm4/item_viewer.php?CISOROOT=/Helbu
        rn&CISOPTR=792&REC=4

Lesson Plan: Depression Photo Essay (Grades 9–12)—Teaching with Digital
    Content, University of Illinois–Urbana-Champaign; Chicago Public Library
    Special Collections Library; Early American Museum; Illinois Heritage As-
    sociation; Illinois State Library; Lakeview Museum of Arts and Sciences;
    Lincoln Home National Historic Site; McLean County Museum of History;
    Museum of Science and Industry; Mystic Seaport
    http://images.library.uiuc.edu/projects/tdc/lessonplans/DepressionPhoto.
        html

Access to these rich collections of digitized primary source material is the
result of many individual library efforts supported by software tools and
services offered by Online Computer Library Center (OCLC) and others.
It is a long-term goal of OCLC and its members to build a global digital
repository that aggregates the metadata of digital items with links and access
to the items. This article discusses the origins of the digital collections tools,
how the evolution of technology and information science has combined
to provide technology solutions, and how the activity of building digital
collections has moved from small initial "special" projects within the library
to large and at times regional efforts with a longer-term focus on digital
access and preservation of these unique and valuable digital resources.

HISTORY

The initial efforts of building digital collections were fueled by the widespread and rapid growth of the Internet. The sharing of digital information in the form of computer text files rapidly extended to images, documents, and other media. During the 1990s, significant advances in computer technology created a wide user base for this information channel. The decade saw a significant improvement in the color quality and resolution of computer displays, a rapid increase in central processing unit (CPU) power, a substantial increase in disc storage capacity, and an ever increasing improvement in network speed—each generation of technology costing less than its predecessor. Easily accessible and relatively affordable software tools to support Web sites were widely used, and the first wave of local collection Web sites sprouted up in many libraries. Typically, these collections were comprised a set of scanned photos posted within a locally designed Web homepage and various navigation designs. While these efforts attracted considerable interest due to their novelty and creativity, there were a number of problems.

First, there were no established standards or set of best practices for organizing this new data medium. Finding particular items was an intellectual challenge. The collections were created in separate silos of effort. They lacked a cohesive connection for comprehensive searches, Web store site maintenance, and consistency in implementation. Second, sustainability was a continual problem. These projects were typically implemented as a special effort by staff that held other full-time jobs. After completing the first instance, they typically returned their focus to these primary jobs. Support and evolution of the Web site were a great challenge because of staff changeover and the lack of common tools. Finally, the existing software for large data sets was designed for text and numbers. The software did not handle images well and was usually priced for the commercial market and beyond the budget constraints of most libraries.

In the mid 1990s, I was director of a research laboratory at the University of Washington in Seattle, whose focus was on nontraditional database applications in medicine. Our group was studying how to handle the mixed data resulting from the relation type of patient name, address, insurance company, etc., and of the visual type with text such as an X-ray or CT scan with the associated text diagnosis. Implementing a mixed data type data solution allowed us to search large repositories of medical images for specific types of patients who were diagnosed with a specific condition.

I was invited to speak at an IBM library forum to present this work as an example of future directions for library systems. My presentation covered the evolving technology, the features of our research systems, and the opportunities of future information systems for library organizations. The second speaker at the forum expressed great concern about the limitations of technology in the context of how difficult it was for end users and professional librarians to implement and utilize these new Internet-connected computer systems. The issues included a lack of understanding of metadata descriptions for the digital data, rapidly evolving technology, difficulty in curating collections because of changing staff and complex tools, the challenge of ever-changing standards, and a lack of search options for multiple and diverse collections.

Over the course of several additional follow-up discussions I identified an opportunity to use the technology from our research efforts and the knowledge of the library community to develop a new kind of software that would handle these challenges. The design included these objectives: simple to use, customizable for local requirements and recognition, internally robust, powerful text search engine, open metadata definition. The software would also support metadata cross walking to allow cross-collection searching while retaining the individual richness in the collection metadata description.

BROADER GOALS FOR THE SOFTWARE

An early challenge was how to identify and support the full range of digital content type found in a special collections library. We wanted to support the full range of special collection content types—images, photos, maps, postcards, historical newspapers, documents, and books. It was also important to provide the ability for each collection coordinator to define and use metadata that was specific to their collection while providing a collection administrator-controlled crosswalk to a common metadata scheme like the Dublin Core.

We were very interested in an architecture that would encourage sharing and support collaborative work in the digital workflow. We achieved this by developing a desktop application—called the acquisition station—that could be used by multiple catalogers working on multiple collections on the same server at the same time. This implementation was successfully used—first by the University of Utah and then by the State Library of Louisiana (LOUIS)—to initiate and support multiple institution digitization and collection building. We called this software suite of tools CONTENTdm.

This version of the CONTENTdm digital collection software was developed by a team at the University of Washington that included Craig Yamashita, Lawrence Yapp, Joe Tavares, Geri Ingram, and Jill Fluvog. The first digital collection implemented on CONTENTdm was done in partnership with the University of Washington Libraries. In 1996, the Libraries launched a campuswide effort to transform the unique scholarly collections of faculty and libraries into a rich multimedia digital archive. The Libraries partnered with the College of Engineering's Center for Information Systems Optimization to develop a high-performance image archive complete with robust metadata capabilities, multiresolution scanning, and a powerful search engine. These features were needed to bring new life to special collections.

About 100,000 digital images were transferred from video discs to the CONTENTdm system. The images were a collection of early Seattle vaudeville and entertainment posters. The online access to these images generated great interest. Over the next 5 years we continued to improve the software with a variety of new features, and as more libraries heard about our efforts they began to request copies of the software. In 2001, the technology was transferred from the university to a new company named DiMeMa (for digital media management). Over the next 5 years the CONTENTdm user base grew from a handful of institutions to over 300 U.S. libraries. In 2002, DiMeMa partnered with OCLC to provide access to libraries and joined OCLC in 2006, as the leading provider of digital collection management software.

CURRENT STATUS

OCLC now has a Digital Collection Services group that provides services for libraries and other cultural heritage organizations to create, curate, and manage digital collections. The services help organizations create and showcase digital collections on the Web and provide long-term archiving of digital master files. The group also works with librarians and other professionals to develop and evolve new and best practices for digital collections.

The CONTENTdm Digital Collection Management Software supports such standards as Dublin Core, JPEG2000, OAI (Open Archive Initiative), Harvesting, PHP (Hyptertext Preprocessor), and API (Application Programming Interface). The software can handle a full range of primary source material types, including images, photographs, posters, postcards, maps, documents, journals, diaries, theses, dissertations, newspapers, yearbooks, and audio and video files.

Another key component of supporting the full cycle of digital collection curation is digital preservation, whose challenges include an increasing volume of digital materials with limited resources.

To address the need for digital preservation in the library community, OCLC has implemented a Digital Archive Service that provides secure managed storage for digital originals and master files. The ISO-9001 certified service integrates disaster recovery into the library's workflow for building digital collections.

This service provides Automated Monitoring, which includes manifest verification, virus checking, fixity check (digital fingerprinting), and format verification. A user of the archive receives regular reports that include storage use and growth, file types, and a record of an access or disseminations.

The digital collections can reside on a CONTENTdm Server, either installed locally or on an OCLC-hosted server. Digital items can be added from anywhere using the CONTENTdm Project Client, which can be distributed among staff and collaborating partners, through the Connexion client using Connexion digital import, or through a Web browser using a simple Web form. Collections can also be managed remotely over the Web.

The digital collections can be searched via the Web using standard Web browsers by any number of end users, unless a library elects to restrict access. With its ability to handle any file type, CONTENTdm can serve as an institutional repository to bring collections together into a cohesive and accessible Web-based environment. For organizations seeking opportunities for broader collaboration in developing and sharing collections, the Multi-Site Server is an option for cross-collection searching on multiple servers.

CONTENTdm is scalable, enabling a library to upgrade and increase capacity without new software installations. Organizations with small, unique collections to statewide groups with hundreds of collections have selected CONTENTdm for their projects. While most users run the CONTENTdm software "out of the box," it also has an API that allows for custom development. The open architecture supports extensions, and the Web interface is fully customizable.

CONTENTdm also facilitates discovery of items in special collections through WorldCat. Metadata for collections can be added to WorldCat to make digital items more visible to searchers on the Web through World-Cat.org and WorldCat Local. Those searchers who go to sites such as Google and Yahoo! Search also will discover WorldCat results for library-owned items among their results.

GOING FORWARD

Recent surveys on the impact and direction of digital library efforts have identified some significant trends. Libraries are increasing their efforts to digitize "reborn" paper material in addition to setting up institutional repositories to capture the born digital material published by their patrons such as electronic theses and dissertations. These efforts focus on digitization first to establish the digital collections with planning for digital preservation a future effort to be determined.

The increase in the digital collection activities within a growing number of libraries also supports the evolution of this type of effort from a special project limited by time and resources to an integral part of the libraries' activity. Best practices are emerging that support more open and flexible metadata creation, the use of social networking and tools to leverage group interest, and a strong interest in the aggregation of the digital collection metadata to support cross-collection searching of these rich resources through sophisticated and robust tools. A common objective is to create, contribute to, and use a universal search and access source. Our experience has demonstrated that every item is special to someone, the aggregate is special to most and the integration with other content is valuable to all.

As digital collection creation and maintenance (curation) becomes mainstream in the library, it is also becoming the focus of more traditional measures of library activity, including assessment and evaluation, both from the collection manager's perspective and the user's point of view, and sustainability, that is, how to move the creation of digital collection resources from a grant-funded, project status into a program with dedicated operating funding.

To respond to these trends, OCLC plans to extend the tools that support digital collection efforts in the library to increase the efficiency of workflow and to reduce the cost of these efforts. Capture and cataloging of digital content will be enhanced through new software tools that support use of terminology services, metadata templates, and batch processing. The CONTENTdm software is fully Unicode compatible, and has extended the support for electronic archival description (EAD) Finding Aids. A new digital collection Gateway service will support collection administrator control of harvesting digital collection metadata into WorldCat. This harvested data will be discoverable through the Open WorldCat.org and the local institutions' view in WorldCat Local.

While there is much work still to be done to create and preserve these valuable digital collections, it is clear that these efforts by the library organizations involved are adding great value to scholarly research and interest at all levels.

The RLG Partnership

JAMES MICHALKO

RLG Programs, OCLC Online Library Center, Inc., Dublin, OH, USA

ABSTRACT. *Created in 2006 with the coming together of RLG and OCLC, the RLG Partnership is a transnational research venue for libraries, archives and museums. In concert with OCLC Research, the RLG Partnership focuses on a work agenda that includes system-wide organization and interactions of libraries, archives and museums; research information management; mobilizing unique materials in collections; metadata support and management; and infrastructure to support metadata flow in the Web environment.*

At the present time the RLG Partnership consists of over 150 institutions that have chosen to affiliate in this special venue sponsored by the Online Library Center (OCLC) and supported by OCLC Research. These institutions support the work of the Partnership through the payment of annual dues and active staff engagement in a program of work. These are self-selected institutions that want to work with similarly motivated institutions to address architectural, workflow, and service issues in the design of their future services.

Within OCLC, the RLG Partnership is unique. It is a transnational research venue for institutions wishing to coordinate their efforts and address the grand challenges (and opportunities) confronting research information organizations. Staff from the OCLC Research division coordinate and support the efforts of these affiliated libraries, archives, and museums. Through active collaboration, these RLG Partners develop shared solutions, participate in innovative experiments, assist in the design and testing of new prototypes, and reach consensus on exciting new approaches to shared challenges.

For libraries and other cultural organizations prepared to invest resources and staff expertise in collaboratively designing innovative programs and future services, the RLG Partnership is a global alliance of like-minded institutions that focuses on making operational processes more efficient and shaping new scholarly services by directly engaging senior managers. Unlike other regional, trade, or issue-driven groups in the community, the RLG Partnership is supported by the full capacities of OCLC Research. The Partnership influences and directs a substantial portion of the OCLC Research effort. It proceeds from an international, system-wide perspective, and it connects to the broad array of OCLC products and services.

Today's libraries, archives, and museums have to manage their collections differently, organize what they deliver more effectively, and create new infrastructures to sustain a new service array in order to be a valued part of the scholarly process. Confronted with disruptive technologies and challenging economics, they must genuinely transform how they make their collections available to their users—a feat that is beyond the ability of an individual institution. Libraries, archives, and museums prepared to invest and lead on these challenges and create a new future find the RLG Partnership an important part of their response.

THE COMBINATION

This special venue within OCLC was created during the merger of the Research Libraries Group, Inc. (RLG) into OCLC in July 2006.

During the discussions leading to the merger it became clear that both organizations wanted to grow their support for research institutions and that what was needed and wanted by research institutions could best be delivered by joining the distinctive capabilities of the two. Moreover, the institutions served by both organizations would benefit from economies achieved through integration of services.

The combined capabilities of both organizations would support an exceptional agenda for libraries, archives, and museums focused on applied research, community building, and prototyping of systems and services.

There were two key components to the combination: (a) the creation of a venue within OCLC Research that would support the RLG Partnership (the programmatic and leadership component of RLG's traditional activities); and (b) the integration of RLG's online products and services with OCLC's service lines.

The goal in establishing a venue for research institutions within OCLC was to reinvent for the 21st century effective forms of collaborative action. Renewed collective effectiveness depended on a broader range of capacities than either could provide alone. Within RLG the emphasis of many decades had been on collective issue identification, community building, and consensus making. OCLC Research provided the community with deep expertise in beta development, tool building, data mining and business intelligence, and broad enabling architectures and infrastructure.

With libraries, archives, and museums challenged by disruptive technologies that have altered information consumer behavior and made our operating environments increasingly uncompetitive, the combination of RLG Programs' experience with OCLC Research's expertise could support collective action with a much broader range of capabilities.

THE CONTEXT

The RLG Partnership shares a point of view about the current information context, the institutional operating environment, and the implications for the future of research collections.

In particular we think that within a generation the library's information sources and delivery services will be largely virtual. Libraries will continue to provide direct access to physical materials, but this will be very much focused on the special demands of their local constituencies. "Comprehensive" research collection building will be done by a very small number of institutions, while special collections of the special or unique materials of research will be maintained and featured at many institutions.

Within 10 years museums and archives will expand their primary missions to emphasize widely disseminated disclosure of their collections and the routine provision of digital surrogates of those collections.

The primary mission of cultural institutions will be to provide access to trustworthy, authoritative information in support of the research, teaching, and learning process.

Providing tools and services that enhance research and learning productivity around those knowledge resources will be a vital part of institutional operations.

Institutions will discharge this mission in new ways and provide alternatives for many of their traditional activities. Redundant physical collections will be consolidated and managed via a centralized system and set of processes. Library purchase or provision of physical materials not held locally will be done largely on demand, based on examination of digital surrogates. Disclosing what an institution collects and licenses in the most efficacious fashion will be a major investment.

Collecting materials that are distinctive to local mission and milieu will define research-focused institutions, while being an activity in which all libraries engage. This includes locally created intellectual assets, as well as those procured externally. As collecting activities become more focused on rare and unique materials, libraries, archives, and museums will increasingly depend on shared standards, processes, and technology. Moreover, there will be major reorganizations of staffing effort and major shifts in the types of staff expertise required to maintain vibrant and valued arrays of teaching, learning, and research support.

Based on this view of the future, the RLG Partnership supported by OCLC Research has committed itself to a continuing work agenda that can impact this future while at the same time preserving and renewing the value of research libraries, archives, and museums, thereby ensuring that they are important in the emerging new processes by which research is done and learning occurs.

THE WAY THE PARTNERSHIP WORKS AND ITS AGENDA

Where the Partnership invests effort reflects key areas for shared attention and collaborative action. The following criteria are consistent with the capabilities of OCLC Research and serve as a way of identifying priorities and maximizing impact as we help libraries, archives, and museums design their future. The criteria include:

- Eliminates a redundant effort or process
- Affects system-wide behaviors
- Creates shared capacity
- Changes community economics
- Cuts across cultural sectors
- Transforms something (process, standard, etc.) into a routine
- Translates something (process, standard, etc.) into community terms
- Responds to a known and shared Partner need
- Provides opportunities for Partner engagement

The actual work agenda is dynamic and influenced by the advisory body elected from staff within RLG Partner institutions. Because of the emphasis on changed operational processes and new services, our advisors usually come from the senior manager cohort within Partner institutions. They are the ones charged with making these changes real and are best positioned to advise on the collective contributions that could make these changes faster, more effective, or more efficient.

The current agenda of the RLG Partnership has five broad themes representing persistent areas of shared uncertainty and change for the communities we serve. They also represent areas where a leadership subset of the Partnership could make an impact, areas where OCLC Research brings distinctive capabilities, and areas where other organizations have not successfully engaged.

Initial program focus areas include the following.

The first program focus is on system-wide organization, where the objective is to provide the evidence and the frameworks that will allow libraries

and other cultural institutions to reshape their services based on a broad understanding of how individual institutions are parts in broad and complex
regional and global systems of service provision. Areas of interest include
user studies; the interactions of libraries, archives, and museums; system-level
risks and challenges; and finally, methods for managing print collections as
a collective resource.

The second area is in research information management. Here, the objective is to reach a collective understanding of the responsibilities of and
opportunities for libraries in an environment where research is done differently and E-research becomes the norm. The Partnership is exploring new
prospects for adding value to the scholarly communication process, helping
scholars get the most out of new technologies that can enhance the quality
of their work, and helping academic institutions with the assessment of their
research outputs.

Mobilizing unique materials is the third area of focus. The objective
is to achieve economies and efficiencies that permit these unique materials in archives and museums to be effectively described, properly disclosed, successfully discovered, and appropriately delivered. Overall the
RLG Partnership wants to bring about greater collaboration among libraries,
archives, and museums by surfacing models for sharing data, services, and
expertise.

The fourth area is in metadata support and management, whose purpose
is to provide new structures for controlled data and improve current metadata workflows. As new service ambitions emerge that allow library, archive,
and museum processes to be done at their most efficient level—locally, re-
gionally, or globally—new structures for controlled data will be necessary
as will changes to the current flows of metadata between the machine systems that consume and depend on these services. We can advance this by
providing prototypes that demonstrate the value of aggregating, enriching,
disclosing, or manipulating structured data for use in different discovery and
metadata creation environments.

Finally, the Partnership is focusing on infrastructure and organization to
enable consistent, reliable metadata flows in the Web environment through
the provision of Web development tools, reference implementations, and
the management of identifiers. All of these provide important scaffolding on
which the library, archive, and museum community can rely as they build
new services.

OUTPUTS OF THE PARTNERSHIP

The outputs of the RLG Partnership efforts may be about creating change
and building community, synthesizing best practices and supporting architecture or standards that embody those practices, delivering beta development

or tools, and providing evidence for decision making and future change, research work, best practices, specifications, and prototypes.

The activities of building change and creating community are associated with mobilizing the library, archive, and museum community in support of collaborative action and reform of inefficient workflows, or building consensus about a preferred set of solutions. They are characterized by direct engagement with members of the RLG Partnership and other research institutions in shared work and expressed in authoritative recommendations or "blueprints" for community change. For example, editorial pieces are created that are intended to stimulate community response and that include specific recommendations for changed practice or investment of resources. Working groups provide direct engagement opportunities for the members of the RLG Partnership to shape outcomes of our work. Partner events are held with a thematic focus on consensus building or agenda planning.

The Partnership's engagement in best practices, architecture, and standards ranges from recommendations to architectural implementations. There is a continuum for many projects, including final recommendations or conceptual frameworks.

Beta development involves the creation of experimental software or systems to explore ideas (proof-of-concept), elicit feedback, and confirm interest in a proposed design. Access to beta software, tools, or systems may be open to the world or limited to select groups of users.

Another important output of the Partnership is developing evidence. This activity is about building context around problems and discussions, including such work as data-mining studies that provide an empirical context for issues of interest and/or support decision making; user studies that illuminate important aspects of information-seeking behaviors; literature reviews/ syntheses that summarize current thinking in a particular area; and technology watch reports that educate the community on important technologies, standards, etc. The common theme to all work in this area is that it is aimed at furthering understanding: of the contours of an issue or problem, of the user community, of a new technology, and so on.

Through deliberate investment and leadership the RLG Partnership can help libraries, archives, and museums design compelling new institutional futures, building and delivering collections and services that are responsive to a dynamic information context. The aim of the Partnership is to enhance the ways in which libraries, archives, and museums create value in the research and learning process.

WebJunction: A Community for Library Staff

MARILYN GELL MASON

WebJunction, OCLC Online Computer Library Center, Inc., Dublin, OH, USA

ABSTRACT. *The author reviews the history, accomplishments and plans of WebJunction.*

INTRODUCTION

WebJunction (WJ) is a Web-based service that provides online learning and community support for library staff. Using Web 2.0 technologies, WJ enables library staff, libraries, and library organizations to form communities, implement learning programs, and share content on topics of specific interest to the library community.

Founded in 2002 with funding from the Bill & Melinda Gates Foundation, WJ launched on May 12, 2003, and has grown quickly into a robust service with 15 community partners, 35,000 course enrollments, and close to 100,000 unique visitors per month. This article describes the background of WJ, the Community Partner Program and other community services, the scope of Online Learning Services, and the latest improvements that enhance user experience.

BACKGROUND

In July 1997, Bill and Melinda Gates founded the Gates Library Foundation, the predecessor to the Bill & Melinda Gates Foundation (BMGF, founded in 2000). In the first 5 years of its existence the Gates Foundation's Library Program almost singlehandedly transformed public libraries. Not since Andrew Carnegie endowed 2,500 libraries has one vision had such a dramatic impact on public libraries and the services they provide. By 2002 the Gates

Foundation had invested over $280 million (more has been invested in the years that followed) to provide computers, training, and Internet access to public libraries in the United States, Canada, and Native American communities. It had placed over 30,000 computers in over 11,000 libraries in low-income communities throughout North America. Because of these efforts over 145 million people were able to enjoy free access to information that would otherwise have been unavailable to them.

The infusion of technology and training enabled public libraries to move from being providers of information in print to providers of information of all types and in all media. The democratizing impact of placing this powerful technology in public libraries brought new life to libraries and to the communities they serve. The BMGF wished to provide a way to support these services going forward and in early 2002 called for proposals to build a self-sustaining online community that would enable library staff to share the knowledge and resources necessary to successfully support public access to information in public libraries.

As a nonprofit membership organization with deep roots in the library community, experience in working with contributed content, and technical expertise needed to develop the architecture and infrastructure necessary to the success of the project, the Online Computer Library Center (OCLC) seemed like the ideal organization to lead the project. Other organizations that were part of the initial project were the Colorado State Library, the Benton Foundation, Isoph, and TechSoup. Each organization extended the range and capabilities of OCLC, and the proposal we put together was funded. The result of those initial development efforts became WebJunction.

Today WJ has several major programs: Community Partner Program, Online Learning, Tools, and an Enhanced User Experience.

COMMUNITY PARTNERS

The Community Partner Program launched in 2004 and is WebJunction's unique offering for state, regional, provincial, and national libraries or similar organizations. Community Partners use this unique blend of Web portal, social tools, helpful content, and online courses to help their libraries and staff share ideas, solve problems, network, develop skills, and stay informed about state resources and programs for libraries. The program includes a co-branded portal, an array of online learning tools, and enhanced community-building capabilities.

Each Community Partner site is individually branded, and community partners have control over content, courses, discussion boards, and groups on their site. Community partners have found this to be an effective way to generate interest in specific issues, develop an active online learning program for library staff across the state, and distribute information quickly and easily. At the end of 2008, WJ had 15 Community Partners: Arizona, Connecticut, Georgia, Idaho, Illinois, Indiana, Iowa, Kansas, Maine, Minnesota, New Hampshire, Ohio, Rhode Island, Vermont, and Washington.

Communities of Practice are less formal than Community Partners and are organized more loosely around topic areas. Current Communities of Practice include Spanish Language Outreach, Rural and Small Libraries, and Government Information in the 21st Century.

ONLINE LEARNING

The power and performance of a library lie with the ability of its staff to deliver the best possible experience to patrons and the community. As technology, community demographics, and culture continue to evolve, it is important to keep library staff on a path of continuous learning through training and development programs. Providing adequate learning opportunities has become more and more challenging as costs for staff to attend offsite courses continue to escalate even while the need to continually update competencies for all staff continues to grow.

E-learning is one way to help reduce costs while increasing participation. Initially WJ offered only self-paced courses. While these continue to be the bulk of the course catalog, WJ has also experimented with live online courses. In fact, WJ is now offering a continuing series of free Webinars. WJ has also done research into the status of E-learning in libraries, and those publications are available for free download on the site. They provide important information about what works in blended learning and ways E-learning can be successfully implemented. Titles include the following:

• Blended Learning Guide
• Continuing Education Survey Results
• Staff Training in Public Libraries: 2007 Fact Sheet
• Staff Training in Academic Libraries: 2007 Fact Sheet
• Sustaining Public Access Computing Programs
• Trends in E-Learning for Library Staff

Courses are an important part of the community partner program, but they are also available through individual purchase or volume purchase. Wimba Classroom provides a professional Web-conferencing capability, allowing individual libraries or library organizations to distribute their own courses. This can also be used for meetings among staff who are geographically dispersed.

New in late 2008, WebJunction's Learning Partner Program is an opportunity for larger libraries and library systems to take advantage of powerful tools and services to help in the implementation and management of training programs, reducing the cost and staff time required to manage training effectively. The Learning Partner Program provides tools that enable individual libraries to create courses, to assign them as part of an overall staff development program, and to track staff progress through the courses.

WJ is working hard to increase the quality and quantity of courses available, especially on topics specific to libraries. Increasingly, WJ expects to work with other library organizations to broker courses that they develop. This will enable those who develop courses to recoup some of the costs of development, and is likely to diversify offerings available. WJ is excited about the opportunity to work closely with the library community to continue to improve and develop this important area.

TOOLS

In addition to some of the E-learning tools described above, WJ provides access to TechAtlas, an important tool for technology planning. Originally developed by N-Power for use by not-for-profits, the tool was acquired by WJ in 2007 and has been customized for use by libraries. Originally used by the Gates Foundation in their grant making to libraries' programs, TechAtlas is now also used by libraries to assist in developing a technology plan that is the basis for E-rate applications.

A PERSONAL PLACE

With the launch of the latest version in August 2008, WJ began offering a suite of tools that enable users to customize their WJ experience. When you register as a member (membership is free) you automatically get a "My Account" page where you can enter information about yourself, find and invite friends, find and create groups, track discussions, and add bookmarks. There are also sections for tracking courses, comments, and activities. All of this content can be shared with all members, shared only with friends, or held privately. As a kind of "Facebook," WJ now offers the only service designed specifically for library staff where members can share information in a positive and supportive environment.

This sharing of content is the key to WebJunction. It is based on the belief that each member has something important to contribute to the group and that we can solve problems and improve library service by sharing our best practices.

LOOKING FORWARD

Throughout its development WebJunction has worked closely with the library community to ensure that priorities for development reflect the priorities of the profession. We pay close attention to team leads in community partner states and regularly survey the membership. In addition we openly solicit comments and suggestions on an ongoing basis.

Although originally founded to support public libraries, the base of users of WJ is broadening. At this point Community Partners are state libraries, which are generally charged with the support and development of all types of libraries throughout their states. With their leadership WJ now offers its services to all types of libraries including academic, school, and special libraries as well as public libraries. We are finding that the need for ongoing training is universal and is not specific to any one type of library. The same is true for community services. We can all learn from each other, and the tools WJ offers to facilitate sharing are available to all library communities.

OCLC Research: Past, Present, and Future

NANCY E. ELKINGTON

OCLC Online Computer Library Center Research, Dublin, OH, USA

ABSTRACT. *From its modest beginnings in the mid 1970s as a small research and development unit of Online Computer Library Center, Inc. (OCLC), OCLC Research has evolved to become a significant research organization, a preeminent laboratory for the exploration of innovative uses of library data and information system technology, and a key agent of change, advancing the state of the art within OCLC and in the global library and information science community. OCLC Research is one of the world's leading centers devoted to exploration, innovation, and community building on behalf of libraries, archives, and museums and is dedicated to helping memory institutions more effectively serve users of information, information systems, and cultural heritage collections.*

ORGANIZATIONAL FOUNDATIONS

Founded in 1967, OCLC is a nonprofit, membership, computer library service and research organization dedicated to the public purposes of furthering access to the world's information and reducing the rate of rise of library costs. More than 69,000 libraries in 112 countries and territories around the world use OCLC services to locate, acquire, catalog, lend, and preserve library materials. OCLC and its member libraries cooperatively produce and maintain WorldCat, the OCLC Online Union Catalog.

The Research and Development Group was formed in 1974 under the leadership of James E. Rush. The OCLC Research Department was formally established within OCLC as a distinct administrative unit on July 1, 1977, and expanded over the next several years by manager W. David Penniman

Neal Kaske (1981–1983), who championed the name change to the Office of Research and led the staff toward a deeper understanding of online catalogs while also securing project funding from the Council on Library Resources and the National Science Foundation. From 1984 to1986 Michael J. McGill served as Acting Director and put in place many of the outreach efforts that served to more widely share the work of the division with colleagues elsewhere. Martin Dillon followed as Director from 1986 to 1994; during his tenure the Office of Research shifted its research focus more directly onto the issues facing the OCLC membership. Research Scientists Edward T. O'Neill and Thomas B. Hickey were co-acting directors from July 1993 to May 1994. In 1994, Terry Noreault (Terry Noreault promoted to Vice President, 1999) was named Director, and in 1999 was named Vice President, Office of Research and Special Projects, dedicating the division "to research that both explores the place of the library in the changing technology environment and develops tools that enhance the productivity of libraries and their users." Thom Hickey, Chief Scientist, was acting Director from 2000 until Lorcan Dempsey (Lorcan Dempsey to head office, 2001) took up the reins of leadership in 2001. When RLG, Inc. (formerly the Research Library Group) and OCLC became a single agency in July 2006 (RLG membership approves move, 2006), RLG's programmatic activities, programs-related personnel, and partner relationships with 150+ leading research-oriented libraries, archives, and museums became part of an expanded division at OCLC initially called OCLC Programs and Research, but now renamed OCLC Research.

CURRENT ORGANIZATION

The Vice President of Research (Lorcan Dempsey, also Chief Strategist) reports to the President and directs the OCLC Research division. The division's formal mission statement reads, "The mission of OCLC Research is to expand knowledge that advances OCLC's public purposes of furthering access to the world's information and reducing library costs" (OCLC, n.d.a). OCLC Research's work serves two primary audiences: (a) the OCLC membership and the global library community, and (b) the RLG Partnership, a transnational group of libraries, archives, and museums supporting research and scholarship (Michalko, 2009). The Vice President, RLG Programs (James Michalko) reports to the Vice President of Research and manages work designed to respond to the needs of the RLG Partnership. The two Vice Presidents serve as part of OCLC's Senior Leadership Team and jointly develop a dynamic and impactful work agenda that is responsive to the needs of the community. The division is composed of nearly 50 staff, including research scientists, program officers, software engineers and architects, a user interface designer, a project manager, and administrative staff, all of whom work in teams in support of the active work agenda.

THE PAST 10 YEARS: CHALLENGE AND CHANGE

OCLC Research has long focused its attention on addressing complex, often intransigent challenges facing libraries and their users (Godby & Richardson, 2003). In the past decade, many projects have been undertaken and completed and most bear the distinctive hallmarks of innovation: leadership, insight, invention, and action. Four initiatives are singled out because they can be seen as exemplars of the quality of investigation and depth of investment that has been made on behalf of the community at large: Dublin Core, PREMIS, VIAF, and Virtual Reference.

Dublin Core

When the World Wide Web was still in its infancy, one of the earliest challenges facing libraries was how to describe resources that lived only in the Web environment. The first Dublin Core workshop was held in 1995 and was cosponsored by OCLC Research and the University of Illinois' National Center for Supercomputing Applications (NCSA). The goal of the workshop was to agree on a simple, modular, extensible metadata scheme for Web-based resources (Weibel, 2005). The result was a core set of data elements for resource discovery.

Since then, the original element set has been expanded, extended, translated, and profiled in myriad ways, always in keeping with the original intent. The core set is an international standard (International Standards Organization, n.d.) and has been adopted in some form by at least seven national governments, by private industry, and by many libraries and other cultural memory institutions around the world. Of all OCLC Research endeavors, this one has had the most sweeping impact on the information community.

In January 2009, the Dublin Core Metadata Initiative (DCMI) established itself as an independent, public, not-for-profit company limited by guarantee in Singapore. DCMI is now the parent organization under which committees and groups work to develop and "support interoperable metadata standards that support a broad range of purposes and business models" (Dublin Core Metadata Initiative, 2009). The DCMI Web site (www.dublincore.org) is managed by the National Library of Korea (http://www.nl.go.kr/nlmulti/index.php?lang_mode=3); administration of the initiative is under the direction of the National Library Board Singapore (http://www.nlb.gov.sg/), and the metadata registry is the responsibility of the Resource Center for Knowledge Communities (http://www.kc.tsukuba.ac.jp/en/divisions.html) at the University of Tsukuba (Japan).

PREMIS—Preservation Metadata

In March 2000, OCLC Research and RLG, Inc. launched a joint initiative to identify and support best practices for the long-term retention of digital objects. (RLG, Inc was an independent consortium of research libraries, museums and archives that operated programs, systems and services for its members from 1974 to 2006. In July 2006, OCLC and RLG combined.) This collaboration facilitated consensus-building activity among key stakeholders in digital preservation; the initiative brought together leading international experts from North America, Europe, and Australia to review existing practices, share expertise, and identify common approaches wherever possible (Lavoie, 2001). In 2002, the group published its final report, "A Metadata Framework to Support the Preservation of Digital Objects" (OCLC/RLG Working Group, 2002).

The framework included a set of metadata elements, mapped to the conceptual structure and reflecting the information concepts and requirements articulated in the Open Archival Information System (OAIS; Consultative Committee, 2002) model. The following year, a new working group (also jointly sponsored by OCLC Research and RLG, Inc.) was formed to develop a data dictionary intended for use by those who were actively engaged in preserving digital information. In 2005, the two organizations published the PREMIS Data Dictionary for Preservation Metadata (PREMIS Working Group, 2005). As a mark of recognition for its contribution to the global digital preservation landscape, the publication and its authors were awarded the 2005 Digital Preservation Award by the British Conservation Awards and the 2006 Society of American Archivists' Preservation Publication Award. The working group was retired.

The Library of Congress now sponsors the PREMIS Maintenance Activity and provides a permanent home for the Data Dictionary, XML schema, and related materials. In 2008, version 2.0 of the Data Dictionary was released by the international PREMIS Editorial Committee.

VIAF: The Virtual International Authority File

During the 2003 International Federation of Library Associations and Institutions (IFLA) World Library and Information Congress in Berlin, the Deutsche Nationalbibliothek (DNB), the Library of Congress (LC), and OCLC agreed to develop a Virtual International Authority File (VIAF) for personal names (Bennett, Hengel-Dittrich, O'Neill, & Tillett, 2007). Since then, the DNB, the LC, OCLC, and the Bibliothèque nationale de France (BnF) have jointly conducted a project to match and link the authority records for personal names in the retrospective personal name authority files of the three national library catalogs. The long-term goal of the VIAF project is to link the authoritative names from many national libraries and other authoritative sources into a shared global authority service for persons, corporate bodies, conferences, places, and more. A prototype (VIAF, n.d.) was developed by OCLC Research and has been undergoing review and improvement for the past several years.

During 2008, the founding partners decided to expand the number of contributing national libraries and invited some two dozen institutions to consider participation. At this writing, a number of national libraries in Europe and the Pacific Rim have indicated their desire to become active members of this project.

The implications of this and related efforts in OCLC Research could be substantial. The techniques and systems that effectively support the management of multiple authority files will be critical to the success of an increasingly international and multilingual, networked community.

Virtual Reference

"Seeking Synchronicity: Evaluating Virtual Reference Services from User, Non-user, and Librarian Perspectives" was undertaken by OCLC Research and Rutgers with grant support from the Institute for Museum and Library Services (IMLS), a U.S. federal agency. The project goals were evaluating the practice, sustainability, and relevance of virtual reference services (VRS). VRS are human-mediated, Internet-based, synchronous library information services. The rapidly increasing use of remotely accessed digital reference resources has increased the demand for librarians to provide reference services online. VRS users, nonusers, and librarians provided data for this research in focus group interviews, online surveys, telephone interviews, and VRS session transcripts. The project provided findings regarding user and librarian preferences, process and usability issues related to technology, and content issues related to information accuracy and query negotiation. In addition, the project results inform the understanding of computer-mediated communication, the impact of virtual relationships, and generational differences in information seeking using live chat technology (Sillipigni Connaway & Radford, 2005–2008; Sillipigni Connaway, Radford, & Dickey, 2008).

CURRENT WORK: GLOBAL IMPACT

OCLC Research works with the community to collaboratively identify problems and opportunities; to model and test solutions; to develop consensus; and to share findings through experimental services, published reports, presentations, and professional interactions. Its vision is global and its impact is profound.

The OCLC Research toolkit includes data, applications, standards, and services; more important, it is composed of an extensive supply of human expertise, ingenuity, creativity, and leadership. Its partners are staff at institutions around the world, who are likewise committed to improving the Web-based information environment for the benefit of users everywhere.

Four areas of focus characterize a wide range of work under way in the division:

- Harnessing the power of terminologies
- Making names work harder
- Mobilizing unique materials
- Understanding and managing the global, collective collection

Harnessing the Power of Terminologies

Controlled vocabularies, such as thesauri and subject heading systems, have been used by librarians for decades to improve the indexing of a wide variety of information resources (including articles, books, movies, music, photographs, and Web sites). The purpose behind this work has been to increase the effectiveness of the end user in locating desired materials.

OCLC Research's Terminology Services (OCLC, n.d.h) prototype uses library and Web standards to make the terms, relationships, descriptions, and other information in controlled vocabularies readily available as resources on the Web. Each vocabulary is fully indexed and searchable and a vocabulary entity can be referenced by its identifier. Data is retrievable in multiple representations including the MAchine-Readable Cataloging (MARC) authority format in (eXtensible Markup Language) XML, used by libraries, and the SKOS (Simple Knowledge Organization System) Core Vocabulary designed for Semantic Web applications.

Librarians and developers of library applications are encouraged to experiment with the vocabularies and services provided by this project. The services may be used in a variety of ways. Some examples:

- as a source of terms for social tagging
- for query refinement in search applications
- to provide context for a search term
- to validate names and subjects in metadata
- to facilitate cross database searching

Making Names Work Harder

OCLC Research has for some time been examining and building experimental services that make data work harder. That is, research scientists have deliberately set out to determine whether there are good ways to make the collective assets of WorldCat deliver even more value because of its very nature and composition. For example, names (personal, corporate, institutional) are a central part of every MARC record.

The idea of WorldCat Identities is simple: create a summary page for every name in WorldCat (Hickey, 2007). Since there are some 125 million records in the database and nearly 25 million names mentioned somewhere, this is a large-scale data mining effort that would have been difficult even a few years ago. In its initial stages, the initiative focused on personal and corporate names; when viewing the beta version (http://orlabs. oclc.org/Identities) of the service, a page for the Beatles can be found as well as for John, Paul, George, and Ringo.

The summary pages are automatically generated and include:

- Most widely held works by the person
- Most widely held works about the person
- Genres of works
- Roles the person plays (e.g., composer, arranger, performer)
- A publication timeline for works both by and about the person
- Languages of publication
- Images of covers (if available)
- Audience level (kids, general, special)
- Related names (linking to WorldCat records and to their own Identities pages)
- Useful links
- Associated subjects

The beta service was tested in 2007 by a group of staff from institutions affiliated with the RLG Partnership (OCLC, n.d.b) and was moved into the production version of WorldCat in 2008. It builds on earlier work in OCLC Research to develop many of the functions behind the page displays. WorldCat Identities is proving to be a valued service for institutions wishing to link to this powerful tool in order to enhance their own users' experiences (Chan, 2008).

Mobilizing Unique Materials

For more than two decades, RLG worked closely with the rare books, archives, and manuscripts community to improve access to unique and special collections (Van Camp, 2003). Moreover, some of the earliest experiments in using digital technologies to effectively disclose special collections were managed by RLG with its members (Erway, 1996).

Today, special collections materials are of increasing interest and importance. As materials from the general stacks become more ubiquitous (through "mass" digitization projects and as institutions move toward joint ownership of books and journals), special collections may become what defines a library collection. With the shift in importance, this is a good time for an examination of the end-to-end process that results in archival and special collections materials being delivered to interested users. The overarching goal of this initiative is to achieve economies and efficiencies that permit these materials to be effectively described, properly disclosed, successfully discovered, and appropriately delivered.

Achieving control over these collections in an economic fashion will mean that current resources can have a broader impact or be invested elsewhere in other activities. The near-term effort is to take a systemwide view that will identify gaps in current operations—missing evidence, needed changes in practice, cumbersome processes, deficiencies in technology platforms that support description and disclosure, and required supporting services (OCLC, n.d.d).

Understanding and Managing the Global, Collective Collection

For many years, OCLC Research scientists have been mining WorldCat in order to better understand the nature of the global, collective collection. Seminal research has been undertaken that has changed the conversation around the ways library collections intersect and overlap and the implications for the community in its approaches to acquisition, description, storage, access, and digitization (Lavoie, 2006).

Chris Anderson first coined the term "the long tail" in an article in *Wired* magazine in 2004, referring to the extensive and elusive, little-known but highly prized materials at the shallow end of the publishing curve (Anderson, 2004). Since then, OCLC Research staff have posed a number of new questions about the systemwide library book collection (Dempsey, 2006) while also conducting research into several aggregations of holdings and gathering evidence to support new forms of interlibrary collaboration (Lavoie & Waibel, 2008. See also Jackson, Sillipigni Connaway, & Loh, 2007 and O'Neill, Sillipigni Connaway, & Prabha, 2006).

Since 2006, new work to engage with members of the RLG Partnership around collective collection issues of overlap, duplication, and last copies has resulted in a set of initiatives to advance the research library agenda by identifying strategies to understand, prepare for, and help advance libraries, archives, and museums in more profoundly cooperative models of acquiring, managing, and disclosing collections (OCLC, n.d.e). Further, specific attention has been focused on the ways libraries, archives, and museums can more effectively work together (Zorich, Waibel, & Erway, 2008).

COMMUNITIES AND OUTREACH

Throughout its history, OCLC Research has engaged with multiple communities and shared the results of its work in a variety of venues. OCLC Research works with the community and affiliates in the RLG Partnership to:

- collaboratively identify problems and opportunities
- develop prototype and test solutions
- develop consensus
- publish insightful and timely reports
- share findings through presentations and professional interactions

Formal publication (OCLC, n.d.f) in the information and library science literature is a frequent route to sharing findings and new insights. Presentations are often given at professional conferences around the world, contributing to a wider understanding of the work underway in the division.

In addition to a range of collaborations both formal and informal, standard forms of outreach also include the following:

- partnering with faculty at library schools and libraries on research topics of mutual interest
- visiting institutions where related work is being undertaken in order to exchange approaches and comingle investigations
- collecting impressions and opinions of professionals in order to shape our work
- inviting leaders in the field to share the results of their work in the OCLC Research Distinguished Seminar Series (OCLC, n.d.c)
- hosting RLG Partnership events (OCLC, n.d.g) that provide a venue for institutions to engage with one another around common interests
- managing groups of experts from around the world who come together to solve common problems
- interviewing key players in the field and conducting Webinars on the use of new tools to explore new challenges (OCLC, n.d.g)
- publishing reports and newsletters to more broadly disseminate our work
- working closely with members, partners, and other agencies on the development, maintenance, and deployment of information system-related standards

FUTURE DIRECTIONS

OCLC Research plays a distinctive role in advancing the library agenda and in collaborating with libraries, archives, and museums that seek to better serve their primary constituencies through the exploration and application of networked solutions.

In the near term, OCLC Research's program officers and research scientists will continue to examine, analyze, and address some of the grand challenges facing the global community in partnership with allied institutions, organizations, and individuals:

- Can libraries share the increasing burdens of managing vast collections of printed works?
- Can we do a better job of managing workflows in research assessment?
- Can we work smarter and faster as we invest in projects and programs to disclose and mobilize our unique collections?
- Can we amplify the value of controlled data and at the same time streamline our collective investments for the ultimate benefit of our users?
- Can we assist in the design of services that are optimized to operate in the network cloud as well as those that span personal, institutional and cloud environments? Current information about OCLC Research and its activities is available on its Web site: http://www.oclc.org/research/

REFERENCES

Anderson, C. (2004, October). The long tail. *Wired 12*(10). Retrieved from http://www.wired.com/wired/archive/12.10/tail.html

Bennett, R., Hengel-Dittrich, C., O'Neill, E. T., & Tillett, B. (2007). VIAF (Virtual International Authority File): Linking the Deutsche Nationalbibliothek and Library of Congress name authority files. *International Cataloguing and Bibliographic Control, 36*(1), 12–18.

Chan, S. (2008, 7 December). OPAC: Connecting collections to WorldCat identities. Fresh + New (blog), Powerhouse Museum. Retrieved from http://www.powerhousemuseum.com/dmsblog/Index.php/2008/12/07/opac-connecting-collections-to-worldcat-identities

Consultative Committee for Space Data Systems (2002, January). Reference model for an open archival information system (OAIS). Retrieved from http://public.ccsds.org/publications/archive/650×0b1.pdf

Dempsey, L. (2006). Libraries and the long tail: Some thoughts about libraries in a network age. *D-Lib Magazine 12*(4).

Dublin Core Metadata Initiative (DCMI) incorporated in Singapore (2009, January). Press release. Retrieved from http://dublincore.org/news/press/DCMI_press_20090105_incorporation.pdf

Erway, R. (1996). Digital initiatives of the Research Libraries Group. *D-Lib Magazine*, December. Retrieved from http://www.dlib.org/dlib/december96/rlg/12erway.html

Godby, C. J., & Richardson, J. V., Jr. (2003). OCLC Office of Research. In M. A. Drake, *Encyclopedia of library and information science* (pp. 2231–2237). New York: Marcel Dekker.

Hickey, T. B. (2007). WorldCat identities: Another view of the catalog. *OCLC NextSpace 6.*

International Standards Organization (n.d.). ISO 15836:2003 and American National Standards Institute/National Information Standards Organization: ANSI/NISO Z39.85.

Jackson, M. E., Sillipigni Connaway, L., & Loh, E. (2007). Changing global book collection patterns in ARL libraries. Report, Global Resources Network. Retrieved from http://www.arl.org/resources/pubs/grn_global_book.shtml

Lavoie, B. F. (Ed.). (2001). Preservation metadata for digital objects: A review of the state of the art (White paper, OCLC/RLG working group on preservation metadata) OCLC research publication. Retrieved from http://www.oclc.org/research/projects/pmwg/presmeta_wp.pdf

Lavoie, B. F. (2006). Books without boundaries: A brief tour of the system-wide print book collection. With Schonfeld, R. C. *Journal of Electronic Publishing 9*(2).

Lavoie, B. F., & Waibel, G. (2008). An 'artful' analysis of the rich holdings of four museum libraries. *NextSpace 8*(February).

Lorcan Dempsey to head office of research (May 21, 2001). OCLC Press Release. OCLC Digital Archive, http://worldcat.org/arcviewer/1/OCC/2006/07/19/0000023368/viewer/file28.html

Michalko, J. (in press). The RLG Partnership. *Journal of Library Administration 49*(6).

OCLC Online Computer Library Center (n.d.a). About research. Retrieved, from http://www.oclc.org/research/about

OCLC Online Computer Library Center (n.d.b). Betatest WorldCat Identities project. Retrieved from http://www.oclc.org/programs/ourwork/renovating/leveragevocab/identities.htm

OCLC Online Computer Library Center (n.d.c). Distinguished seminar series. Retrieved from http://www.oclc.org/programsandresearch/dss/default.htm

OCLC Online Computer Library Center (n.d.d). Effectively disclose archives and special collections program. Retrieved from http://www.oclc.org/programs/ourwork/collectivecoll/archives/default.htm

OCLC Online Computer Library Center (n.d.e). Managing the collective collection. Retrieved from http://www.oclc.org/programs/ourwork/collectivecoll/default.htm

OCLC Online Computer Library Center (n.d.f). Publications 2000–2009. Retrieved from http://www.oclc.org/research/publications/default.htm

OCLC Online Computer Library Center (n.d.g). RLG Programs events. Retrieved from http://www.oclc.org/programs/events/default.htm

OCLC Online Computer Library Center (n.d.h). Terminology services. Retrieved from http://www.oclc.org/research/projects/termservices/default.htm

OCLC/RLG Working Group on Preservation Metadata (2002, June). Preservation metadata and the OAIS information model: A metadata framework to support the preservation of digital objects. Retrieved from http://www.oclc.org/research/projects/pmwg/pm_framework.pdf

O'Neill, E., Sillipigni Connaway, L., & Prabha, C. (2006). Last copies: What's at risk? *College and Research Libraries 67*(4), 370–379.

PREMIS Editorial Committee (2008, March). PREMIS data dictionary for preservation metadata, version 2.0. Retrieved from http://www.loc.gov/standards/premis/v2/premis-2-0.pdf

PREMIS Working Group (2005, May). Data dictionary for preservation metadata. Retrieved from http://www.oclc.org/research/projects/pmwg/premis-final.pdf

RLG membership approves move to combine with OCLC. (2006) http://worldcat.org/arcviewer/1/OCC/2007/01/09/0000057113/viewer/file17.html

Sillipigni Connaway, L., & Radford, M. L. (2005–2008). Seeking synchronicity: Evaluating virtual reference service from user, non-user, and librarian perspectives. Final project report, Institute of Museum and Library Services.

Sillipigni Connaway, L., Radford, M. L., & Dickey, T. J. (2008). On the trail of the elusive non-user: What research in virtual reference environments reveals. *Bulletin of the American Society for Information Science and Technology, 34*(2), 25–28.

Terry Noreault promoted to vice president (January 8, 1999). OCLC Press Release. OCLC Digital Archive, http://worldcat.org/arcviewer/1/OCC/2003/07/08/0000003706/viewer/file77.html

Van Camp, A. (2003). RLG, where museums, libraries, and archives intersect. *LIBER Quarterly 13*(3/4).

VIAF: The Virtual International Authority File (n.d.). Retrieved from http://orlabs.oclc.org/viaf/

Weibel, S. L. (2005). Border crossings: Reflections on a decade of metadata consensus building. *D-Lib Magazine, 11*(7/8) [July/August]. Retrieved from http://www.dlib.org/dlib/july05/weibel/07weibel.html

Zorich, D., Waibel, G., & Erway, R. (2008). Beyond the silos of the LAMs: Collaboration among libraries, archives, and museums. Dublin, OH: OCLC Research.

Advocacy and OCLC

CATHY DE ROSA

OCLC Online Computer Library Center, Inc., Dublin, OH, USA

ABSTRACT. *Promoting the evolution of library use, of libraries themselves, and of librarianship is one of OCLC's chartered objectives. The author discusses nonprofit business models and new approaches for advancing their missions through advocacy. OCLC's recent advocacy programs are described.*

One of the truly wonderful benefits of working for a mission-based organization such as the Online Computer Library Center (OCLC) is the opportunity to engage with many extraordinary individuals and organizations. During the course of any given year, OCLC staff members meet and work with hundreds of passionate library leaders, information professionals, researchers, entrepreneurs, political leaders, trustees, students, and patrons—all of whom are working to advance research, scholarship, education, community development, information access, and global cooperation. The ideas exchanged are often the catalysts for program ideas at OCLC and increasingly, it is hoped, at partner organizations and groups outside the library community. This cooperative approach to value creation has been a practice at OCLC since the earliest days of the Cooperative. Yet in an environment rapidly being transformed by remarkable innovations in advancing information access and knowledge sharing that have originated far outside the definition of the traditional library community, collaboration, strategy development, and advocacy are being redefined by OCLC and many others in the last decade.

New nonprofit "business" models and value creation approaches are being developed that promise new frameworks for nonprofits to meet the growing challenges of advancing their mission in a world increasingly reshaped by social practices and policy. One such advocacy-in-action model was presented at an OCLC Symposium at American Library Association (ALA) Midwinter in 2008 New Leadership for New Challenges (more about symposiums later). Leslie Crutchfield, coauthor of *Forces for Good: The Six Practices of High-Impact Nonprofits*, presented a very new framework for maximizing the potential of nonprofit organizations. Her extensive research found that the nonprofit organizations that have the largest impact and create the greatest force for good are the organizations that have learned to balance the challenges of providing great services while also advocating for change in the larger environment to as many constituents as possible.

Crutchfield's advice and framework suggest that nonprofit organizations should build core business practices that focus not simply on building their own products, services, or mission, but equally on connecting to the products, services, and missions of the greater community. Serve and Advocate. Crutchfield and coauthor Heather McLeod Grant suggest that nonprofits that want to maximize their mission should actively work to integrate strategies that not only provide great services, but strategies and programs that can "Share Knowledge," "Grow the Pie," "Develop Leadership," and "Leverage Others."

Although advocacy programs have been a part of OCLC's mission since its founding in 1967, it is clear to OCLC trustees, management, employees, and members that OCLC is just beginning to really put in place the programs that will be required to meet the goal of service and advocacy for libraries. The past decade has seen some strong advancement. In the remainder of this article, I will provide a brief overview of several of the advocate-to-serve programs that have been launched at OCLC over the past decade that are aimed at Sharing Knowledge, Growing the Pie, Developing Leadership, and Creating Leverage.

> Being an extraordinary nonprofit isn't about building an organization or scaling it up. It's about finding ways to leverage other sectors to create extraordinary impact. Great nonprofits are catalysts; they transform the system around them to achieve greater good.
>
> — Leslie Crutchfield, *Forces for Good*

SHARING KNOWLEDGE

Library and Information Research

The OCLC Office of Research, founded by Frederick G. Kilgour in 1978 (see "OCLC Research: Past, Present, and Future," this issue) has been the largest program of its kind in the library community for 30 years. In the last decade, the number of partnerships has grown beyond libraries to touch archives, museums, and national and international standards bodies. The library community has benefited greatly by sharing issues and needs in communities such as Open Archives Initiative, Society of American Archivists, Institute for Museum and Library Services, International Organization for Standardization, National Information Standards Organization, the World Wide Web Consortium, Internet Engineering Task Force, and Internet2. One of the greatest contributions is the Dublin Core Metadata Initiative, an open forum of libraries, archives, museums, technology organizations, and software companies working together to develop interoperable online metadata standards that support a broad range of purposes and business models.

Information Landscape Research and Reports

In 2003, OCLC launched a major initiative aimed at creating a market research function within OCLC. The goal of the initiative: build a body of international market research that analyzes information from the perspective of the information consumer and to share that research both inside and outside the library field. In the last 6 years, OCLC has conducted a series of environmental scans that identify and communicate trends of importance to the community. In compiling these reports, OCLC staff have worked with library and information experts throughout the world as well as global enterprises such as Gartner, Outsell, Pew, and Amazon.com. Among the reports that have been published are these:

- *From Awareness to Funding: A study of library support in America*
- *Sharing, Privacy and Trust in Our Networked World*
- *Perceptions of Libraries and Information Resources*
- *Information Format Trends: Content, Not Containers*
- *Environmental Scan: Pattern Recognition*

In total, more than 40,000 printed copies of these reports have been shared with the community worldwide. In addition, since the release of the OCLC *Environmental Scan* in 2003, users have downloaded well over 150,000 membership report files.

Growing the Pie

WORLDCAT.ORG

Certainly one of the significant ways to advocate for libraries is to find ways to promote the value of library services to the patrons and researchers they serve. The launch of WorldCat.org in 2006 represented an important advance in both the availability of library resources and the promotion of value in the Web world. Through WorldCat.org, OCLC is experimenting with various models for integrating the collections and services of libraries into the consumer Web space to reach Web users who are now more likely to turn first to their Web browser—not their library—for information. OCLC is partnering with Google, Yahoo, and other Internet companies to put library records and holdings in the results lists of search engines, online bibliographies, and online booksellers in order to drive traffic to libraries. Each month, there are about 13 million page views of WorldCat.org that originate from search engine sites and other partners. Traffic from WorldCat.org to library services—online public access catalogs (OPACs), interlibrary loan (ILL) services, full-text articles, virtual reference services—average some 700,000 per month, with approximately 80% of click-throughs going to library OPACs. As this issue is printed, new partnerships are under investigation with cellular phone providers and others to help grow the reach and impact of library services and increase the impact of mobile devices.

AMPLIFY THE VOICE OF LIBRARIES TO THE WORLD THEY SERVE

One of OCLC's chartered objectives is "to promote the evolution of library use, of libraries themselves and of librarianship." In pursuit of that objective, OCLC champions libraries to increase their visibility and viability in the communities they serve. Programs include advertising and marketing materials that OCLC creates and libraries can use in their planning and advocacy efforts to reinforce the idea of the library as relevant. OCLC's modest annual advertising spending has been transitioned from promoting services to libraries to advocating for libraries to those they serve. OCLC ads feature extraordinary stories from people who tell how libraries changed their lives. Two such people were Neal Peterson and Gregory Maguire. Petersen is a world-class yachtsman from South Africa who learned navigation and boat design at his public library. Maguire, the author of *Wicked: The Life and Times of the Wicked Witch of the West*, which is now a Broadway musical, credits libraries with engaging his imagination, fueling a passion for literacy, and effectively starting his writing career.

PARTNERSHIPS FOR ADVOCACY

Since 2002, OCLC has partnered with the Bill & Melinda Gates Foundation to expand services to libraries and to research ways to more effectively communicate library value in an era of rising costs and increased competition for funding and mindshare. The Foundation and OCLC created WebJunction, an online learning community for librarians and library staff. The community helps members share knowledge and experience in order to provide the broadest possible public access to information technology for library users. The site contains a range of online courses along with content creation and social tools, such as friends, public profiles, groups, discussions, tagging, and recommendations. The community has attracted more than 30,000 registered members, and some 275,000 individuals have visited the site to become engaged or take courses since its launch in May 2003.

In November 2006, the Bill & Melinda Gates Foundation awarded OCLC a $1.2 million grant to evaluate the potential of a national library support campaign to increase public library funding in the United States. The grant funded extensive quantitative and qualitative research among voters and elected officials. The findings were published in the 2008 report *From Awareness to Funding: A study of library support in America*. The research confirms that most Americans hold the library in high esteem, a part of one's national identity in a democracy. The freedom to access information and increase both personal and community knowledge is highly valued. The findings suggest that promoting these core beliefs to the right sectors of the community can increase library awareness and library funding. But without action, the research suggests that libraries will continue to fall short of the funding needed to achieve their mission. In response, in 2009 the Foundation awarded OCLC a $5 million grant to put the research into action, creating a national library support campaign and community materials to increase funding support for libraries.

DISTINGUISHED SEMINAR SERIES

The Distinguished Seminar Series, started in 1978, helps develop leadership at OCLC and across the broader community by encouraging the exchange and debate of ideas across disciplines and industries that are shaping the information landscape. Each year, OCLC invites two to five distinguished individuals from the information community and beyond to Dublin to make presentations on topics of current interest. Speakers may discuss recently completed or early-stage research that they have undertaken and report on professional activity or involvement in commercial ventures, standards activities, or social change initiatives. The topics sometimes align closely with activities within OCLC, but also may represent areas of interest to the library and information science community not formally under study. Past speakers have been from Microsoft, IBM, and the National Archives and Records Service as well as from libraries. Marketing consultant Ben McConnell, author of *Citizen Marketers: When People are the Message* and *Creating Customer Evangelists: How Loyal Customers Become a Volunteer Sales Force*, spoke in 2006.

INTERNATIONAL LIBRARY LEADERSHIP DEVELOPMENT

Working with the International Federation of Library Associations and Institutions (IFLA) and the American Theological Library Association, OCLC provides career development and continuing education for library and information science professionals from countries with developing economies through the Jay Jordan IFLA/OCLC Early Career Development Program. Up to six individuals are selected for participation in an intensive 5-week program. Four weeks are based at OCLC headquarters in Dublin, Ohio, USA; one week is based at OCLC in Leiden, Netherlands. The program gives Fellows opportunities to meet with leading information practitioners, and to visit libraries and explore topics including information technologies, library operations and management, and global cooperative librarianship. Since its inception in 2001, the program has welcomed 44 librarians and information science professionals from 28 countries.

OCLC SYMPOSIUMS

Twice a year, OCLC hosts symposiums at conferences of the American Library Association to explore new ideas and present new thoughts emerging in business and popular culture. Each symposium features well-known speakers who analyze cutting-edge industry trends, technology developments, and social change initiatives, and invites a discussion and debate on how these trends will impact libraries. Previous topics covered include branding, customer service, social networking, new technology platforms (Web 2.0), new digital economic models (the Long Tail), new market segments and lifestyles (Gamers and Life 2.0), new learning tools (iPods and cell phones), and personalization technologies (MyLibrary). To encourage interactivity with the audience, handheld devices are distributed to attendees to take quick polls on questions and responses. Since the inception of the twice-a-year symposium program in 2004, more than 30 speakers and about 5,000 librarians and library directors have participated in OCLC symposiums. In addition, OCLC is expanding this program to other parts of the world. In 2008, there were OCLC symposiums in the United Kingdom and Canada.

CREATING LEVERAGE THROUGH OTHERS

As librarians well know, collective action (cooperation) is a powerful strategy for increasing effectiveness and advancing change and social action. More and more, collaboration for social change means working with both nonprofit and for-profit organizations, which together can create tensions that did not exist before or could not reach scale without the support of the other. As the work of organizations increasingly occurs over the Internet, across geographic boards, and beyond traditional markets or communities, achieving lasting impact may no longer be possible without finding ways to partner with organizations that have very different objectives, missions, or commercial goals. As Crutchfield advocates, greater forces for good can more often be created through unlikely partnerships than traditional approaches.

Over the past decade, the range and number of OCLC partnerships have grown significantly. OCLC works with hundreds of publishers and materials vendors, search engine providers, online booksellers, and corporations that sell local computer systems to libraries. Through formal alliances with these companies, OCLC is working to advance library services and message by bringing library services and information to people through avenues that often don't start at the library.

GOOGLE, YAHOO!, ASK.COM

Beginning in 2003, OCLC partnered with search engine providers to share the world's information and to advocate for libraries across the broadest possible Internet landscape. Today, OCLC shares WorldCat records with Google to better facilitate discovery of library collections through the Google Book Search program, which makes the full text of over 7 million digitized books searchable. Working with Yahoo!, OCLC developed a special edition on the Yahoo! Toolbar, which provides always-there access to WorldCat records via Yahoo! Search, plus the full complement of Yahoo! services. Ask.com also utilizes WorldCat records for inclusion in their indexes. These nontraditional partnerships are an important, and likely only a first, step in creating increased value by for libraries by advancing not only library missions but business value of partners.

SERVE AND ADVOCATE

Maintaining a dual purpose—to allocate resources to deliver services and to spend resources to advocate for a community—creates issues of balance, focus, and organizational identity. It is not easy for an organization to max-imize the impact and manage the costs across these overlapping objectives. During much of its 40-year existence, OCLC has worked to balance, yet fully engage, in both service and advocacy. OCLC has been described as an orga-nization with a dual (or in some eyes a dueling) identity. OCLC is a vendor that delivers services for a fee. OCLC is a cooperative that advocates for and serves libraries. As the Crutchfield and Grant model explains, the two together are more powerful in achieving a mission than either is alone. At times the model requires organizations to make sacrifices and choose path-ways that they otherwise would not pursue. It requires a longer-term view to see activities and partnerships that will ultimately create more benefit for the community. A serve-and-advocate strategy is a more highly leveraged approach to achieving change. The traditional way to scale an organization's impact is to build and fund new locations one by one. Expansion takes longer, requires more capital, and attains results slowly. But by leveraging the serve-and-advocate model, nonprofits distribute the costs, scale more quickly, and have more immediate impact through collective action. The lesson from Crutchfield and Grant's research is that organizations seeking to scale their impact should embrace the serve-and-advocate model as an engine of change.

In many ways, it is essential that OCLC, as a cooperative, continue to find ways to be the catalyst for this advocacy model—serve and advocate—and partner with increasingly diverse organizations and groups to find new ways to advance the mission of libraries. When the next decade of OCLC's work is chronicled, it is the author's hope, and strong belief, that the role of advocacy will be even more effectively integrated with the services of OCLC—that there will be no need for a separate chapter on "Advocacy"; it will be the essence of every chapter.

OCLC 1998–2008: Weaving Libraries into the Web

JAY JORDAN

OCLC Online Computer Library Center, Inc., Dublin, OH, USA

ABSTRACT. *The author briefly reviews OCLC's history form 1967 to 1998, then focuses on the accomplishments and activities of the OCLC cooperative from 1998 to 2008. Particular attention is given to OCLC's strategy of weaving libraries into the World Wide Web and the transformation of WorldCat from a bibliographic database into a globally networked information resource.*

WorldCat began operation on August 26, 1971. Since then, two generations of librarians have helped to build the WorldCat online union catalog, entering records into the database keystroke by keystroke. Online Computer Library Center (OCLC) cataloging and resource-sharing services are embedded in the workflows of many libraries. In many parts of the library community, OCLC is taken for granted, as if it were a utility that, instead of providing electricity or water, delivers bibliographic information 24/7.

It is no exaggeration to state that OCLC has become a vital part of the global information infrastructure that supports research, scholarship, and learning around the world. How did that happen? And where does OCLC go from here? To understand the OCLC of today and its future directions, it is useful to start with a condensed history.

ORIGINS

OCLC's roots are in academe. OCLC was founded as the Ohio College Library Center in 1967 by Frederick G. Kilgour and the presidents of Ohio's colleges and universities. They sought to establish a computer library network for "the fundamental public purpose of furthering ease of access to and use of the ever expanding body of worldwide scientific, literary and educational knowledge and information" (Ohio College Library Center, 1967, p. 1).

The founders established OCLC as a nonprofit corporation and a membership organization. Libraries that joined OCLC agreed to do all their current Roman alphabet cataloging online and to create original cataloging records for items they could not find in the database. Membership was a commitment to contribute to the cooperative as well as to use the OCLC system for its stated objectives of reducing the rate of rise of per-unit library costs and increasing the availability of library resources. The members who used OCLC services had an institutionalized role in the governance of the organization by electing members of the Board of Trustees. From the beginning, member institutions and their librarians saw themselves as stakeholders in OCLC.

As a nonprofit corporation, OCLC's objectives were not to maximize profits or return on shareholders' investments, but rather to pursue its broad public purposes of increasing availability of library resources and reducing the rate of rise of library costs. From the beginning, the founders believed that OCLC should be self-sustaining and pay its own way.

OCLC's financial policy was expressed in its first annual report, which called "for each institution to pay for operational costs prorated on the amount of use each member makes of the system" (Ohio College Library Center, 1968, p. 1). OCLC's most recent annual report echoed that theme:

> OCLC is a nonprofit, membership, computer library service and research organization whose public purposes of furthering access to the world's information and reducing library costs dominate its plans and activities. In support of these purposes, OCLC strives to maintain a strong financial base by operating in a business-like manner in order to accommodate growth, upgrade technological platforms, conduct research and development and still subsidize worthwhile projects for the benefit of libraries and their users (Online Computer Library Center [OCLC], 2008, p. 50).

As OCLC's founder and first president, Frederick G. Kilgour oversaw the growth of the Ohio College Library Center from an intrastate network of 54 Ohio academic libraries to an international network of libraries of all types and sizes. He led the development of the OCLC online union catalog and shared cataloging system (1971) and the OCLC Interlibrary Loan (ILL) system (1979). He created the OCLC Office of Research in 1978, which in the early 1980s experimented with the home delivery of library services through cable television and electronic publishing, and which today pursues a broad program of research and activities aimed at extending the value of libraries, archives, and museums. Today, Kilgour is widely recognized as one of the leading figures in 20th-century librarianship.

On August 26, 1971, after 4 years of research and development, the OCLC online union catalog and shared cataloging system began operation. Ohio University in Athens, Ohio, was the first institution to catalog online. On the first day of operation, Ohio University's staff cataloged 147 items. In its first year as an OCLC member, Ohio University was able to increase the number of books it cataloged by a third, while reducing its staff by 17 positions through attrition.

The Online Union Catalog and Shared Cataloging system pioneered the computer revolution in libraries. It enabled libraries to rapidly and efficiently catalog books and order custom-printed catalog cards. It was a new library tool that was dynamic. Libraries would either use the information that already existed in the database to catalog an item, or they would put it in themselves for other libraries to use. The economies of scale increased as the database and number of users grew. There were huge increases in library productivity.

Word of this innovation quickly spread, and by 1979, OCLC would have participants in all 50 states of the United States as well as the first participant in Canada.

The original design of the OCLC online system called for six subsystems:

1. online union catalog and shared cataloging
2. interlibrary loan
3. acquisitions
4. serials control
5. subject access (reference)
6. circulation control

From 1971 to 1981, OCLC focused on creating and expanding the online cataloging system and telecommunications network and adding subsystems to complete the original system design. Serials Control was added in 1975, Interlibrary Loan in 1979, and Acquisitions in 1981. A prototype circulation control subsystem was also developed in 1981. The acquisitions and serials control subsystems were migrated from the online central system to standalone systems in the 1980s, and circulation control was implemented in a series of local library systems rather than on the centralized system. As will be seen later in this article, by 2007, with the implementation of WorldCat.org and WorldCat Local, OCLC was finally realizing the integrated system design envisioned by Kilgour in 1967!

It is interesting to note that when the OCLC online system began operation, the principal tool for accessing the library's collection was the card catalog, which was expensive to maintain. Preparing the cards for a single title would cost a library somewhere between $30 and $60 (1970 dollars).

The OCLC system enabled a library to order custom-printed catalogs. The cards would arrive in boxes or envelopes, already in alphabetical or call number order, ready for filing in individual receiving catalogs. OCLC significantly reduced the costs of maintaining card catalogs. OCLC's card production peaked at 131 million cards per year in 1985 and by 2008 had dropped to 1.8 million cards. Most libraries have long ago shut down their card catalogs and now have local library systems and online public access catalogs in which they get their cataloging information in electronic form.

In the 1980s, OCLC adapted distributed and microcomputing technologies and expanded its product line to some 60 offerings. By 1985, OCLC was offering the following local system products: LS 2000 local library system, which provided an online public access catalog and circulation control; and SC350 and ACQ350, which were microcomputer-based systems for serials control and acquisitions, respectively.

At the same time, OCLC announced its intent to move "beyond bibliography" and provide full-text information to people when and where they wanted it. OCLC Founder Frederick G. Kilgour had stepped down from management of OCLC in 1981, but he continued to work on research projects at OCLC. One of his pet projects was EIDOS (Electronic Information Delivery Online System). The EIDOS prototype enabled a library user to search for a book, browse its table of contents and index pages, and then request the actual text and graphics. These electronic books would be maintained online at OCLC. EIDOS was launched in1986, well before the World Wide Web was invented, and 16 years before OCLC acquired NetLibrary, a provider of electronic books.

Throughout the 1990s, OCLC continued to pioneer in electronic publishing. With the American Association for the Advancement of Science, OCLC launched the world's first peer-reviewed electronic journal, *The Online Journal of Current Clinical Trials*. OCLC researchers developed the Guidon graphical user interface and launched the Electronic Journals Online program, both of which were discontinued when newer technology became available. In 1990, OCLC introduced Electronic Collections Online, whose Web interface provided access to a large collection of academic journals.

While OCLC was indeed moving beyond bibliography, it also continued to build and maintain the WorldCat database and its core systems in cataloging and interlibrary loan. In the 1990s, OCLC put in place a new online system (PRISM) for cataloging and resource sharing and implemented two new telecommunications networks, an X.25 network in 1991, and 6 years later, a TCP/IP (Transmission Control Protocol/Internet Protocol) network as the Internet became the communications medium of choice for libraries and information seekers.

As technology changed, so did OCLC, adapting distributed computing and microcomputing technologies to its products and services. OCLC also made significant investments in the infrastructure that supported its computer systems. As early as 1978, OCLC had installed an uninterruptible power system to support its online system in the event of a power outage.

OCLC also introduced new services throughout the decade. In 1991, OCLC sparked another revolution, this time in online reference services. FirstSearch was the first online service to provide end users of libraries with access to bibliographic, abstract, and full-text databases.

In 1990, OCLC sold its local systems division and left the standalone local library systems business, where it had achieved only 8% of the market in the United States. This was in line with OCLC's announced strategy to focus on core services in cataloging and resource sharing, to eliminate marginal operations, and to focus on building a new core service in reference. OCLC would continue to be active in local systems, but its emphasis changed from providing hardware and software installation to linking its central system with local area networks on campuses and in regions.

For example, OCLC introduced SiteSearch software (see below), which enabled groups of libraries to share resources and support large-scale projects such as the University System of Georgia's GALILEO statewide system. OCLC also enhanced its cataloging service with PromptCat, which provides automated delivery of cataloging information, and its resource sharing service with ILL Fee Management, which processes debit/credit interlibrary loan transactions, thereby saving libraries the costs of writing checks.

Thus, OCLC entered its fourth decade with a great deal of momentum. Libraries continued to set new records in cataloging and resource sharing, and the new core service in online reference was growing dramatically.

By 1998, the Internet had taken some giant leaps. Web browsers, search engines, and E-commerce roiled society in general and put new pressures on libraries. Libraries themselves were embracing the Internet and looking forward to adapting it to their services. That momentum would help propel OCLC and its participating libraries into a new era of digital librarianship.

OCLC: THE FOURTH DECADE

In 1999, as part of an ongoing strategic planning process, the Board of Trustees and OCLC management reaffirmed the commitment to the basic principles set forth in OCLC's charter and articulated a vision of how OCLC would pursue its public purposes over the next decade. That vision was stated as follows: "OCLC will be the leading global library cooperative, helping libraries serve people by providing economical access to knowledge through innovation and collaboration."

In 2000, OCLC shared with its membership a new global strategy designed to extend the OCLC cooperative and provide services around the world, based on the needs of libraries in their regions. The strategy that guided OCLC over the next decade could be summarized as "weaving libraries into the Web, and the Web into libraries."

The plan called for OCLC to transform WorldCat from a bibliographic database and online union catalog to a globally networked information resource of text, graphics, sound, and motion. (Recall OCLC's earlier efforts to move beyond bibliography!) The new WorldCat would interweave the World Wide Web with the physical and electronic collections of the world's libraries, archives, and museums. "It will help information professionals better manage their collections and services. More important, it will help people navigate the world's constantly expanding body of knowledge and find the information they need" (OCLC, 2000, p. 44).

The salient features of OCLC's strategy were to extend the cooperative, build a new technological platform, transform WorldCat from a bibliographic database and online union catalog to a globally networked information resource, introduce new services, and, ultimately, weave libraries into the Web. As will be seen in the remainder of this article, OCLC has made considerable progress toward each of these objectives.

EXTENDING THE COOPERATIVE

As noted above, the members of OCLC have always wanted to make the cooperative as inclusive as possible, with the more libraries attached to the network generating economies of scale and benefits for both libraries and their users. Table 1 shows that OCLC has indeed extended the cooperative over the past decade. This growth is attributable to a combination of factors including new services such as CatExpress (see below), which made it easier for small libraries to catalog on OCLC. OCLC has also extended the cooperative through strategic alliances and mergers with WLN, Pica, CAPCON, and RLG.

GOVERNANCE

In 2008, the membership adopted a new governance structure for the OCLC cooperative. The new structure is designed to extend participation in the OCLC cooperative to an increasing number of libraries and cultural heritage

TABLE 1 The OCLC Cooperative 1998–2008 (Members, Participants, Countries in 1998 and 2008)

	2008	1998
participating libraries	60,000	30,000
participants outside U.S.	11,900	3,200
participant countries	111	64
WorldCat records	100 million	38 million
WorldCat holdings	1.2 billion	668 million

institutions around the world. It includes regional councils that send delegates to a Global Council, which in turn elects 6 members of a 15-member Board of Trustees. The transition to the new structure was under way in 2009 and was coordinated by representatives of the 2008/2009 Members Council and the Board of Trustees. OCLC's governance is discussed elsewhere in this volume.

WLN

In 1999 OCLC merged with WLN (originally the Washington Library Network), a nonprofit corporation serving 550 libraries in the Pacific Northwest region of the United States and Canada. Subsequently, OCLC matched 4.2 million bibliographic records and added 17.4 million location listings from WLN libraries into WorldCat. OCLC also integrated WLN services such as authority control and collection development into its own offerings. WLN libraries joined OCLC's digital global community for cataloging, resource sharing, and reference services, while OCLC member libraries benefited from the inclusion of libraries from the Pacific Northwest in the OCLC network.

PICA

A series of alliances between OCLC and the Pica Foundation in the Netherlands has extended the OCLC cooperative to new libraries and users in Europe. The Pica Foundation was created in 1969 as a cooperative, not-for-profit organization by the Royal Library of the Netherlands and a number of university libraries. In 1978, the Royal Library of the Netherlands signed OCLC's first international agreement, whereby OCLC provided the Royal Library with 750,000 records from WorldCat (with holdings removed) for nine Dutch libraries. That same year, 1978, Pica's central online database was established to reduce library cataloging costs. Over the next 20 years, Pica implemented new services in local library systems, reference, and end-user access. Pica also moved beyond the Netherlands, extending its services to hundreds of academic, public, and other libraries throughout Europe.

In 1999, the Pica Foundation and OCLC established Pica B.V. to better serve the European library community. In 2002, Pica B.V. merged with OCLC Europe, the Middle East, and Africa to form OCLC PICA, and in 2007, OCLC acquired full control of the organization, which is now called OCLC Europe, the Middle East, and Africa (OCLC EMEA). OCLC's activities in Europe are discussed elsewhere in this volume.

CAPCON

In 2003, the CAPCON Library Network became the OCLC CAPCON Service Center (renamed OCLC Eastern in 2007). CAPCON provided OCLC training and support to more than 300 libraries in the District of Columbia, Maryland, and Virginia. The move to establish CAPCON as an OCLC service center was initiated by the CAPCON Board of Trustees and was approved by the CAPCON membership. During the transition, the CAPCON Board of Trustees served as an advisory council to the new service center.

RLG

On July 1, 2006, Research Libraries Group (RLG) and OCLC combined operations. RLG was a nonprofit organization of over 150 research libraries, archives, museums, and other cultural memory institutions. Over the next year, OCLC integrated RLG's services in online cataloging, resource sharing, and digitization/imaging with OCLC's. The RLG Union Catalog was integrated with WorldCat by processing more than 50.4 million records and adding approximately 7.8 million records to WorldCat.

RLG's program initiatives are being continued as RLG–Programs, a new division of OCLC Programs and Research. This unit, based in San Mateo, California, combines RLG's successful tradition of identifying issues and building consensus among research institutions with OCLC's research capacities and robust prototyping capabilities. Both RLG Programs and Research are discussed elsewhere in this volume.

The author has noted before that the coming together of RLG and OCLC could only have happened at the board level and through the resolve of its leaders, OCLC Board Chair Lizabeth Wilson, Dean of Libraries, University of Washington, and RLG Board Chair James Neal, Vice President for Information Services, Columbia University. Their efforts have helped to expand OCLC's horizons in the museum and archive community as they strengthen the cooperative's deep roots in libraries and librarianship.

BUILDING A NEW TECHNOLOGICAL PLATFORM

The computer industry and OCLC faced a major challenge as the year 2000 approached. There was a worldwide problem in that many computers and applications could only track dates in a two-digit year and six-digit date format (YYMMDD). The two-digit year had been devised in the 1950s to save memory space, which was expensive in the early days of computing. This solution proved to be a time bomb, however, that ticked away quietly until the first early warnings began to appear—when the year 1999 turned to 2000, many computers would erroneously read the date as 1900 rather than 2000. As the year 2000 drew closer, the news media ran countless stories about what could conceivably go wrong shortly after midnight on January 1, 2000—from people not being able to access their bank accounts to planes falling from the sky. In short, anything that had a computer chip in it or relied on a computer system was imperiled at the turn of the century.

The March/April 1998 *OCLC Newsletter* carried a special report on how OCLC was preparing for the Year 2000, or Y2K. OCLC had started work on the problem back in 1996. By December 31, 1999, OCLC staff had modified, tested, and reinstalled approximately 7.2 million lines of code in its systems at a cost of about $8 million. At 7 p.m. Eastern Standard Time on New Year's Eve, OCLC suspended access to its online user systems for 24 hours as a precaution during the rollover to the Year 2000. It also posted status reports on the OCLC Web site during the transition. The rollover went so smoothly that OCLC was able to make its systems available 2 hours earlier than planned, restoring service at 5 p.m. on January 1, 2000. Clearly, the advance preparations of OCLC, libraries, networks, indeed the entire computing industry, paid off. It should also be noted that OCLC had the financial strength and technological wherewithal to do what needed to be done over a 4-year period. In retrospect, Y2K was not just about accommodating two digits in the date field; it also showed how interconnected the world had become.

Having cleared the Y2K hurdle, OCLC faced yet another project vital to the future growth of the cooperative—the online system was running out of institution holding symbols. Since 1971, the OCLC system had identified libraries/institutions via a three-character institution symbol and holding libraries within the institution with a unique four-character symbol. There were 39,000 three-character symbols available, and by October 1999, OCLC had used 29,689 of them, with the remaining symbols projected to be depleted by October 2002. Fortunately, OCLC completed the $2.8 million holding symbol expansion project ahead of schedule, and by August 2001, began assigning five-character symbols to new institutions joining the cooperative. The present method of assigning symbols is expected to accommodate OCLC's growth well into the future.

Y2K and holding symbols notwithstanding, as part of the new strategic plan, OCLC simultaneously embarked on a series of major projects to build a new technological platform. In March 2000, OCLC decommissioned its 10-year old X.25 network and all OCLC services became Internet based. Libraries were now using Internet protocols to communicate with each other, and the OCLC cooperative became truly part of the global, digital network of the World Wide Web.

That same year, OCLC began to move from an environment in which it had built and maintained its own proprietary system for over 30 years to one of hardware and licensed software with widespread industry adoption. The new system was based on Oracle database technology with open architectural models that allowed better interoperability within OCLC services and also with external services. In building the new platform, OCLC used rapid-application development techniques and continuous improvement based on user feedback.

The OCLC FirstSearch service was migrated to the new platform in 2004, and the cataloging and resource-sharing services in 2005.

The OCLC computer network has evolved constantly since the OCLC online system began operation on August 26, 1971. The online union catalog and shared cataloging system began with a Xerox Sigma 5 computer; a telephone network of four dedicated, synchronous lines running at 2400 bits per second; and 54 cathode-ray-tube terminals specially designed to handle the ALA character set. When OCLC moved into its present main office in Dublin, Ohio, in 1981, the computer facility comprised 44,400 square feet on three stories and housed 17 mainframe computers. At the time, the computer facility was built to reclaim heat produced by the mainframes and use it to help heat the rest of the building. By 1994, the last mainframe had been decommissioned, and OCLC had to install a gas-fired boiler to heat the building.

In 2008, OCLC implemented a second data center in Westerville, Ohio, about 15 miles from the Dublin center. As OCLC launches new services, it must have an information technology infrastructure in place so that its library services are always on and always accessible. In addition, OCLC must provide a global development platform that meets the needs of eight engineering centers in Australia, Germany, the Netherlands, the United Kingdom, and the United States.

TRANSFORM WORLDCAT

The WorldCat that emerged in 2005 on the new technological platform contained the following information in addition to the bibliographic information of an LC-MARC (Library of Congress Machine Readable Cataloging) record:

- book jackets
- tables of contents
- articles
- reviews
- readers' advisories
- E-books
- OPAC (online public access catalog)/Open URL links
- electronic holdings data
- graphics, sound, motion

The Unicode standard enabled WorldCat to support access in a number of languages and character sets in the vernacular. By 2008, WorldCat was supporting 12 language scripts: Arabic, Bengali, Chinese, Devanagari, Greek, Hebrew, Japanese, Korean, Latin, Tamil, and Thai. This made it practicable for an increasing number of international organizations to merge their

TABLE 2 Major Batchloads into WorldCat (Year Ended June 30, 2008)

| | Major Batchloads in Fiscal 2008 | | |
Institution	Records processed	Holdings set	Records added
Bavarian State Library	11,043,448	8,511,210	4,316,151
National Library of Australia	22,617,313	41,404,542	4,085,801
National Library of Sweden	2,131,097	2,033,396	1,926,700
HEBIS (Germany)	7,840,014	11,442,064	1,806,285
National Library of New Zealand	7,395,497	16,186,678	924,394
Defense Technical Information Center	668,706	668,631	631,597
Toshokan Ryutsu Center (Japan)	732,484	695,782	572,559
Bakers Taylor	1,535,577	1,146,435	514,133
University of Toronto	5,365,115	5,596,509	456,740
German National Library	507,642	475,212	410,617
GGC Dutch Union Catalogue	498,079	554,871	240,084
University of Pennsylvania	6,777,334	6,175,610	211,077
National Library of Israel	211,490	205,457	205,348
Glasgow University	463,592	227,143	172,712
Library of Congress	2,046,988	1,756,006	158,217
University of Calgary	257,529	175,252	149,977
American Antiquarian Society	1,077,399	706,048	140,898
University of California, Berkeley	6,140,703	5,810,597	137,194
University of Manitoba	605,232	397,762	126,532
NUKAT National Union Catalog of Poland	125,999	125,267	123,346
University of California, Santa Barbara	2,357,410	2,204,831	113,571
Huntington Art Library and Botanical Garden	571,065	570,464	106,474
Museum of Natural History (London)	440,831	226,135	103,628

national union catalogs or other large files with WorldCat via automated batch processes (see Table 2). In addition, OCLC has made technological enhancements and workflow improvements to its batchloading processes to accommodate the loading of large files into WorldCat (see Table 3).

The new platform supports not only LC MARC 21 and Anglo-American Cataloguing Rules 2, but Dublin Core and other standards such as OpenURL, LDAP (Lightweight Directory Access Protocol), EAD (Encoded Archival Description), SOAP (Simple Object Access Protocol), XML (Extensible Markup Language), SRU (Search Retrieval via URL), OAI-PMH (Open Archives Initiative Protocol for Metadata Harvesting), and Shibboleth. The platform has reusable components that can be embedded in local library applications (see below). It can create custom views of holdings for groups of institutions. A

TABLE 3 Batchloading/Processing.

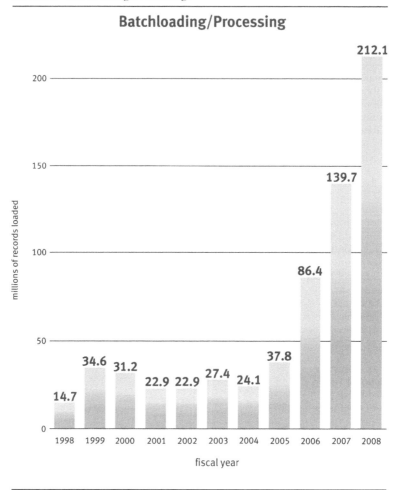

user in WorldCat can now link to evaluative content, digital documents, and objects in other knowledge repositories.

Going forward, the new technological platform provides a solid foundation for sustained growth and innovation. These new capabilities enable OCLC to be more inclusive, to support more institutions in more countries and more languages around the world. As will be seen below, OCLC has introduced a series of new services and capabilities that were not possible on its proprietary, legacy systems.

As WorldCat became bigger and better, it became more attractive to libraries around the world (see Table 4). Indeed, non-U.S. libraries now have six reasons to load their holdings into WorldCat:

TABLE 4 WorldCat at June 30, 2008

	Records by Format			
Format	Total LC Records	Total Participant-input	Total LC-created Participant-input	Total Records
Books	7,174,988	81,633,366	1,774,796	90,583,150
Serials	632,354	3,892,448	37,558	4,562,360
Visual Materials	180,293	3,369,556	18,239	3,568,088
Maps	264,449	1,343,184	8,348	1,615,981
Mixed Materials	49,403	807,437	4,255	861,095
Sound Recordings	303,023	3,393,161	64,197	3,760,381
Scores	88,063	2,255,404	57,603	2,401,070
Computer Files	10,383	828,018	424	838,825
Totals	8,702,956	97,522,574	1,965,420	*108,190,950

*Reflects total unique records after duplicate detection resolution is complete.

- Unicode support
- Ability to FRBRize (Functional Requirements for Bibliogrphic Records) a catalog
- Open WorldCat on the Web (see below)
- Group catalog capability and its customized views
- WorldCat Collection Analysis service
- International resource sharing

In 2008, a new record was being added to WorldCat approximately every 10 seconds. On April 1, 2008, the number of records in WorldCat surpassed 100 million. It took the OCLC cooperative 31 years, from 1971 to 2002, to add the first 50 million records; it took just 6 years to add another 50 million by April 1, 2008. Between then and March 31, 2009, libraries added 27 million records, bringing the total to 135 million records and 1.4 billion location listings. Clearly, WorldCat is growing at a rate that is approaching exponential.

In April 2008, for the first time, the number of records in languages other than English exceeded those for English-language materials. Table 5 shows the growth of languages in WorldCat over 10 years.

QUALITY CONTROL

WorldCat is the world's premier bibliographic database, not only in terms of the depth and breadth of information, but in the quality of that information. OCLC's cataloging system is based on cooperation and a commitment to the quality of the information that is shared among users. And, as new uses for WorldCat are developed for new groups of users, the quality of its bibliographic information becomes even more important. Quality control of

TABLE 5 Multilingual WorldCat

	1998: 37.5 m records	2008: 108.2 m records	Percentage of Non-English Records
Multilingual WorldCat: 1 April 2008			
Total Records	37.5 m records	108.2 m records	
English	23.9 m	55.2 m	36% 1998
French	2.3 m	6.2 m	
German	2.2 m	12.3 m	
Spanish	1.6 m	3.6 m	
Japanese	.8 m	2.5 m	
Russian	.8 m	1.8 m	
Chinese	.7 m	2.3 m	
Italian	.7 m	1.7 m	
Latin	.3 m	1.2 m	50¼%
Portuguese	.3 m	.9 m	
Dutch	.2 m	2.7 m	
Hebrew	.2 m	.7 m	2008

WorldCat is an ongoing effort that involves both the OCLC membership and OCLC itself.

The Enhance Program, established in 1983, now involves 229 institutions (359 OCLC holding symbols), including one in the United Kingdom and two in South Africa, that have volunteered to do quality control work for the OCLC cooperative.

These institutions are authorized to lock, edit, and replace records in WorldCat in one or more bibliographic formats. (An OCLC member library may edit a record that it contributed but not those contributed by another member, unless they are an Enhance participant.) Ninety of these Enhance participants are National Level Enhance participants, chiefly selected Library of Congress (LC) cataloging staff and Program for Cooperative Cataloging (PCC) participants, and these institutions may additionally replace most national-level records, i.e., records provided by the Library of Congress, National Agriculture Library, or National Library of Medicine.

Since 1983 OCLC has provided more than 2.9 million credits for Enhance transactions, including 1.6 million transactions since 1998. Put another way, these 226 Enhance libraries have voluntarily invested their time and expertise to make nearly 3 million improvements to records in WorldCat.

OCLC also devotes human and machine resources to monitoring and enhancing quality in WorldCat. For the year ended June 30, 2008, WorldCat Quality Management staff corrected 2,137,903 bibliographic records. During that same period, CIP (Cataloging-in-Publication) Upgrade Unit staff enhanced 20,501 CIP records, added 1,006 new authority records, and updated 857 authority records. CIP records are bibliographic information supplied by the Library of Congress to book publishers prior to publication for inclusion in the book. Loaded into WorldCat at the same time, the records must have their bibliographic data updated after publication. OCLC's CIP upgrading program makes certain these records are ultimately complete. Libraries find the CIP records useful for ordering books in advance of their publication, and CIP speeds up technical processing so that materials get on the shelves faster for access by patrons.

OCLC also maintains quality in WorldCat through duplicate detection and resolution software. Between June 1991 and July 2005, this software went through WorldCat 16 times, deleting a total of 1,592,586 duplicate book records. OCLC was preparing to implement a new version of this software for its new technological platform in 2009.

OCLC also participates in the Program for Cooperative Cataloging (PCC), which is coordinated jointly by the Library of Congress and PCC participants and seeks to increase the supply of quality records, increase the number of catalogers and cataloging institutions contributing national-level records, and develop and maintain mutually acceptable standards for records. The PCC encompasses other programs whose records are contributed either directly to WorldCat or indirectly via the OCLC Authority File database: NACO for name authority records, SACO for subject authority records, BIBCO for bibliographic records, and CONSER for serial records.

VIRTUAL INTERNATIONAL AUTHORITY FILE

In 2003, Die Deutsche Bibliothek (German National Library), the Library of Congress, and OCLC began work developing a Virtual International Authorities File (VIAF). OCLC builds and maintains the file by using its matching algorithm software to process bibliographic and personal name authority records from the participants. The VIAF is updated regularly with metadata harvested automatically from participating national authority files using OAI (Open Archives Initiative) protocols. The Bibliothèque nationale de France and the National Library of Sweden are now participating in this landmark project for international library cooperation, which virtually combines multiple name authority files into a single name authority service. The long-term goal of the VIAF project is to include authoritative names from many libraries into a global service that will be freely available via the Web to users worldwide.

SERVICES

OCLC services help libraries manage their collections and provide reference services to end users. The services are designed to reduce costs and/or improve services in these areas. Since 1998, OCLC has launched a number of new services, enhanced existing services, and discontinued some services.

CATALOGING AND METADATA

Cataloging remains at the heart of OCLC services and is OCLC's principal source of revenue. In 1998, it generated 40% of OCLC's cost-sharing revenues of $136.2 million, and 34.8% of $246.4 million in 2008. The 11,674 governing members of OCLC have contributed their cataloging records to WorldCat and have worked with other members and OCLC over the years to create an incomparable library resource. As noted earlier, these members have also wanted to include as many libraries as possible in the cooperative, and they have consistently asked OCLC to do more to make it possible for small libraries to participate.

In response to that concern, in 1999, OCLC introduced CatExpress, a Web-based copy cataloging service designed for school and public libraries with low volumes of cataloging. A low subscription price allowed small libraries to obtain quality MARC records in a timely fashion and at a minimal cost. There were 359 subscriptions in the first year, and in 2008, there 2,119 subscriptions.

While OCLC has made progress in recruiting small libraries, much remains to be done if WorldCat is to connect more libraries. In 2008, at the recommendation of the Members Council, OCLC established a Small Libraries Advisory Committee of librarians from member institutions to advise OCLC on ways to provide small and rural libraries around the world with improved access to OCLC services.

Throughout its history, OCLC member libraries have volunteered to participate in experimental programs and pilot projects. In 1980, for example, the Columbus Metropolitan Library volunteered to participate in OCLC's Channel 2000 project, which delivered the world's first electronic library catalog to the television sets of 200 households in Columbus, Ohio.

In 1999, more than 350 libraries and OCLC embarked on an effort to cooperatively catalog Internet resources. The Cooperative Online Resource Catalog (CORC) grew from work in 1998 that OCLC research scientists were doing in metadata, linked authority control, the Web version of the Dewey Decimal Classification, and automated tools for finding, harvesting, and classifying electronic resources (Jordan, 2001). CORC was designed to encourage and enhance the description of Web resources to better serve library users.

CORC went online in 1999, and by 2001 about 350 libraries had contributed 500,000 bibliographic records and Web bibliographies for Internet resources. As the new technological platform took shape, however, it became clear that CORC should not continue as a standalone service, but instead should be integrated into the new cataloging service that was under development.

In 2002, OCLC launched the Connexion cataloging service on the new technological platform. It combined functionality from existing OCLC services such as CORC, CatExpress, the Cataloging Micro Enhancer, Passport, and WebDewey. Connexion supports cataloging of all materials and formats from a single interface that the library can customize. It provides access to WorldCat, linked authority control, automatic classification, and the ability to build subject guides.

OCLC also looked for ways to increase the utility of records in WorldCat. In 2005, WorldCat Collection Analysis was introduced. It provides data mining and manipulation that enable libraries to determine subject coverage in their collections and compare their collections with peer libraries to identify titles held in common and gaps in their collections. The service provides a way for libraries to routinely evaluate collections and communicate collection decisions to faculty, boards of trustees, and administrators as well as to demonstrate financial needs and responsible stewardship of library acquisitions, budgets, and collections.

Also in 2005, OCLC acquired Openly Informatics, which provides linking software and a database of 1.2 million metadata records with links to electronic resources. This acquisition accelerated development of OCLC's eHoldings Service, which was launched in 2006. It streamlines the labor-intensive task of managing E-serials collections by automatically setting and updating WorldCat holdings each month for E-serials. The service uses the OCLC Openly Informatics knowledge base of E-serials to keep WorldCat informed of full text available electronically via aggregated databases and individual E-journals. (OCLC works with WorldCat Link Manager, EBSCO LinkSource, Serials Solutions 360 Link, and the TDNet e-Resource Manager to automate the process of setting and maintaining holdings for ISSN [International Standard Serial Number]-based electronic serials in WorldCat without adding to a library's cataloging workload.)

OCLC partnered with Cornell University Library in 2006 to implement the WorldCat Selection service. Based on the Integrated Tool for Selection and Ordering at Cornell University Library (ITSO CUL), the service streamlines the selection and order process for libraries acquiring new materials. Selectors of library materials can now view new title data from multiple vendors in one central, comprehensive system and get WorldCat records for new purchased materials into their integrated library systems early in the technical services process. They can also share selection decisions with others in their institutions. Holding symbols can be automatically set in WorldCat at the point of order or added later in the cataloging process.

In 2007, OCLC introduced a Terminologies service, which provides access to multiple controlled vocabularies to enable creation of consistent metadata for library, museum, or archive collections. The vocabularies include the Dublin Core; the Art & Architecture Thesaurus of the Getty Vocabulary Program, which describes objects of art as well as the processes and materials from which the objects are made; Newspaper Genre List from the University of Washington; Māori Subject Headings/Ngā Ūpoko Tukutuku from the National Library of New Zealand; and Thesauri for Graphic Materials I and II from the Library of Congress. One goal of the Terminologies service is to make it easier for museums and archives to participate in the OCLC cooperative.

In 2008, OCLC implemented SRU (Search Retrieval via URL) Update. In non-technical terms, SRU Update makes it easier for national libraries and others to keep their union catalogs synchronized with WorldCat. In 2008, the Dutch Union Catalogue started updating WorldCat in real time using SRU technology. In 2009, the second implementation occurred with Libraries Australia. Records appearing in the Australian National Bibliographic Utility now show up 5 seconds later in WorldCat. This machine-to-machine process is introducing system-wide efficiencies that benefit the entire cooperative.

NEXT GENERATION CATALOGING

In 2008, OCLC began the Next Generation Cataloging pilot, which explored the viability of capturing ONIX metadata upstream from publishers and vendors and enhancing that metadata in WorldCat. A variety of academic and public libraries participated in the pilot.

Capturing metadata earlier in the cataloging process will result in workflow efficiencies and greater upstream availability of metadata for use in library technical processing and end-user interfaces. The process will also allow output of enriched metadata in ONIX format, providing value and efficiencies in publisher supply-chain metadata creation and maintenance in support of library, wholesale, and retail markets. OCLC published case studies and findings from the pilot. After the pilot, OCLC began to routinely ingest, create, and enhance metadata in WorldCat and output enhanced data in MARC and ONIX.

The start of the Next Generation Cataloging pilot coincided with the release of a "Report on the Future of Bibliographic Control" by the Working Group on the Future of Bibliographic Control, which was formed by the Library of Congress to address changes in how libraries must do their work in the digital information era. The ability to leverage upstream publisher data effectively is central to the Working Group's recommendations, and OCLC is moving in the same direction as the Working Group's recommendations.

In 2008, OCLC was pursuing two general objectives in cataloging and metadata. The first was to help libraries innovate and reduce the labor costs of their selection, acquisitions, and cataloging practices. Unlike staff-intensive manual methods of the past, OCLC is assembling a set of services based on mining WorldCat to optimize the value of metadata, whether it comes from a library, publisher, or vendor, and to lower staff costs while enhancing the library user's information-seeking experience.

The second objective was to create a WorldCat global metadata network for libraries, museums, archives, and other organizations that want to make their rich collections highly visible to a worldwide audience. To accomplish this, OCLC was developing services to bring a wide variety of metadata into WorldCat and create reliable linkages to print, media, licensed electronic, and digital collections, from the general to the highly specific.

RESOURCE-SHARING AND DELIVERY SERVICES

OCLC's online interlibrary loan system was 30 years old in 2009 and going strong. Over the years, the system has not only increased the availability of library resources, it has also inspired a generation of resource-sharing librarians, some even to write poetry about it (Adams & Kaiser, 1999, p. 7):

> Another day gone.
> I cannot find what I need.
> Check OCLC
> I stand before a shelf
> And see there is an empty space,
> Where the book should be.
> Can you loan it now?
> I need it for a paper
> Not quite last minute.

The system supported more than 10 million interlibrary loan transactions in fiscal 2008. In the past decade, the percentage of OCLC revenues generated by resource sharing has increased from 13.5% to 19.1%. OCLC has continuously enhanced the interlibrary loan system over the years, including such notable additions as direct delivery of ILL requests for patrons in 1993 and ILL Fee Management in 1995.

ILL Fee Management has significantly reduced administrative costs for libraries at the same time that interlibrary loan has increased the availability of library resources. The number of ILL Fee Management participants has increased from 1,070 in 1996 to 2,938 in 2008. These institutions used the service to exchange over $13.9 million in interlibrary loan fees in fiscal 2008, avoiding processing charges for about 967,000 invoices and a similar number of checks.

Another major enhancement to OCLC's resource-sharing capabilities occurred in 2000, when OCLC began distributing OCLC ILLiad Resource Sharing Management software, which was developed by Virginia Polytechnic Institute and State University (Virginia Tech) and maintained by Atlas Systems. This software automates routine interlibrary loan functions and provides sophisticated tracking statistics to library staff. In 2008, there were about 940 libraries in the United States using ILLiad, of which 527 were academic libraries and 89 were ARL (Association of Research Libraries) libraries. There were eight ILLiad users in Hong Kong, and one each in Canada, Egypt, Qatar, Scotland, and Sweden. It is interesting to note that about 50% of the total interlibrary loan requests on WorldCat Resource Sharing in 2008 were initiated by ILLiad users. In 2008, OCLC began providing server hosting to ILLiad users. OCLC and Atlas Systems have also signed an agreement that enables the two organizations to continue to support ILLiad and to integrate the software more fully into OCLC delivery services in the coming years.

OCLC must continuously make decisions about aligning its limited resources with almost unlimited opportunities. Is it in the best interests of the cooperative to continue to offer a service that is used by only a small portion of the membership? At what point do the costs of providing a service outweigh the benefits? Is the current service the best solution? In the last decade, OCLC faced a number of these issues as it pursued its strategy to weave libraries into the Web.

For example, in 2001, OCLC announced that it would discontinue development of its SiteSearch suite of products. It would also discontinue technical support for the service 18 months later, at the end of 2002. OCLC also released a source code license to SiteSearch users so they could continue community development if they so desired. Developed in 1992 by OCLC Research, this suite of software helped libraries integrate and manage their electronic library collections and deliver information resources through a Web-based environment. Although the service was launched with high hopes in 1992, after 10 years there were only about 100 installations, including several statewide consortial implementations. The search engine supporting SiteSearch had become dated, and in the meantime, new technological alternatives had appeared.

In 2004, OCLC introduced Group Services, which provided an integrated solution for searching, cataloging, and resource sharing for consortia and other groups of libraries. A library consortium could have its own union catalog in WorldCat that offers a single, unified view of the group's collections. Since the group catalog is a Web-based service, the institutions did not have to invest in hardware or software to provide their users with a union catalog.

By 2005, about 5,700 libraries were using customized group views of WorldCat as the online public access catalogs for the groups. As these group catalogs and services moved forward, however, it became increasingly clear that OCLC needed to more tightly integrate its resource-sharing and delivery services. Thus, in early 2009, OCLC further refined its consortial borrowing service with the introduction of WorldCat Navigator, which combined the group catalog with the VDX (Virtual Document eXchange) document delivery and interlibrary lending management system (see below) and WorldCat Resource Sharing. The service handled both returnable and nonreturnable items and had circulation interoperability with ILS (Interlibrary Library System) systems.

At the same time that OCLC was developing Navigator, it was winding down a year-long WorldCat Delivery Pilot program with 12 libraries in the state of Montana. In this test, users could generate requests for library-held materials via the library's local system, WorldCat Resource Sharing, or ILLiad. Libraries had the option of delivering items directly to the requesting users instead of to borrowing libraries. Users received the items at home and could return the items in enclosed specially designed mailers. During the pilot, libraries sent more than 10,000 items to patrons' homes. Based on the results of the pilot, OCLC is not pursuing home delivery as a separate offering, but will include aspects of home delivery, such as tracking for major shippers, in a future release of WorldCat Resource Sharing.

Besides in-house development of new resource-sharing services, OCLC also added new capabilities through acquisitions. In 2003, OCLC EMEA acquired V3.Web, an ILL requesting and management system used by 70 public libraries in the United Kingdom and using the V3 database of more than 5 million bibliographic records and 40 million location listings for materials in U.K. public and special libraries.

In 2005, OCLC EMEA acquired Fretwell-Downing Informatics, an information discovery, library management, and knowledge delivery organization, to strengthen and extend their combined worldwide network for information delivery to libraries. Based in Sheffield, United Kingdom, Fretwell Downing Informatics services included OLIB, an integrated local library system (see below); ZPORTAL, a federated search service; and VDX, a document delivery and interlibrary loan management system.

OCLC's long-term objective is to integrate WorldCat Resource Sharing, ILLiad, and VDX into a new model of resource sharing that is changing from the traditional patron model of discover, locate, request, deliver to an automated model based on patron experience. This new model is based on the assumption that the patron does not care where the information comes from. Hence, the order of actions is discover, request, then locate and deliver. The idea is to get the item into the patron's hands as soon as possible.

REFERENCE

As noted earlier, in 1991, OCLC introduced the FirstSearch service, which was the first service to provide users with access to online databases that did not require the intermediation of a professional librarian. FirstSearch required no training. Library users could easily plunge in and consult over 65 databases, including WorldCat. By 1997, FirstSearch ranked number one among online reference services in terms of connect time. The number of online searches done annually on FirstSearch peaked in fiscal 2003 at 99.8 million and by fiscal 2008 had declined to 79.7 million. There are two main reasons for this decline. First, some database providers are now offering access to their databases directly. Second, search engines such as Google and Yahoo now provide access to articles and materials available in the databases.

In 2000, OCLC merged with Public Affairs Information Service, Inc. (PAIS), a nonprofit organization that publishes the PAIS International database of public policy literature from more than 120 countries. The database was added to the OCLC FirstSearch service, and OCLC/PAIS editors were using CORC (see above) to devise subject bibliographies for electronic resources. In 2004, OCLC sold PAIS to Cambridge Scientific Abstracts (CSA). Since the merger, OCLC had made some course adjustments in its strategic directions and determined that PAIS would benefit from greater focus and additional investment as part of CSA. PAIS continues to be a valuable information resource and is still available on the OCLC FirstSearch service.

In 2002, OCLC acquired NetLibrary, a leading provider of electronic books, which at the time was providing 42,000 titles from 315 publishers. About 7,300 libraries were using NetLibrary content in 2002. Since then, OCLC has developed a new technological platform for NetLibrary and made it easier for libraries to integrate eBooks into their collections. Librarians can now consult an online catalog of all eContent titles available from NetLibrary to order individual eBook titles. Patron-Driven Acquisition (PDA) lets patrons participate in the selection of new content. OCLC-MARC records are provided for every eBook title. In late 2008, NetLibrary offered about 170,000 eBook and eAudioBook titles. A new NetLibrary Media Center was being prepared for introduction in 2009. It would allow library patrons to easily search, manage, transfer, and listen to eAudiobooks from their local library.

GOING VIRTUAL

The 2001 ALA Midwinter Meeting was held in Washington, DC. There, on January 12, more than 600 persons attended a symposium at the Library of Congress on "Building the Virtual Reference Desk in a 24/7 World" that was sponsored by LC and OCLC. It is interesting to note that following the symposium, there was a reception labeled "A Celebration of Anniversaries," at which OCLC Founder Frederick G. Kilgour and Winston Tabb, Associate Librarian for Library Services, Library of Congress, spoke on the respective anniversaries of WorldCat (30 years) and the Library of Congress (200 years!). At the symposium, the Library of Congress and OCLC announced they would develop a prototype for a new reference service based on the Collaborative Digital Reference Service (CDRS) pilot begun in early 2000 by the Library of Congress and 16 participating libraries (Library of Congress and OCLC to collaborate, 2001). That prototype developed into a production system that OCLC launched in 2002 as QuestionPoint.

In 2008, there were more than 1,900 libraries in 23 countries using the QuestionPoint virtual reference service. More than 1,500 libraries were participating in the 24/7 reference cooperative, which enables libraries to offer reference service to their communities 24 hours a day, 7 days a week. The reference cooperative included 13 statewide services in the U.S. and nationwide services in the United Kingdom and the Netherlands. Qwidget (a chat widget) was released in 2008; it enables libraries to embed QuestionPoint on their Web pages and in a variety of user environments. Since the QuestionPoint service began in 2002, librarians have used it to answer more than 3 million reference questions.

DIGITIZATION AND PRESERVATION

In 1997, Deanna Marcum, President of the Commission on Preservation and Access and the Council on Library Resources, wrote:

> While the number of information producers grows steadily, libraries, archives and museums have assumed primary responsibility for collecting systematically the information that has lasting value and for taking steps to preserve that information for subsequent generations. Meeting this obligation for print materials has been difficult. The challenge of preserving materials in digital form is even greater. Libraries, archives and museums are now able to provide their users with access to information resources they do not own. But who is responsible for preserving this digital information? Libraries, archives and museums must work with organizations that are willing to help overcome the technical and financial challenges to creating and maintaining digital archives. Such partnerships are not yet common but are critical if cultural repositories are to meet their obligations in the future (OCLC begins electronic archiving, 1997, p. 21).

In the 1990s, OCLC had studied electronic archiving and digital preservation and made occasional forays into this challenging area. In 1993, the board of trustees of MAPS (Mid-Atlantic Preservation Service) voted to transfer control of the organization to OCLC. MAPS was created in 1985 by Princeton, Cornell, and Columbia Universities, the New York Public Library, and the New York State Library to develop and test operating strategies for producing high-quality microfilm in a high-productivity environment. MAPS had a 17,150-sq. ft. facility in Bethlehem, Pennsylvania, designed specifically for high-quality microfilming and storage of micrographics.

OCLC changed the name of MAPS to Preservation Resources and invested in high-quality microfilming and digitization infrastructure. In 1997, the Library of Congress selected Preservation Resources to digitize the microfilmed papers of George Washington, Thomas Jefferson, and Abraham Lincoln. That same year, OCLC and Preservation Resources embarked on eight projects involving the digitization of microfilmed images for electronic access, including the Schomberg Collection of the New York Public Library, perhaps the premier collection of African Americana in the United States.

OCLC's strategy for digital archiving and preservation was to proceed cautiously, on a realistic, step-by-step basis, with an eye toward solutions consistent with OCLC's mission of furthering access to the world's information and reducing library costs. At that time, OCLC and others believed that the problems surrounding digitization and archiving were too big for any single organization to tackle on its own: long-term, inexpensive storage; access for both content providers and users; scanning; indexing; and technology migration. Meanwhile, technological advances were about to accelerate OCLC's involvement in digitization and archiving.

In 2002, OCLC launched a new core service in digital and preservation resources. A digital co-op was created to share information and resources on digital preservation projects. The OCLC Digital Archive service began operations, facilitating capture of Web documents, creation of preservation metadata for digital objects, ingest of objects into the archive, and long-term retention of those assets. With the Royal Library of the Netherlands, OCLC opened Strata Preservation N.V. in The Hague to provide digitization and preservation services for institutions in Europe. (OCLC and the Royal Library sold Strata to KMM Group in the Netherlands in 2008.)

Also in 2002, OCLC began distributing CONTENTdm software which helps libraries manage digital objects and surface their special collections on the Web. In 2006, OCLC acquired DiMeMa (Digital Media Management), the organization that developed and supported CONTENTdm. The software grew from an effort by the University of Washington Libraries to transform the unique scholarly collections of faculty and libraries into a rich multimedia digital archive. The Library partnered with the College of Engineering's Center for Information Systems Optimization to develop a software package for multimedia digital collection management. The Library brought its expertise in cataloging standards and guidelines and end-user searching behavior, while the College of Engineering provided systems knowledge for archiving, retrieval, and display. CONTENTdm is discussed elsewhere in this volume.

In 2004, the Indiana Historical Society became the first institution to add records from a digitized CONTENTdm collection to WorldCat via metadata harvesting. By 2008, there were 456 institutions with CONTENTdm licenses, and they had over 3 million objects under CONTENTdm management. However, only about 200,000 of the objects had MARC records in WorldCat. These records were also available via WorldCat.org, thereby increasing the visibility of libraries' special collections. The harvesting of records from these collections is obviously a future growth area for OCLC.

At this writing in 2009, the University of Michigan and OCLC formed an alliance to ensure continued public access to open-archive collections through the OAIster database. OAIster was started in 2002 with grant support from the Andrew W. Mellon Foundation to test the feasibility of building a portal to open archive collections using the Open Archives Initiative Protocol for Metadata Harvesting (OAI-PMH). OAIster has since grown to become one of the largest aggregations of records pointing to open archive collections in the world with over 19 million records contributed by more than 1,000 organizations worldwide.

Under the partnership, OAIster.org will continue to function as the public interface to OAIster collections, through funding provided by OCLC to the University of Michigan. OCLC also provided a hosted version of OAIster on the FirstSearch platform and made it available through subscriptions to the FirstSearch Base Package at no additional charge. At this writing, metadata harvesting operations were to be transferred from the University of Michigan to OCLC in late 2009.

Also in 2009, OCLC signed an agreement with the Hathi Trust to collaborate in adapting OCLC's WorldCat Local as a public discovery interface for its digital repository, which contains more than 2.5 million digitized volumes from some 25 research libraries in the United States. The initial members of the Hathi Trust were the 13 universities of the Committee on Institutional Cooperation and the University of California system, which wanted to establish a repository for these universities to archive and share their digitized collections.

INTEGRATED LIBRARY SYSTEMS

With the merger with Pica BV in 1999 and the formation of OCLC EMEA, OCLC reentered the local systems business. Pica was a well-established local systems provider, primarily in Europe with its LBS and CBS systems. LBS is an integrated local library management system that supports acquisitions, cataloging, and circulation. The CBS system (Central Library System) provides the infrastructure for the creation and management of union catalogs and tools for regional interlibrary loan. There are CBS installations at the Royal Library of the Netherlands, the German National Library, and the National

Library of Australia, and at ABES (Agence bibliographique de l'enseignement supérieur) in France, to name a few.

OCLC EMEA also develops and maintains three other local library systems acquired through acquisitions. The OLIB (originally developed by Fretwell Downing Informatics) library management system is installed in about 250 organizations worldwide. In 2008, OCLC EMEA completed a 5-year project to create a new public catalog site for the U.S. National Archives and Records Administration based on OLIB. The SunRise library system (originally developed by Sisis) is installed in more than 150 libraries, primarily in Germany, Switzerland, and the Netherlands; the Bavarian State Library is a SunRise user. The Amlib system has some 500 installations in Australia, Africa, and the United States.

OCLC's long-term strategy for the ILS is to create an infrastructure to deliver a large-scale, network-based workflow solution to manage library business processes. The design of the future library management environment will comprise a number of important aspects. It will be an evolutionary process, with new service implemented in a building block process that will eventually become a unified solution. The new services can also be integrated into a library's existing infrastructure and current ILS. The notion is to preserve the functionality of the ILS, but at the same time enhance it by placing it in a network environment and extending it to manage print, licensed, and digitized material with one solution.

OCLC TODAY: WEAVING LIBRARIES INTO THE WEB

In 2004, OCLC published the *2003 Environmental Scan: Pattern Recognition*. This report to the OCLC membership identified trends that are affecting libraries, museums, and archives in five landscapes: social, economic, technology, research and learning, and library. The Scan was based on interviews with 100 information professionals and a review of 300 relevant articles and papers. Four patterns emerged.

First, there continues to be a decrease in guided access to content. Today's information seekers are relying less on traditional guides to information, such as reference librarians, databases, reference guides, and library catalogs. Instead, they are going to the Internet for their information needs, and they are taking new paths to information that do not rely on shapes of information containers—books, journals, or other formats—to guide them. As a result, libraries and OCLC are changing how libraries present information, perform reference, and provide customer service.

Second, information is being disaggregated and provided to users when and where they need it. People are seeking a table, a fact, a quote, a picture, or a single song from what used to be aggregated content in books, journals, or CDs. Libraries are changing the way they manage and provide access to their collections in order to meet the new expectations of information consumers.

Third, there is an increase in collaboration in the information community as advances in collaborative technologies enable organizations to work together in new ways. Open-source software, wikis, Web conferencing, blogging, instant messaging, learning objects, and gaming are new forms of technology-assisted collaboration that allow people to work together and talk to one another seamlessly. Libraries must continue to combine technology with collaboration to weave their services into the new information environment and meet users at the point of need.

Fourth, information has become globalized. More and more people around the world are coming online to read, download, copy, distribute, or link to information. Institutions are now challenged to manage and provide access to information across boundaries of language, culture, and geography.

In 2005, OCLC published another study, *Perceptions of Libraries and Information Resources*. Based on surveys of information users across six countries, this report has been well received and widely quoted in the professional literature. The report included some findings that did not bode well for libraries' Web presence, including:

- 84% of respondents use search engines to begin an information search
- 1% begin an information search on a library Web site
- 90% are satisfied with search engines
- People think that libraries are about books
- A majority do not consider the library a source for readily available information, especially digital content

Given the environmental trends and the habits of information seekers noted above, it is obvious that the challenge for libraries is to define and market their relevant place in the information environment—their services and collections, both physical and virtual.

At the same time, the pace of technological change has continued unabated. Libraries have added more systems to support online public access catalogs, acquisitions, and access to licensed databases. As a result, libraries have made significant investments in computer resources and infrastructure. They now incur the costs of supporting an array of systems across workflows for print, licensed, and digital materials. Similarly, libraries have a fragmented presence on the Web, where they must compete with search engines and other information resources in meeting the information needs of people.

Meanwhile, the focus of computing has moved from the personal computer to the Internet. The current trend is cloud computing, where applications and data are stored on the Internet rather than on a local computer. This presents OCLC with the opportunity to provide libraries with computer infrastructure in the cloud, where they use the applications they need.

Rather than buying, implementing, and maintaining software themselves, libraries can use an application without having to worry about the technology that supports the applications. Instead, they can focus on running their organizations and serving their users. Accordingly, OCLC is building its next-generation services in a Web environment, one that will greatly amplify the power of library cooperation.

OPEN WORLDCAT

OCLC began weaving libraries into the Web in 2003 with the Open WorldCat pilot. This program studied the feasibility of making WorldCat records and library holdings available to the general public on the open Web via search engines such as Google and Yahoo! Search. The notion was to make it easy for a person who is looking for information via a search engine to end up finding it in a nearby library. To do this, OCLC would make WorldCat records directly available to the general public for the first time. Heretofore, WorldCat had been available only through participating libraries.

OCLC began the pilot after extensive consultations with the Board of Trustees, Members Council, regional service providers, and member libraries. There was consensus that this was something the OCLC cooperative had to try, given the habits of information seekers noted above. The pilot offered the possibility of raising the visibility of libraries on the Web. It was indeed consistent with OCLC's chartered objective of increasing availability of library resources.

In the first phase, users could access links to Open WorldCat through selected Web sites, including Alibris, Abebooks, Antiquarian Booksellers Association of America (ABAA), BookPage, and HCI Bibliography. For example, a person searching the ABAA Web site for an out-of-print book would have the option of finding libraries holding the item if the search came up with no hits among ABAA members. "Find it in a WorldCat library by pressing the button below," the message read.

The second phase of the pilot involved making WorldCat records available to search engines. Before doing so, OCLC directly informed the membership of its intention to make a subset of 2 million abbreviated records available on Google and Yahoo! with links to the Web-based catalogs and sites of 12,000 academic, public, and school libraries participating in OCLC.

In 2005, the Open WorldCat pilot became an ongoing program, and that first year there were 59.6 million referrals from partner sites to the Open WorldCat landing page, and from there 1.7 million click-throughs to library services. Put another way, 1.7 million searches that started on the open Web brought people to library Web sites and services. By 2008, the referrals from partner sites were running at an annual rate of 134.5 million with about 8.9 million click-throughs to library services.

OCLC was also helping libraries increase the visibility of their special collections by automatically harvesting metadata from CONTENTdm-supported collections for subsequent conversion at OCLC to the MARC format for loading into WorldCat. In 2004, the Indiana Historical Society became the first institution to register one of its special collections for metadata harvesting by OCLC for addition to WorldCat. Thus, people could gain access over the Web to the "Postcards of Indiana" collection through links from WorldCat.

WORLDCAT.ORG

On August 8, 2006, OCLC launched the WorldCat.org Web site. The site offered a search box that people can download and use to search all the records in WorldCat and identify libraries that hold an item.

This was one of the signal achievements in the history of the OCLC cooperative. It was a tribute not only to the vision of OCLC Founder Frederick G. Kilgour, but to the perseverance and hard work of catalogers and librarians who have built WorldCat record by record since 1971. The OCLC database had begun life as a cataloging and resource sharing tool, but Fred Kilgour and the OCLC pioneers always dreamed that one day it would be widely available to the general public.

Indeed, the first OCLC public use terminals began appearing in libraries as early as 1974. Back then, users grappled with the derived search keys (an author-title search was 4,4—the first four letters of the author's last name, first four letters of the title; a title search was 3,2,2,1). An OCLC study noted that "most of the recorded use of the terminal was done by young, registered, frequent patrons of libraries." People still had to go to the library to use the library, but OCLC and its member libraries were making progress (Ohio College Library Center, 1976).

As noted above, in 1980, OCLC and Columbus Metropolitan Library combined WorldCat with cable television in a home delivery of library services experiment. People in 200 households could access the library's catalog and order books. The remote control device was bigger than a breadbox and was attached to the TV set by a 10-foot cable, but no matter, the future was just around the corner!

In 1991, OCLC made another leap forward with FirstSearch. For the first time, people could search WorldCat by subject, and they did not have to bother with derived, truncated search keys. OCLC hailed this latest advance as "a revolutionary new concept in providing the general public with online reference information." (OCLC, 1991)

In 2005, as noted above, OCLC launched the Open WorldCat program, which let people search a subset of WorldCat through popular search engines such as Google and Yahoo!

Then, in August 2006, people could search the entire OCLC database on the Internet through the OCLC Cooperative's search site—WorldCat.org—and find the item in a nearby library (Jordan, 2006).

Ten years from now and millions of records and billions of location listings later, WorldCat will likely be available in new ways that are now only dimly perceived through the haze of emerging technologies. But with WorldCat.org, the OCLC cooperative had become part of the Web and the global information infrastructure in a new and profound way.

Subsequently, OCLC has added a series of enhancements to World-Cat.org, all designed to help libraries create a compelling user environment. WorldCat Identities creates a summary page for the more than 25 million personal and corporate authors mentioned in WorldCat. Each Identities page presents a summary for the individual identified, including: total works, genres, roles, classifications, a publication timeline, and an audience level indicator. Additional features enable users to create lists, tag records with their own category descriptions, build bibliographies, and install search plug-ins on Facebook and Firefox. By 2008, WorldCat.org also contained more than 58 million records linked to full-text journal articles. The WorldCat database is indeed moving beyond bibliography.

WORLDCAT LOCAL

WorldCat Local is yet another example of a new OCLC service that began as a pilot program. The pilot began at the University of Washington Libraries in April 2007. Initial pilot participants included the Peninsula Library System in California, Lincoln Trail Libraries System and eight other libraries in Illinois, and the Ohio State University Libraries. WorldCat Local provides a single interface to the collections of a library. It interoperates with locally maintained services such as circulation, resource sharing, and resolution to full text to create an integrated experience for library users. WorldCat Local searches the entire WorldCat.org database and presents local and group library holdings at the top of the results list, as well as ownership details for WorldCat libraries outside the local library and consortium.

With the implementation of WorldCat Local, OCLC began providing a local connection to cloud computing. It is a service provided to the library across the Internet that eliminates costs to the library for hosting, operating, and maintaining software. WorldCat Local is "activatable," which means that library staff configure the service from their library using their library's policies. This configuration is done using an online questionnaire that ideally requires the involvement of staff from both public services and technical services.

WEB SERVICES

Web services enable applications to interconnect over the Web through machine-to-machine interfaces. They cover a wide range of activities that let people tap into the computing power on the Web. In addition to WorldCat. org, WorldCat Local, and the WorldCat Identities mentioned above, OCLC has also introduced these Web services in the past 5 years.

The xISBN service, developed by OCLC Research, supplies International Standard Book Numbers (ISBNs) associated with an individual intellectual work, based on information in the WorldCat database. It finds all related editions of a book, including paperback, hardback, audiobook, foreign, and out of print. Easily incorporated into library catalogs, the service is available free to OCLC cataloging members and for a fee to others.

The WorldCat Registry enables a library to manage its institutional identity more efficiently. On a secure Web platform, a library can create and maintain a single profile that includes information of use to the library's consortium members, technology vendors, E-content providers, funding agencies, and other partners. This access enables the library to automate routine tasks such as activation of a new subscription service or renewal of an existing one. In 2008, the Registry included more than 120,000 institution records for OCLC and non-OCLC members.

In 2008, OCLC established the WorldCat Developers Network by inviting a small group of developers from OCLC cataloging institutions in North America and Europe to use the WorldCat API (Applications Programming Interface) to build applications that would guide people from the Web to library services. These developers could then link WorldCat information to Internet applications as well as presentations, blogs, and E-mails. This shared development will enhance the creativity and usage of WorldCat.

The Developers Network sponsored events such as the WorldCat Hackathon held at the New York Public Library in 2008 and a Mashathon in Amsterdam in 2009. These events bring developers together in a creative, collaborative environment. This open-source, code-sharing infrastructure improves the value of OCLC data for all users by encouraging new Web services uses.

As noted above, the Qwidget is another Web service that gives libraries the ability to embed a snippet of HTML code throughout their Web pages and in a variety of environments such as Facebook or MySpace.

In 2008, OCLC and Google agreed to exchange data that will facilitate the discovery of library collections through Google search services. OCLC member libraries participating in the Google Book Search(tm) program, which makes the full text of more than one million books searchable, may share their WorldCat-derived MARC records with Google to better facilitate discovery of library collections through Google. Google will link from Google Book Search to WorldCat.org, which will drive traffic to library OPACs and other library services. Google will share data and links to digitized books with OCLC, which will make it possible for OCLC to represent the digitized collections of OCLC member libraries in WorldCat.

INCREASE OCLC'S GLOBAL RELEVANCE AND POSITION OF TRUST

Since 1967, OCLC has been building trust in the library community by providing reliable, cost-effective services that reduce costs and improve services. Continued strong use of these services has enabled the cooperative to undertake programs that benefit the library community in general. OCLC Programs and Research, WebJunction, and advocacy are described in detail in other articles. Each of these programs works to increase OCLC's global relevance and position of trust.

Outside the United States, OCLC operates offices in Australia, Canada, France, Germany, Mexico, the Netherlands, Switzerland, and the United Kingdom and maintains relationships with distributors in numerous countries.

Even though OCLC connects some 69,000 libraries and other institutions in 112 countries, it is still far from being the center of the bibliographic world, let alone the much larger universe of library cooperation. OCLC has a number of strategic partners—IFLA, LIBER, ARL, the Bill & Melinda Gates Foundation, consortia, and 34 national libraries, to name a few—and their constituencies and memberships frequently overlap with OCLC's.

In 2006, OCLC celebrated the 20th anniversary of its partnership with the Kinokuniya Company, which distributes and supports OCLC services in Japan for approximately 400 institutions. Kinokuniya worked with OCLC and Japanese publishers to develop the first Japanese eBook collection available through NetLibrary. Kinokuniya has been instrumental in promoting the growth of Japanese language records in WorldCat and has helped to make it a more global database in content and reach.

In 2007, OCLC was honored to host the fourth China-U.S. Library Conference in Dublin, Ohio. This prestigious scholarly event brought together 60 leaders from research libraries, museums, and archives in China and the United States for 3 days of presentations and meetings regarding cooperation among their institutions. The conference provides an exceptional forum for collaboration between libraries in the two countries and for China scholars worldwide.

In 2008, OCLC Research opened an office at the University of St Andrews in Scotland to represent RLG Programs in Europe, working with partner institutions as well as allied organizations on issues and topics of common interest. About 60 persons attended the RLG Programs European Partners Meeting in Paris in November 2008.

In the United States, the vast majority of libraries that participate in OCLC do so through a regional network or service center. These organizations share similar goals and are committed to advancing research, scholarship, education, and open access to information. As the library environment has changed over the past 40 years, the products and the service models deployed by OCLC and its partners have also evolved. Since 1971, there have been 26 regional service providers that have contracted with OCLC to provide services to libraries in the United States. At this writing there are 15 regional service providers. Today, OCLC offers over 40 products to its libraries in the United States, and most of the U.S. networks now market and support dozens of products in addition to, or as alternatives to, OCLC services.

At this writing, OCLC and its U.S. Regional Service Providers are implementing new programs designed to increase value and reduce overall service costs for OCLC member libraries. (See "The OCLC Network of Regional Service Providers: The Last 10 years," by Brenda Bailey-Hainer in the previous issue of this journal.) The new service initiatives include streamlined billing statements, more account information online, simplified account administration, a centralized training calendar offering easy access to national training and education opportunities, and strengthened product support infrastructure. The programs are designed to take full advantage of current technologies and collaborative programs, to enhance access to OCLC products and services, and to improve cost efficiencies for libraries. OCLC and its U.S. Regional Service Providers continue to strive to deliver consistent, high-quality services to all member libraries, regardless of location, size, or type.

OCLC looks forward to continuing its long-term partnerships with the U.S. Regional Service Providers in working together to grow the community of OCLC partners and offer new programs and service options to OCLC libraries and users.

The OCLC Members Council has been a key driver in increasing OCLC's global relevance and position of trust. In May 2009, the OCLC Members Council held its 90th and final meeting as the OCLC cooperative began to implement its new governance structure of Regional Councils and a Global Council. Eleven years earlier the author had attended his first meeting of the then Users Council in May 1998. Interestingly enough, the theme of that meeting was "Internationalize: The Value of OCLC Membership in a Global Library Community."

Over the next decade the OCLC did indeed become more global. From 1998 to 2009, the number of participating libraries increased from 30,000 to 71,761, and the number of institutions participating outside the United States rose from 3,200 to 16,140. In 1998, there were two delegates on the Users Council from outside the U.S.: Ellen Hoffman, York University, Canada, and Ian Mowat, Edinburgh University, United Kingdom. Since then, the Council has indeed internationalized itself. In 2008–2009, there were 16 delegates from Australia, Canada, Denmark, France, Germany, Mexico, the Netherlands, Singapore, Taiwan, Trinidad and Tobago, and the United Kingdom. Thirty-two delegates from outside the U.S. have served on the Council since 1978.

Of course, the vast majority (525) of Users/Members Council delegates have come from U.S. institutions. Elected by their regional networks or service centers, these delegates have represented libraries of all types and sizes. While they have brought many diverse viewpoints to Council's discussions, they have been consistent on one issue, which is that the OCLC cooperative should be as inclusive as possible. That is a theme that runs throughout OCLC's history, from the Ohio pioneers to the nationwide network of 1978 to the international OCLC of today. The more libraries and cultural heritage institutions in the OCLC network, the better.

GOING GLOBAL

As information continues to flow across national boundaries, as technological barriers continue to dissolve, OCLC's biggest challenges continue to be economic, legal, and political. Therefore, it is more important than ever for OCLC to be steadfast in its public purposes of furthering access to the world's information and reducing the rate of rise of per-unit library costs. Over the past decade, the goal has been to make OCLC services and programs available around the world to as many libraries and other cultural heritage organizations as possible. To do so, OCLC must simultaneously scale up and scale down to meet the needs of both the largest and smallest of institutions.

To be truly global, OCLC must be responsive at the national level by building into products/services more support for local languages as well as other local variations that meet the needs of specific users in each country. OCLC must also build community across various markets by facilitating forums with representatives from a variety of countries.

Being a global library cooperative is not about exporting U.S.-based products, OCLC's strategy is to leverage the knowledge, research, and experience of its members around the world in order to build useful services, develop international standards, facilitate sharing of library resources, and provide end users with information when and where they need it.

Effective globalization is localization on a wide scale, and localization is more than translation of interfaces. Effective globalization requires localization at every point of use. It is about providing access to non-English content. It is about building local alliances so that marketing, support/service, and market research are done locally. It is about joint development projects that utilize local technical resources. It is about partnerships to provide training and education with local language partners.

Finally, OCLC's strategy recognizes that institutions participate in OCLC to increase the availability of their resources and to reduce the rate of rise of their costs. Outside the United States, OCLC offers pricing tailored to the specific needs and economic situations facing prospective OCLC members. Moreover, OCLC strives to keep its prices as low as possible while at the same time maintaining a strong financial base in order to sustain growth, upgrade technological platforms, and conduct research and development.

CONCLUSION

Since 1971, OCLC has provided libraries with $3.7 billion in products and services. WorldCat is in the workflows of most parts of the library, including acquisitions, cataloging, reference, resource sharing, and circulation. OCLC products and services have not only been at low cost, but have saved libraries millions of dollars. Clearly, the OCLC cooperative has worked well for 37 years.

Throughout its history, OCLC has been fortunate to have people in libraries and other knowledge institutions willing to get involved not only in governance, but in research, product development, and testing of new services and programs. The last 10 years has seen OCLC weave libraries into the World Wide Web in a variety of ways. WorldCat has been transformed from a bibliographic database and online union catalog into a globally networked information resource of text, graphics, sound, and motion. As OCLC enters its fifth decade, the shared vision of thousands of librarians and knowledge workers in thousands of institutions is manifesting itself in new levels of cooperation and an ongoing commitment to connecting people with information.

The author believes that the OCLC cooperative continues to have an exciting future. That future will require more collaboration, more institutions, more Web-scale services, more synchronization, and, of course, more innovation. Going forward, people around the world will have dramatically improved access to the rich resources so effectively stewarded by the world's memory institutions.

REFERENCES

Adams, S., & Kaiser, N. (1999). "Interlibrary loan haiku": What the OCLC interlibrary loan service means to me, Dublin, OH: OCLC Online Computer Library Center.
Jordan, J. (2001). Preface, CORC, New tools and possibilities for cooperative electronic resource description. New York: Haworth Press.

Jordan, J. (2006, September). WorldCat goes public. *Next Space*, OCLC Online Computer Library Center, p. 3.

Library of Congress and OCLC to collaborate on digital reference project (2001). *OCLC Newsletter*, March/April 2001, pp. 8–9.

OCLC begins electronic archiving project (1997). *OCLC Newsletter*, March/April 1997, p. 21.

Online Computer Library Center. (1991). *OCLC Newsletter No. 193,* September/ October 1991, p. 19.

Online Computer Library Center, Inc. (1999). *Annual report 1998/1999*. Dublin, OH: Author.

Online Computer Library Center, Inc. (2000). *Annual report 1999/2000*. Dublin, OH: Author.

Online Computer Library Center, Inc. (2008). *Annual report 2007/08*. Dublin, OH: Author.

Ohio College Library Center (1967, 5 July), Articles of incorporation of the Ohio College Library Center. Columbus, OH: Author.

Ohio College Library Center. (1968). *Annual report 1967/68*. Columbus, OH: Author.

Ohio College Library Center. (1976). OCLC Public Use Terminals: report of a survey of users OCLC public use terminals 1974–1975. W. Stuart Debenham, Kunj Rastogi, Philip Schieber.

Chronology: Noteworthy Achievements of the Cooperative 1967–2008

PHIL SCHIEBER

OCLC Online Computer Library Center, Inc., Dublin, OH, USA

ABSTRACT. *This chronology lists programs, activities and accomplishments of OCLC and its members from its founding in 1967 as the Ohio College Library Center through 1998.*

1967

OCLC (Online Computer Library Center) articles of incorporation signed

1968

MARC II (Machine Readable Cataloging) format created at Library of Congress

1969

First LC-MARC II Distribution Service tape, containing approximately 1,000 Library of Congress records, issued

1970

Xerox Sigma 5 computer installed at OCLC for online system

1971

Online shared cataloging system begins operation on August 26, 1971
Online system starts accepting member-input cataloging on October 18, 1971

1972

Three networks join OCLC: Cooperative College Library Center (CCLC), New
England Library Information Network (NELINET), Pittsburgh Regional Li-
brary Center (PRLC)
Standards for Input Cataloging issued
OCLC control number access

1973

M100 Terminal, manufactured by Beehive, introduced
Extended search function is activated—users may now retrieve and view up
to 256 database entries under a specific search key

1974

Dial access to OCLC system
Four networks join OCLC: Five Associated University Libraries (FAUL), Fed-
eral Library Committee (FEDLINK), Interuniversity Council of the North
Texas Area (AMIGOS Bibliographic Council), Pennsylvania Area Library
Network (PALINET)
CONSER (Cooperative Online SERials) program begins building database of
authoritative serials records using OCLC database

1975

First Xerox Sigma 9 installed on online system
Four networks join OCLC: Higher Education Coordinating Council of
Metropolitan St. Louis (Missouri Library Network Corporation-MLNC),
Illinois Research and Reference Center Libraries (ILLINET), Southeastern
Library Network (SOLINET), State University of New York (SUNY, Nylink)

1976

Five networks join OCLC: Bibliographical Center for Research (BCR), Con-
sortium of Universities of the Washington Metropolitan Area (CAPCON),
Indiana Cooperative Library Services Authority (INCOLSA), Michigan
Library Consortium (MLC), Wisconsin Library Consortium (WiLS)
OCLC Western Service Center (PACNET) established

Implementation of card production for MARC II formats in addition to books

Corporate name index added to online system

ALL PRODUCE function

U.S. Government Printing Office starts producing Monthly Catalog of Government Publications from OCLC-MARC tapes

1977

Four networks join OCLC: OCLC Western Service Center (PACNET, OCLC Pacific), Minnesota Interlibrary Teletype Exchange (MINITEX), Nebraska Library Commission (NEBASE), Midwestern Regional Library Network (MRLN)

OCLC adopts new governance structure (Members, Users Council, Board of Trustees)

Ohio College Library Center changes name to OCLC, Inc.

1978

OHIONET established

OCLC Users Council meets for first time

OCLC Office of Research formed

M105 terminal introduced

1979

Interlibrary Loan (ILL) Subsystem introduced

Alberta (Canada) Alcoholism and Drug Abuse Commission becomes first member of OCLC outside the United States; participates via Tymnet

OCLC has participating libraries in all 50 United States

1980

Online name-address directory activated

OCLC Online Union Catalog converted to Anglo-American Cataloging Rules 2 (AACR2) form

Online retrieval by U.S. Government Document number is added

Serials Union List

Holdings in Online Union Catalog display alphabetically by state or region

1981

Acquisitions subsystem introduced
OCLC Europe formed

1982

University of Minnesota becomes first tape-loading member of OCLC
Linked Systems Project begins

1983

OCLC Online Union Catalog becomes host database for U.S. Newspaper
   Program
Merge Holdings capability
LS/2000 local library system launched
Interlibrary Loan subsystem linked to Name-Address Directory
OCLC Online Union Catalog totals 10 million records

1984

Major Microforms
Uninterruptible power system installed for Online System
M300 Workstation introduced
Interlibrary Loan Micro Enhancer introduced
Enhance Program

1985

MICROCON introduced

1986

Second AACR2 conversion of OCLC Online Union Catalog
TAPECON and Group Access Capability

1987

CJK350 system introduced for cataloging Chinese, Japanese, and Korean materials
Online access to Library of Congress subject authority records
Search CD450 introduced

1988

Forest Press, publisher of the Dewey Decimal Classification, becomes part of OCLC; OCLC Forest Press publishes 20th edition of the *Dewey Decimal Classification*
CAT CD450 introduced
OCLC/AMIGOS Collection Analysis System

1989

OCLC receives U.S. patent for Graph-Text
M386/16 Workstation introduced

1990

American Association for the Advancement of Science and OCLC begin joint electronic publishing venture
EPIC service introduced
New technological platform for cataloging and resource sharing (PRISM service) introduced
GOVDOC service
OCLC assumes control of MAPS (Mid-Atlantic Preservation Service), later known as Preservation Resources

1991

FirstSearch service introduced
M386sx Workstation introduced
X.25 telecommunications network installed

1992

Online Journal of Current Clinical Trials, world's first peer-reviewed electronic medical journal, is launched by American Association for the Advancement of Science and OCLC

Preservation Resources receives patent for preservation camera exposure system

Migration to new OCLC cataloging and resource sharing system (PRISM) completed

1993

Keyword searching on Online Union Catalog
Interlibrary Loan subsystem link to FirstSearch service
Sunday hours for OCLC Cataloging and Resource Sharing services
Automated authority corrections software applied to Online Union Catalog
Automated tape management system installed at OCLC
M486DXI Workstation introduced
Electronic Dewey introduced
Telecommunications Linking Program
OCLC acquires Information Dimensions (IDI) from Battelle Memorial Institute; IDI develops text management systems

1994

OCLC SiteSearch software introduced
Electronic Journals Online program starts
Gateway software for local systems interface to OCLC
Name-Address Directory, Union List, and Chinese-Japanese-Korean (CJK) Plus are available on PRISM technological platform
Internet Cataloging Project
OCLC Interlibrary Loan Transfer
E-mail submission of error corrections for Online Union Catalog

1995

Authorities capabilities
PromptCat introduced
Internet access to OCLC Cataloging and Resource Sharing
ILL Fee Management introduced

OCLC WebZ Server
Preservation Resources scanning/indexing service
Harvard Resource File
Interlibrary Loan Custom Holdings
NetFirst database of Internet resources

1996

MARC Format integration completed
OCLC Authority Control service
OCLC CatCD for Windows
Custom Holdings for Union List
World Wide Web access to FirstSearch
21st edition of *Dewey Decimal Classification*

1997

Name of OCLC Online Union Catalog changed to WorldCat
OCLC ILL Micro Enhancer for Windows software
Electronic archiving projects under way in seven libraries
FirstSearch Electronic Collections Online
TCP/IP telecommunications network installation starts
OCLC sells IDI (Information Dimensions)

1998

OCLC introduces Z39.50 Cataloging
Library of Congress (LC) and the International Federation of Library Associations and Institutions (IFLA) agree to use OCLC ILL Fee Management to reconcile coupon payments for all international loans from LC
OCLC FirstSearch service and Electronic Collections Online become available 24/7
Korea Research Information Center (KRIC) begins delivering OCLC cataloging and reference services to 164 universities and research institutions in South Korea
OCLC introduces dial-up and dedicated TCP/IP (Transmission Control Protocol/Internet Protocol) access to the Internet

1999

OCLC Users Council unanimously adopts a resolution, "Shared Commitments to the OCLC WorldCat Principles of Cooperation," that reaffirms the commitment of OCLC, the regional networks, and member libraries to cooperation and shared responsibility for building access and content for digital libraries

OCLC expands Internet access to the equivalent of more than 300 T-1 lines

OCLC receives ISO 9001 registration for Design and Development of Automated Library Services, Databases and Telecommunications Facilities with provisions for User Documentation and Technical Support

OCLC merges with Public Affairs Information Service (PAIS)

OCLC and Pica Foundation in the Netherlands establish Pica B.V., a jointly owned organization that will lead to closer cooperation among libraries in Europe

OCLC releases French and Spanish language interfaces for the OCLC First-Search service

SABINET Online, an OCLC distributor in South Africa, and OCLC announce plans for the 400-plus libraries of SABINET Online to migrate to the OCLC Cataloging service

OCLC and Washington Library Network (WLN) merge

National Library of Australia and OCLC reach an accord that enables 1,300 Australian libraries to become full or partial members of OCLC

OCLC Preservation Resources delivers digitized images of the George Washington Presidential Papers to the Library of Congress National Digital Library Program

2000

OCLC Board of Trustees retains consulting firm of Arthur D. Little to conduct a study of OCLC's strategic directions and governance structure; the Board also appoints a special advisory council to guide and direct the study

More than 7,500 librarians at 350 downlink sites in North America and Europe tune in for a videoconference of the final 2 hours of the OCLC Users Council Meeting, the first virtual meeting of the 60 delegates who represent the worldwide OCLC membership (May 2000)

OCLC Cataloging Express Service introduced

OCLC decommissions its proprietary X.25 network; all OCLC services are now Internet-based

OCLC installs new power system in its Dublin, Ohio, data center

OCLC begins distributing OCLC ILLiad Resource Sharing Management software

In collaboration with the Library of Congress and the Research Libraries Group, OCLC adopts the pinyin romanization scheme for Chinese characters in authority and bibliographic records in WorldCat

Pica B.V. introduces new LBS local library system and migrates its CBS central system for cataloging and interlibrary loan to a Unix environment

Pica B.V. launches PiCarta International, an end-user information service

OCLC acquires Library Technical Services (LTS), a library cataloging service based in Winnipeg, Manitoba, Canada

2001

The OCLC Users Council unanimously ratifies changes to OCLC Articles of Incorporation and Code of Regulations that change its name to Members Council and add six new delegates from outside the United States

First four Fellows in the IFLA/OCLC Early Career Development Fellowship Program spend 4 weeks at OCLC in Dublin, Ohio

OCLC Arabic Cataloging Software is introduced

OCLC converts 152,000 Chinese language authority records and 710,000 Chinese language bibliographic records in WorldCat from the Wade-Giles transliteration scheme to pinyin

OCLC Asia Link service changes its name to Language Sets and adds Spanish materials to the Chinese, Japanese, Korean, Vietnamese, and Russian sets already available; the service selects, acquires, and catalogs sets of library materials for libraries

OCLC FirstSearch services enhanced with descriptive item content and format icons

Bill & Melinda Gates Foundation awards OCLC a 3-year, $9 million grant to create a Web-based computing portal for public libraries (WebJunction)

2002

OCLC Connexion cataloging service launched

OCLC and the Research Libraries Group sponsor Preservation Metadata Implementation Strategies (PREMIS), a working group to develop recommendations and best practices for implementing preservation metadata in digital preservation systems

QuestionPoint virtual reference service launched

OCLC acquires NetLibrary

OCLC begins distributing CONTENTdm digital collection management software

OCLC and Royal Library of the Netherlands establish Strata Preservation N.V.

2003

OCLC launches WebJunction computing portal for public libraries

Die Deutsche Bibliothek, Library of Congress, and OCLC agree to develop a Virtual International Authorities File

OCLC Pica acquires V.3 Web, an ILL requesting and management system previously provided by LIBPAC

22nd edition of the *Dewey Decimal Classification* is published

OCLC Research makes available at no charge an algorithm to convert bibliographic databases to the Functional Requirements for Bibliographic Records (FRBR) model, in which individual records are brought together under the concept of a work

The ILL Policies and Technology Directory replaces the Name-Address Directory and provides users of the OCLC Interlibrary Loan service with a Web-based central source for entering and retrieving information on interlibrary loan policies

Connexion Client, a Windows-based interface to OCLC Connexion, debuts

OCLC launches Open WorldCat Pilot to make library resources available from nonlibrary Web sites

Integrated resource sharing interface added to OCLC FirstSearch service

OCLC E-learning Task Force issues white paper on *Libraries and the Enhancement of E-learning*

OCLC Members Council and OCLC release *Library Training & Education Market Needs Assessment Study*

OCLC introduces Group services, which enable consortia to build group online union catalogs and provide resource sharing and reference services under one locally customized interface

OCLC publishes *2003 OCLC Environmental Scan: Pattern Recognition*

CAPCON (originally Consortium of Universities of the Washington Metropolitan Area) becomes part of OCLC

2004

OCLC Research launches ResearchWorks, a demonstration lab that showcases prototypes, interactive tools, and other experiments of OCLC researchers

Indiana Historical Society is the first organization to add records from a digitized CONTENTdm collection to WorldCat via metadata harvesting

To make the copyright permissions process more convenient for librarians, OCLC and the Copyright Clearance Center (CCC) form a partnership to provide direct access to the CCC's copyright permissions services from OCLC FirstSearch databases

OCLC Research provides open-source software programs that implement the Open Archives Initiative (OAI) protocols for data storage and harvesting in support of institutional repositories—OAICat and OAIHarvester

OCLC acquires 24/7 Reference Services from Metropolitan Cooperative Library System, Los Angeles, California

OCLC Online Service Center is launched, enabling libraries to manage their OCLC accounts more efficiently with self-serve ordering and other account management tools on a secure, online site

WorldCat supports Cyrillic, Hebrew, and Greek script records

OCLC sells PAIS to Cambridge Scientific Abstracts

OCLC Pica acquires Sisis Informationssysteme, a provider of library management systems and portal software based in Oberhaching, Germany

OCLC Pica acquires Fretwell-Downing Informatics, a provider of library management systems based in Sheffield, England, with offices in Australia, the Netherlands, and the United States

Worthington (Ohio) Libraries contributes 1 billionth holding symbol to WorldCat on August 11, 2005

Thai and Tamil script support for WorldCat

2006

OCLC joins CLOSKSS (Controlled LOCKSS—Lots of Copies Keep Stuff Safe), a nonprofit community approach to securing access to electronic scholarly content for the long term

OCLC, LIBER (Association of European Research Libraries) exchange bibliographic records to support digital preservation efforts

OCLC Founder Frederick G. Kilgour dies on July 31 at age 92

WorldCat Collection Analysis Service is introduced

OCLC acquires Openly Informatics, which provides linking software and a database of 1.1 million metadata records with links to electronic resources

OCLC acquires DiMeMa, Inc., the organization that developed and supports CONTENTdm software

OCLC Pica starts Open WorldCat pilot for libraries in Germany, the Netherlands, and the United Kingdom

RLG and OCLC combine organizations to integrate services and create RLG Programs (originally Research Libraries Group), a new division within OCLC Programs and Research

Terminologies service launched

OCLC launches WorldCat.org Web site, making collections in OCLC member libraries visible on the Internet to people everywhere

Amazon.com becomes OCLC PromptCat participant

Bill & Melinda Gates Foundation awards OCLC $1.2 million grant to develop
   library marketing campaign
OCLC Cataloging Partners program merges with OCLC PromptCat service to
   form WorldCat Cataloging Partners, a collaborative effort with materials
   vendors to reduce cataloging costs for libraries
OCLC to host Consortium of European Research Libraries Hand Press Book
   database
OCLC Members Council meets outside the United States for the first time, in
   Quebec City, Quebec, Canada
Free Web-based WorldCat Registry is introduced; enables libraries and
   groups to manage organizational data for vendors, third parties in one
   place
OCLC launches a pilot test of WorldCat Local, which lets libraries customize
   WorldCat.org as a solution for local discovery and delivery services

2007

WorldCat Delivery Pilot starts in 12 Montana libraries
OCLC hosts fourth China–U.S. Library Conference, which brings together
   leaders from libraries, museums, and archives in China and the United
   States
Bibliothèque nationale de France joins the Virtual International Authority File
   Project with Deutsche Nationalbibliothek, Library of Congress, and OCLC
OCLC Programs and Research opens office at the University of St Andrews,
   Scotland, United Kingdom
OCLC acquires the remaining shares of OCLC Pica Group B.V., the European-
   based library and information systems supplier, to become the sole share-
   holder of the organization

2008

OCLC begins Next Generation Cataloging Pilot to explore viability of captur-
   ing metadata from publishers and vendors
OCLC acquires EZProxy authentication and access software
WorldCat.org adds Facebook application
Mellon Foundation awards OCLC $145,000 grant to conduct data exchange
   study with seven RLG Programs art museum partners
University of Washington Libraries enters 100,000,000th bibliographic record
   into WorldCat on April 1
QuestionPoint virtual reference service introduces Qwidget, a new chat
   widget

OCLC launches Digital Archive service for long-term storage of libraries' digital collections

OCLC Members Council ratifies changes to the Articles of Incorporation and Code of Regulations recommended by the Board of Trustees that will transform the current Members Council into a Global Council that connects with Regional Councils around the world (May 18–20)

WorldCat Local is introduced

Google and OCLC agree to exchange data, link digitized books to WorldCat

OCLC issues new membership report, *From Awareness to Funding: a Study of Library Support in America* (funded by Bill & Melinda Gates Foundation)

OCLC introduces Web Harvester, which enables libraries to capture and add Web content to their digital collections through CONTENTdm software

xISSN service introduced; supports management of serials information

OCLC pilots WorldCat Copyright Evidence Registry

WorldCat tagging introduced

WebJunction publishes *Latinos and Public Library Perceptions* report

WorldCat.org links to digitized content in Google Books

Questia and OCLC link records from WorldCat to E-book previews

Bibliothèque nationale de France to add records to WorldCat

OCLC develops experimental WorldCat iPhone application

OCLC, Syracuse University, and University of Washington receive Mellon Foundation grant to help develop a new Web search experience based on expertise from librarians

50 library developers attend first WorldCat.org Hackathon at New York Public Library, November 7–8

Novanet and University of New Brunswick become first Canadian institutions to use OCLC WorldCat Local

OCLC and the Royal Library of the Netherlands sell Strata Preservation N.V. to KMM Groep

National Library of Sweden joins Virtual International Authority File project

National Library of Israel and OCLC complete pilot project resulting in the addition of more than 788,000 new bibliographic records and 1.1 million holdings from the national library to WorldCat

Index

Page numbers in *Italics* represent tables.
Page numbers in **Bold** represent figures.